The Gospel of Jesus

WILLIAM R. FARMER

The Gospel of Jesus

THE PASTORAL RELEVANCE OF THE SYNOPTIC PROBLEM

Westminster/John Knox Press
Louisville, Kentucky

Book design by Drew Stevens

Cover design by Susan E. Jackson

Cover illustration: Miracle of Christ Healing the Blind. *El Greco. Metropolitan Museum of Art, New York. Courtesy of Superstock.*

First edition

Published by Westminster/John Knox Press
Louisville, Kentucky

This book is printed on acid-free paper that meets the American National Standards Institute Z39.48 standard. ♾

PRINTED IN THE UNITED STATES OF AMERICA
9 8 7 6 5 4 3 2 1

Library of Congress Cataloging-in-Publication Data

Farmer, William Reuben, date.
    The gospel of Jesus : the pastoral relevance of the synoptic problem / William R. Farmer —
1st ed.
        p.   cm.
    Includes bibliographical references and indexes.
    ISBN 0-664-25514-0 (alk. paper)
    1. Two source hypothesis (Synoptics criticism) 2. Bible. N.T. Mark—Sources. 3. Q
hypothesis (Synoptics criticism) 4. Jesus Christ—Teachings. I. Title.
BS2555.2.F298 1994
226′.066—dc20
                                                                93-43359

TO
NELL COCHRAN FARMER

Contents

Part 6
Summary and Conclusions

Preface

This book appears at a time of great perplexity over the question of what can be said with confidence about Jesus. Because of the controversial nature of this question, I have tried to be particularly careful not to speculate as to the motives that may account for what scholars are writing about this. However, I make no claim to have eliminated bias altogether from my treatment of the work of those with whom I am in disagreement. In general in this book I have tried to focus on the consequences of following certain research hypotheses. So much seems to hinge on the question of Q. If there ever was such a document, the case for giving weight to *Thomas* and other apocryphal gospels becomes more plausible. However, if we go in that direction we are led to a different Jesus than the church has ever known, a Jesus who is closer to the model of a wandering Cynic philosopher. It is important to note that not all scholars who believe in Q would necessarily agree with scholars (like John Dominic Crossan) who see Jesus in this way. But scholars who see Jesus as a wandering Cynic philosopher presently seem to be getting the greatest public attention for their reconstructions based on Q. Whether they represent a new trend remains to be seen.

As a young visiting instructor at DePauw University in 1954, I recall vividly the experience of standing before a blackboard with my back to a class of college students. I was lecturing on the synoptic problem. After inscribing on the board the traditional diagram for the Two-Source Hypothesis with Mark to the upper left, Q to the upper right, and Matthew and Luke below with the appropriate arrows indicating the dependence of these later Gospels upon Mark and Q, I began to explain why we needed to hypothesize the existence of Q, an otherwise (I had to admit) completely unknown document. Q was necessary to explain the agreements between Matthew and Luke where these agreements could not be explained as having been drawn from Mark.

As I reviewed the reasons for the view that Mark was the earliest Gospel, I became conscious that what I was saying was not logically persuasive. I remember saying to myself, "Bill, you did not make adequate preparation for this lecture." But instead of turning to my class and acknowledging that I was unable to give them any conclusive reason for the priority of Mark, I instead began to raise my voice and speak with greater authority in hopes of discouraging anyone from asking me to explain why I thought the facts I was citing led to the conclusion I was asserting.

The eventual realization that I was passing on to my students a tradition that deserved to be questioned has set the course for much of my research in the past forty years. This book represents the fruit of a prolonged struggle with one of the great intellectual problems of the twentieth century. How is it possible to explain that competent scholars in an unquestioning manner continue to base what they say about Jesus on such problematic premises as the priority of Mark and the existence of Q? This book goes further than anyone has ever gone before in offering an answer to this question.

In the meantime, thanks to the work of the Jesus Seminar, the consequences of inquiring about Jesus utilizing the ideas of Markan primacy, and the existence of Q are beginning to have an impact on the public. Newspapers have announced to the world the chief results of the work of this seminar, including, for example, the conclusion that Jesus did not teach his disciples the Lord's Prayer. These scholars have broken out of their ivory towers, and through books like Crossan's *The Historical Jesus: The Life of a Mediterranean Jewish Peasant*, public awareness of the importance of critical scholarship is reaching new levels in our time.

The Gospel of Jesus is designed to reach a wide readership. With this book read and digested, anyone can now participate in the debate. Where is Q leading us? What reason is there to believe that Q ever existed?

During the past forty years, interest in the historical Jesus has waxed and waned. At the moment, there appears to be an upswing of interest in the subject. The publications that have come from the Jesus Seminar, bolstered on the one hand by books following the *Thomas*-Q line by scholars like Crossan and, on the other hand, by a steady fixing of the text of Q by Professor James Robinson and the International Q Project, serve to provide (assuming Q) a credible basis for the claim that what the church has to say about Jesus is all wrong. In fact, the combined work of these scholars, whatever their intentions, suggests that he probably was a very different Jesus. But was he?

Scholars who refuse to adhere to the *Thomas*-Q line and insist on giving the church's Gospels great weight in their historical reconstructions continue to produce portraits of Jesus that are recognizable as developed variations of the church's traditional teaching about Jesus. Why does this not settle the matter? Is it not more credible to think that new research, taking account of new insights, would produce results that stand in some intelligible relationship to earlier understandings?

Could the answer to this question be that highly unlikely reconstructions are capturing the attention of the public precisely because their authors are perceived as being more objective. Do not these *Thomas*-Q adherents represent themselves to the public as scholars who are willing to let the chips fall where they may? But, is the public being misled? A lot hinges on how much reliance should be given to the source theories upon which the *Thomas*-Q scholars depend.

Perhaps scholars who are turning their backs on the *Thomas*-Q line and prefer to remain methodologically closer to the Gospels of the church are being responsible in doing so, in view of the undeniable fact that good grounds exist for questioning the priority of Mark and the existence of Q. Q is hypothetical, the church's Gospels actually exist.

In any case, the time has come for pastors and interested laypeople, including students, to begin participating in the dialogue. This book is written precisely for that wider audience. With this book in hand it is now possible for any discerning nonspecialist to enter the discussion. Those equipped with the insights and arguments of this book can now call the hand of all interpreters of the Gospels who ask readers to follow them out onto the thin ice of speculation based on the Two-Source Hypothesis. This book prepares the reader to see through the argument from authority ("Most scholars hold") and to recognize those who tend to raise their voices and speak with greater authority, when they really cannot give convincing arguments for Markan priority and the existence of Q, for what they are—adherents of outdated ideas.

An important work by Elaine Mary Wainwright, *Towards a Feminist Critical Reading of the Gospel according to Matthew* (Berlin and New York: Walter de Gruyter, 1991), came to my attention after the manuscript for this book had been sent to the publisher. No footnote or series of footnotes referring to Wainwright's work would do justice to what she has accomplished. Readers will find their reading of chapter 7, "The Faithful Witness of Women," considerably illuminated by a reading of Wainwright's work.

Acknowledgments

Once . . . we accept the faith perspective of the authors of the New Testament and the judgment of the Church which has canonized this apostolic faith response as a witness guaranteed by God, a new avenue of knowing the reality of Jesus is opened up for us. This faith is then pursued not merely as a safeguard against reducing the figure of Jesus to pre-fabricated clichés, but as a positive hermeneutical tool which can answer the question raised by the quest for the historical Jesus: who is this man? We also begin to understand that it is not a great tragedy for us—in fact it might be providential—that we do not have personal writings by Jesus himself (or transcripts of his discourses for that matter). *God's intention was to bring about a community of faith around Jesus so that the understanding of Jesus would become inseparable from accepting the witness of this archetypal community. In fact, the reality of Jesus, "who he was and what he intended," or more precisely, who he was in God's plan of salvation and what God revealed to us through his person, deeds, and words, becomes accessible to us only through the divinely guaranteed documents of the apostolic Church, that is, the New Testament. If Jesus wanted to reach all humankind through a community whose faith, life, and ritual are to continue the faith, life, and ritual of this archetypal apostolic community, then the fact that Jesus himself authored no book or letter makes complete sense. If Jesus' reality could be reached without the faith response embodied in the documents of the apostolic Church, an individualistic relationship between isolated individual believers and Jesus would become a distinct possibility. Then our faith would not necessarily be an ecclesial faith.*
—*Roch Kereszty, O.Cist.**

I wish to begin by acknowledging my indebtedness to that church which formed the New Testament canon and made the decision (against Marcion) to retain the Law and the Prophets within the Christian canon. Kereszty's statement clarifies the way in which the church can critically appropriate the work of historians who empathetically wish to enter into the world of the

---

*From his article "Historical Research, Theological Inquiry, and the Reality of Jesus: Reflections on the Method of J. P. Meier" (*Communio* 19 [Winter 1992]: 595). Fr. Kereszty wrote this in response to Meier's book *A Marginal Jew: Rethinking the Historical Jesus*, vol. 1 (New York: Doubleday & Co., 1991). In a footnote, Kereszty makes it clear that he also has in view J. D. Crossan's *The Historical Jesus: The Life of a Mediterranean Jewish Peasant* (San Francisco: HarperCollins, 1991).

biblical authors and, sharing the faith perspective of those authors, seek to interpret the biblical text for contemporary readers.

I also wish to acknowledge those who, sharing membership in the living body of Christ, have assisted in various ways in the production and perfection of this book without any attempt to define the exact nature of the assistance each of them has rendered me: Lee Cary, Lamar Cope, David Dungan, Susan Earl, Alexander Evans, Denis Farkasfalvy, William Frank, John Gibbs, Tim Gollob, Linda Hajak, Paul Hinnebusch, Virgil Howard, Roch Kereszty, John Kloppenborg, Carrie Jane Loftis, James McKenna, Alan McNicol, Ben Meyer, Luis A. Payan, David Peabody, Patricia Ridgley, Philip Shuler.

None of these persons is responsible for any statement in this book except where his or her own work is explicitly cited.

I wish to acknowledge the efforts of the editorial staff of Westminster/John Knox Press to assist me in writing this book in such a way as to reach a wider readership. Specialists are prone to write for specialists, and if this book succeeds in reaching that wider readership which the author and the publisher are seeking, then the credit in no small measure will go to my editor Jeff Hamilton, to whom I am specially grateful for the suggestion to begin every chapter with a quotation from scripture. On my own I have adopted the practice of beginning even smaller units of the book with some pertinent quotation.

While I am responsible for all translations in this book, I have made extensive use of the Revised Standard Version. I have consulted critical editions of the original texts and other translations as well, chiefly the New English Bible.

W.R.F.

University of Dallas

PART 1

Why This Book?

CHAPTER 1

Introduction

The Truth of the Gospel

> One of the most striking features of the *Gospel of Thomas*[1] is its silence on the matter of Jesus' death and resurrection—the keystone of Paul's missionary proclamation. But Thomas is not alone in this silence. The Synoptic Sayings Source (Q), used by Matthew and Luke, also does not consider Jesus' death a part of the Christian message. And it likewise is not interested in stories and reports about the resurrection and subsequent appearances of the risen Lord. The *Gospel of Thomas* and Q challenge the assumption that the early church was unanimous in making Jesus' death and resurrection the fulcrum of Christian faith. Both documents presuppose that Jesus' significance lay in his words, and in his words alone.[2]
>
> —*Helmut Koester*

The statement by Harvard University's influential Professor Helmut Koester points up the need for this book. At issue in Gospel studies today is what the apostle Paul called "the truth of the gospel."[3] Do we end up with a credible story of Jesus that is adequate to account for the faith of those who bear his name, or do we end up with the teaching of some Mediterranean philosopher who has no idea of what must be done to turn the world upside down and to set the human family on a different path?

In Paul's day, circumcision and related matters of Jewish law were the concrete problems. Those are not issues today. At issue today is whether the death of Jesus should be regarded as an unnecessary or an essential part of the Christian message. To put the matter in other terms, should Jesus' significance be sought in his words and in his words alone, as we see in Professor Koester's reading of *Thomas* and the synoptic sayings source Q? Or should Jesus' words be taken together with the story of his death and resurrection as found in the church's Gospels?

The trend among New Testament scholars who follow the *Thomas*-Q line is to represent Jesus as one whose disciples had no interest in any redemptive consequence of his death and no interest in his resurrection.[4]

Because *Thomas* is a late-second- to fourth-century document, by itself it could never be successfully used to lever the significance of Jesus off its New

Testament foundation. Similarly, the sayings source Q, allegedly used by Matthew and Luke, by itself could never be successfully used to achieve this result. But used together, as they are by a significant number of scholars, *Thomas* and Q appear to reinforce one another. As a consequence, what is impossible to achieve using either *Thomas* or Q alone may be possible to achieve when the two are used together.

Similarly, by itself the sayings source Q would never be regarded as a document of greater authority than the Gospels of the church. But with *Thomas*, the Q document appears to take on greater historical authority. This is because *Thomas*, which contains only sayings of Jesus, proves that the sayings of Jesus were once collected and circulated separately from the story of Jesus' ministry. This fact weighs significantly in the minds of those who give greater authority to the Q document than to the canonical Gospels. According to the Two-Source Hypothesis, Q is earlier than Matthew and Luke and therefore is chronologically closer to Jesus, the authority for all who base their religious beliefs on his teachings.

It is obvious that a great deal hangs on Q, including the question of whether such a document ever existed. It is significant that many scholars today would deny that Q ever existed.[5] Since this book does not address the synoptic problem, but rather the *pastoral relevance* of that problem, no attempt will be made to review all the arguments against Q. The reader will be given instead an explanation of how one can reach the position held by those who end up with a Jesus who is the teacher of "the Q Community," a very different Jesus from the Jesus known in the church.

On the Koester-Robinson School

Professor Koester offers a solution to the synoptic problem that places the Gospel of Mark before Matthew and Luke and hypothesizes that Matthew and Luke have independently copied Mark. Because Matthew and Luke have in common many sayings of Jesus not in Mark, this solution proceeds to hypothesize the use of a "sayings source" to explain these shared sayings in Matthew and Luke. One then can argue, as does Professor Koester's close associate Professor James M. Robinson, that it is "appropriate" for us to refer to this hypothetical sayings source as an authoritative "sayings Gospel."[6] One could also hold, as Professor Robinson does, that this so-called Gospel, its hypothetical character notwithstanding, is "the most important Christian text we have."[7] Assuming the validity of this analysis, Q becomes a chief source, if not *the* chief source, for understanding Jesus. Because Q contains no reference to the cross or resurrection, it follows that the New Testament emphasis on the cross and resurrection is theologically misleading. To further explore this possible solution to the synoptic problem, one must do no less than reconstruct Christian origins, beginning with Jesus as teacher of the Q community, and recognize that the result may be a different Jesus from the one the church has always known.

On the other hand, if one reads the New Testament in light of a different development in Gospel studies that places Mark after Matthew or Luke, or both, it makes a difference. To begin with, there is no need for a hypothetical Q. One can explain everything with a much less complex hypothesis, the Two-Gospel Hypothesis. This hypothesis presumes that Luke made use of Matthew. The Jesus one comes to know in reading the Gospels in this way is not significantly different from the Jesus the church has known since the time of the apostles. This is the Jesus who, with the Holy Spirit, enables the church to raise up saints and martyrs.[8]

To the nonspecialist in the field of contemporary scriptural interpretation, the program of the Koester-Robinson school seems, at best, implausible. In simple terms, it seems odd that anyone would hold to the hypothesis, let alone that the theory might ever become a threat to dominate the academy. Most people would ask how an apocryphal *Thomas* and the nineteenth-century Q hypothesis would ever be given greater credence than the New Testament canon, with its early witness of the pre-Pauline community! The fact is, however, that the Koester-Robinson school is quite active, and may be expected to continue to exercise scholarly influence so long as the academy grants this school its chief premise—the reliability of the Two-Source Hypothesis.

On the Case Being Made

The case being made in this book is developed according to the following plan: In part 1 this question is asked: "Why this book?" The answer to this question has been presented in this introductory chapter. In essence, we argue that our understanding of Christian faith is vitally affected by the research paradigm we use when we interpret the Gospel texts. Specifically, we argue that the Two-Source Hypothesis, especially in the hands of the *Thomas*-Q school of exegesis, gives us a different Jesus than the Jesus that has been transmitted by the church since the time of the apostles. On the other hand, the Two-Gospel Hypothesis, with all hypotheses that recognize the primary character of the Matthean text, presents a Jesus who stands in a more meaningful relationship to the Jesus of apostolic teaching.

In part 2, it is then appropriately asked: "What is the Two-Gospel Hypothesis?" This question is answered in chapter 2 in terms of a systematic overview of this hypothesis. This is followed in chapter 3 by going about the same matter from a different angle, namely, by expounding the Two-Gospel Hypothesis through a set of texts.

In part 3, the argument is advanced by asking this question: "What difference does it make whether one uses the Two-Source Hypothesis or the Two-Gospel Hypothesis?" This question is answered by examining another set of texts:

Chapter 4. The Lord's Prayer
Chapter 5. The Lord's Supper
Chapter 6. Justification by Faith
Chapter 7. The Faithful Witness of Women
Chapter 8. God's Special Commitment to the Poor
Chapter 9. The Keys of the Kingdom

In part 4 a new point is raised. The reader now deserves a reasoned answer to the question: "How, why, where, and when did the idea of Markan primacy arise?" Readers of this book will naturally begin their reading with whatever point of view they bring to the book. In most cases, this means that the reader will begin to read the book with a predisposition toward the view taught in most textbooks and transmitted in most classrooms, namely, the priority of Mark and the existence of Q. But many who read on, especially through chapter 9, will have reason to ask: "What can have been the circumstances under which the idea of Markan primacy originated?" This question is answered in chapter 10 in relation to the general theme of "The Idea and Reality of Markan Priority." This theme is discussed in terms of (1) the Criterion of Length, (2) the Argument from Order, (3) the Minor Agreements, (4) Luke's Use or Disuse of Matthew.

This more technical discussion is followed by chapter 11, "A Social History of Markan Primacy." Here, the reader is taken back into the chaotic and conflictive period of the *Kulturkampf* in Germany 1870–1878. At that time, important ideological needs were present in German society that help us to understand how the simple romantic conjecture of Markan priority was dramatically transformed for Protestants into a fixed idea that appears to resist rational refutation—an idea in which many people, now including many Roman Catholics, have come to believe. Convincing arguments and compelling evidence challenging the validity of this idea appear to have had little power to change this belief. The way the earlier phase of belief in Markan priority, represented by the romanticist Johann Gottfried von Herder, was blended with the dogmatic phase associated with the *Kulturkampf* is well brought out in the story about a Tübingen scholar of the twentieth century, who upon hearing a colleague from abroad express doubt about the priority of Mark, turned to him and said, "But, my dear friend, Mark must be first because it is so beautiful!"

Later, at a conference on the Gospels at that same university, an American scholar questioned belief in Q. His paper was published, but none of his

German colleagues joined him in expressing doubts about the Two-Source Hypothesis.[9] More recently, conferences have been held at various German universities where the Two-Source Hypothesis has been questioned, not only by Americans but also by scholars of other nationalities. But, in general, the hypothesis has not been challenged by German scholars. As late as August 1993, at an International Conference of New Testament scholars meeting in Chicago, a German professor referred in his lecture to the consensus on Markan priority and the existence of Q. When confronted on the point, he defended his right to this opinion and cited his own unpublished research. Chapter 11 helps the reader understand this situation.

The first German professor to break ranks with her colleagues on the priority of Mark and the existence of Q is Dr. Eta Linnemann, who exposed how German university students are brainwashed on the synoptic problem. Explaining how some colleagues cite the early nineteenth-century work of Christian Gottlob Wilke and Christian Hermann Weisse as proving the priority of Mark while providing "not one argument to illustrate how Wilke and Weisse arrived at their findings," Linnemann observes: "The students must take it on blind trust that the required proofs for the Two-Source Hypothesis have been set forth in those books, to which it would be quite difficult to gain access." A well-researched study of nineteenth-century Gospel research, she noted, documents that Wilke and Weisse did not prove the priority of Mark. Linnemann criticizes her colleagues for failing to bring attention to the "untenability" of the hypothesis (the Two-Source Hypothesis) with the result that the "student is hoodwinked."[10] It must be understood that these "hoodwinked" students are the university professors of the future, so the process repeats itself. This condemnation of her colleagues' academic procedures will privately be discounted by some, not only because Linnemann is a woman, but also because she has left her university position to work more closely with the church and teach Bible on the mission field in Indonesia. But Linnemann's academic credentials are equal to those of her male colleagues who remain at their university posts. Moreover, her specific charges against representative scholars are well documented. Neither Linnemann nor any of her colleagues whose work she specifically criticizes (Strecker, Schnelle, Marxsen, Conzelmann, Lindemann, Koester, and Zimmermann) indicate that they are aware of the role of Germany's state-controlled universities in implementing government policy during the *Kulturkampf* outlined in chapter 11.

In part 5 we raise the question: "What is behind the current interest in Q?" This question is answered in chapter 12 by analyzing the critical basis for the upswing in scholarly interest in Q. At the conclusion of this chapter, titled "A Dismantling of the Church's Canon," the reader is given some idea of what the church has at stake in the outcome of this debate.

In part 6 we then formally ask the question: "What is at stake?" This question is answered clearly in the concluding chapter, "The Gospel of the Lord Jesus." This chapter is not an attempt to summarize the book. Yet, in it the reader will find that much of what has gone before will begin to fall into place. The argument of the book as a whole is cumulative. But the argument in this final chapter is a tour de force. By this point in the book, the reader does not need a pedantic restatement of what has gone before. In its place is a "go for broke" demonstration of the difference it makes whether one ends up with a credible story of a Jesus who with the Holy Spirit has the power to raise up saints and martyrs in the church or whether one ends up with some amorphous philosophy that fails to explain anything.

The final chapter of this book attempts to address the question of what difference it makes whether one adheres to the commonly accepted Two-Source Hypothesis or the less popular, but perhaps more credible, Two-Gospel Hypothesis. The church at its best will always strive to "get it straight." We must never forget what happened to the "quest for truth" in the universities of the Third Reich. A "critically correct" civil religion, pushed by university-trained German-Christian theologians like Emanuel Hirsch, gloried in the idea of Markan priority with its understanding of Christian theology based on the Two-Source Hypothesis, while Christians who witnessed unto blood and resisted unto death the Nazi horrors that led to the Holocaust drew spiritual support from a reading of the Gospels that called them to be saints and martyrs of the church (an understanding of Christ called for by any hypothesis that recognizes the primary character of the Matthean text). This is the difference. This is what is at stake for the church.

I invite you to consider whether the idea of Markan priority and the established world of biblical scholarship based upon this idea, in the past or present, could be considered culpable in maintaining the status quo at the expense of human rights. The saints and martyrs of the church included those who have witnessed unto blood on behalf of the poor and oppressed. They care very little for our university-based critical tradition, and thus have been free to read the Gospels as they were first read by oppressed Christians in the pre-Constantinian church, and as they have been read by oppressed Christians throughout the ages. This is the way I would encourage all readers to approach the Gospels. I have reflected long and hard on this matter and have taken it to heart. This book details my journey. The conclusions follow naturally as a sequel to my previous work.[11]

I am told that my previous work makes it clear that I think the New Testament canon is a martyr's canon. If that is so, then it can be said that this book is aimed to drive one more nail in the coffin of the academic case used to support a "critically correct" civil religion that has been at the throat of the church for over a century—that is, the church that grows from the seed of the martyrs.

Obviously, I am as opposed as anyone to the social and ecclesiastical perversions of Christianity that have existed in the past and exist today. But that is for theologians and committed journalists to expose. The student of scripture has a more fundamental task to perform: With a firm grasp of the Gospel and the sharp point of the pen, that task is to delineate interpretive error where it appears and, as far as possible, to lay bare the source of the confusion. If in the process the student of scripture can illuminate the text for the benefit of the homilist, preacher, teacher, or moralist, so much the better. In fact, this kind of practical concern goes hand in hand with the apostolic concern to "get it straight." As with Paul's visit with Peter in Jerusalem and his confrontation with Peter in Antioch, all is in service of expediting the Gospel.[12]

How to Read This Book

A word of advice to the reader: There is no one way to read this book. The reader who has reached this point in the book may well proceed directly to a later chapter. Each reader will be guided by a different set of priorities and bring a unique perspective to the task of reading this work. Some may dip into part 3 before reading about the Two-Gospel Hypothesis in part 2 to satisfy themselves that adherence to one or another hypothesis can make a difference in how one understands the Gospels.

Other readers may choose to go from this opening chapter, where the work of Koester and Robinson is mentioned rather briefly, directly to chapter 12, where relevant parts of their work are analyzed in detail. Still others, having learned something in advance of what is said about the *Kulturkampf*, may now want to go directly to chapter 11.

For readers with no particular reason to depart from reading in sequence, the chapters will move forward in a logical manner.

The reading won't all be easy going. However, much effort has been expended by many people to make this book suitable for a wider reading public than normally deals with the arcane topic of the synoptic problem. To repeat, this book is not primarily a book on the synoptic problem.[13] It is more specifically a book on the *pastoral relevance* of that problem. This book also spells out in detail the differences it makes whether, in living or in teaching the Gospel, one follows one or the other of the two most widely accepted solutions of the synoptic problem used by scholars today. The attentive reader will learn something about the synoptic problem, but more important the attentive reader will learn about its pastoral relevance.

A Final Word

This is a philosophical work. It invites the reader to think. To think deeply.

How do we come to believe what we believe? What is the best way to test our beliefs? Is there another example of an idea that was essentially correct giving way to a false idea for a period of time, only to reassert itself in the end? Yes. The ancients had evidence that the earth was a sphere. Yet, for a long period, this idea lay dormant and the Ptolemaic theory was dominant. Finally, with great difficulty, the idea that the earth was a sphere replaced the flat-earth idea. So in the history of ideas this is nothing new. (Galileo would confirm this observation!)

The idea that the Gospel of Mark was composed after the Gospels of Matthew and Luke was well regarded by the best scholars at one time. Yet, it was replaced for one hundred years by the idea that Mark was the earliest Gospel, and only now has the earlier idea, that Mark was a later Gospel, reasserted itself. No less a scholar than Helmut Koester acknowledges that the text of Mark appeared in its present form after the Gospels of Matthew and Luke and cannot have been known by the evangelists Matthew and Luke because too much evidence exists that the present text is secondary to the texts of Matthew and Luke.[14] Professor Koester presents the best example of how the priority of Mark has resisted rational refutation. In the face of evidence he himself has cited against the Two-Source Theory, rather than give up the idea of Markan priority and the concomitant idea of the existence of Q, he is willing to propose that several versions of Mark once existed, each one serving to explain evidence that would be more simply explained if the original Gospel of Mark were acknowledged to be later than Matthew and Luke.[15] Professor Koester is not alone in this denial. Adherents of the idea that a Q document once existed, encountering evidence difficult to explain, now hypothecate more than one earlier edited version of Q.[16]

This indicates that the ideas of both Q and Markan priority are privileged ideas. It is sometimes said in defense of holding on to the discredited ideas of the priority of Mark and the existence of Q that they have proven useful and should not be discarded too hastily. This book will provide a sustained argument against the view that usefulness is a reliable criterion. The reader should ask at every point: "In what way can it be said that the ideas of the priority of Mark and the existence of Q are useful?" If they are useful, they should be useful to someone or in some way. Let the reader make a special effort to note exactly in what way and for whom these ideas have been and remain useful.

On the other hand, it should be readily admitted that advocates of the Two-Gospel Hypothesis realize that their paradigm can be useful. For example, it can be useful for anyone interested in combating racism, or poverty, or oppression. It can be useful for anyone interested in the question of the faithful witness of women in the ministry of Jesus. It can be useful for anyone interested in the relevance of the Lord's Prayer, the Lord's Supper, justification by faith, and the keys of the kingdom passage in Matthew. This usefulness, however, does not settle the question of the validity of this hypothesis. The validity of any Gospel hypothesis depends upon arguments based on historical and literary evidence. Regrettably, this evidence is still in dispute, and it is understandable that many have turned away from the synoptic problem without hope of its ever being solved. At this time, many otherwise serious scholars irresponsibly shrug their shoulders and dismiss the matter with the rhetorical question: "What difference does it make?" This book aims to answer that question in such a manner as to widen the circle of those who are able to recognize what is at stake, and in this way throw light on the importance of resolving this question.

PART 2

What Is the Two-Gospel Hypothesis?

CHAPTER 2

A Systematic Overview
of the Two-Gospel Hypothesis

The Tradition of the Church

The Two-Gospel Hypothesis proposes that Matthew and Luke were written before Mark and John. This proposal receives support from widely respected and highly regarded patristic sources.

1. This hypothesis is supported by the testimony of Clement of Alexandria who, according to Eusebius of Caesarea, wrote that the Gospels with genealogies were written first. Subsequent interpreters in the church have understood this to mean that Matthew and Luke, each with a genealogy, were written before Mark and John, neither of which has a genealogy.

Eusebius certainly accepted Clement's testimony. He states that Clement is handing on a tradition from the primitive elders "concerning the order of the Gospels." After mentioning the sequential priority of the Gospels with genealogies, Clement next mentions Mark and then John. This suggests that Clement regarded Mark and John as chronologically following Matthew and Luke.

All scholars familiar with the nature and value of tradition will be interested in Clement's Testimonium which may be found in Eusebius, *Ecclesiastical History* 6.14.5–7.

> And, again in the same books [*Hypotyposeis* 6], Clement has inserted a tradition from the primitive elders with regard to the order of the Gospels as follows: he said that those Gospels were written first which include the genealogies, and that the Gospel according to Mark came into being in this manner: . . .

Eusebius's report of Clement's Testimonium is quite clear. It tells us plainly that Matthew and Luke were earlier than Mark.

Moreover, this tradition is not to be understood as originating with Clement's immediate teachers, whom he also calls "elders," but from the primitive elders, "the elders who lived in the first days." It is not unreasonable to suppose that some of these primitive elders themselves had living contact with the Gospel writers or at least with their disciples. Much depends, of course, on when the Gospels were written. The point is that the burden of proof in this matter rests upon the critic who would discount this tradition as having no historical value.

It is not unreasonable to imagine that the observation that the Gospels with genealogies came before the Gospels without genealogies referred at first to shorter versions of Matthew and Luke where the genealogies were omitted, as for example with Marcion's shorter version of Luke.[1] However, whatever occasioned the origin of this tradition, its transmission suggests that the church believed *ipso facto* that Mark and John without genealogies along with any other Gospels without genealogies were also composed after Matthew and Luke.

This Testimonium from the primitive elders, which has come to us through Clement and Eusebius, was accepted in the church according to the plain sense of the text as Eusebius understood it, all the way down into the ninth century. This is made certain by the learned ninth-century Irish monk Sedulius Scotus. He explains that Mark omitted the birth narratives because he knew that they had already been recorded "in the first two evangelists." Sedulius makes this comment while explaining a passage from the "monarchian" prologue of Mark. This fourth- or fifth-century prologue also shares the view that the Gospel of Mark was composed after Matthew and Luke and that Mark had seen both of these earlier Gospels. This testimony, well attested from the second until the ninth century, flatly contradicts the theory of Markan priority.

There is also a tradition in the church that the Gospels were composed in the order Matthew, Mark, Luke, John. One finds support for this tradition in various places, including the monarchian prologue of Luke. According to this prologue, Luke was written in Achaia after Matthew had been written in Judea and after Mark had been written in Italy. This tradition also flatly contradicts the theory of Markan priority. Mark is always represented as later than Matthew. The only question concerns whether Mark came after Matthew or after both Matthew and Luke. We have two differing traditions; Luke before Mark, and Mark before Luke. How can this apparent discrepancy in church tradition be resolved?

There are, of course, certain practical pedagogical advantages in placing Mark before Luke in the canon. For example, this sequence serves the principle of incremental gain. If Matthew is read first, then by also reading Mark one can learn more; after reading Matthew and Mark, one can learn still more by reading Luke, and finally still more by reading John. If one reads Mark after having read Matthew and Luke, one learns very little that has not already been covered by Matthew and Luke. Again, when read in the canonical order, Mark carries the reader forward from the very Jewish account of Matthew to the more universal account of Luke. Moreover, one notes that, in the process, Mark's account remains essentially faithful to that of Matthew while it fittingly prepares the reader to take up Luke's quite different account. These practical advantages may not have contributed to the origin of the canonical order, but they would have commended this order once adopted. The canonical order Matthew, Mark, Luke, and John is an ecclesiastical order. It never caused any confusion in the mind of writers like Clement and Origen. The chronological order Matthew, Luke, Mark, and John was for them on a different level from the ecclesiastical order.

Defenders of Markan priority cannot accept this evidence and hold to their theory. If they hold to their theory they must ignore, explain away, or deny the value of this important external evidence. Yet, sound historical method requires that the historian give a balanced weight to both external evidence and to the internal evidence based solely on a study of the texts of the Gospels themselves.

In sum, it is a distinct advantage of the Two-Gospel Hypothesis that it enjoys the support of the historical evidence. The Gospel of Matthew and the Gospel of Luke were, as far as this external evidence is concerned, clearly believed to have been composed before the other Gospels—certainly by Clement and presumably by all scholars who accepted Clement's Testimonium, including Eusebius, clear down to the ninth century.

2. The Two-Gospel Hypothesis is also supported by Augustine of Hippo, who first laid out in detail the results of a prolonged and exhaustive comparative study of the internal evidence of all four Gospels (*The Harmony of the Gospels*). From his painstaking study of the texts of the Gospels, Augustine concluded that each succeeding evangelist made use of the work of his predecessor or predecessors.

Clement's view that Mark was sequentially composed after Matthew and Luke would have meant for Augustine that Mark had made use of both Matthew and Luke. Indeed, Augustine's preferred view agrees with, though it may not strictly require, the conclusion that Mark knew both Matthew and Luke.

After mentioning his earlier view set forth in book 1, that Mark was second and had abbreviated Matthew, Augustine himself in book 4 turns to another view that he says is more probable:

> [I]n accordance with the more probable account of the matter he [Mark] holds a course in conjunction with both [Matthew and Luke]. For although he is at one with Matthew in the larger number of passages he is nevertheless at one rather with Luke in some others . . .[2]

When we consider this excerpt within its larger context and in relation to all other relevant passages in *The Harmony of the Gospels*, one can be led to the conclusion that it was Augustine's final opinion that "Mark is literarily dependent upon both Matthew and . . . Luke."[3]

Augustine supplements his literary analysis by recognizing the theological themes that characterize both Matthew and Luke. In the human face of Mark's Gospel, says Augustine, the reader discerns the figure who fulfills both the kingly office of Christ emphasized by Matthew and the priestly image of Christ emphasized by Luke. Although Augustine makes no direct reference to the Testimonium of Clement, his preferred view does not contradict that important piece of external evidence.

Literary Evidence

The internal evidence, considered as a whole, confirms that Mark used both Matthew and Luke.

First: The Two-Gospel Hypothesis does not require the critic to deny the existence of earlier sources used by the evangelists, written, oral, or both. In fact, advocates of the Two-Gospel Hypothesis fully recognize the importance of oral tradition in the development of the Jesus traditions utilized by the evangelists. Moreover, oral tradition continued alongside the compositional activity of the evangelists, no doubt exercising its influence upon each evangelist even as he was making use of the written compositions of his predecessors.

But the Two-Gospel Hypothesis makes it quite unnecessary to appeal to hypothetical documents like Q to explain close agreement among the Gospels. As Augustine saw, no one of the evangelists did his work in ignorance of that of his predecessor(s). Thus, according to the Two-Gospel Hypothesis, Matthew wrote first, making extensive use of existing sources (oral and written); Luke wrote second, making extensive use of Matthew and other source material (oral and written); Mark composed his Gospel making extensive use of both Matthew and Luke as well as a limited amount of other source material (oral and written). All three evangelists exercised their authorial freedom in different ways, and all three made distinctive contributions to their compositions.

Second: It was not until the eighteenth century that scholars in general began to note the internal evidence that Mark had artfully combined the texts of Matthew and Luke. By this time, Augustine's view in book 1 of his *Harmony of the Gospels*, that Mark was the epitomizer of Matthew, had mistakenly become fixed as the traditional view of the church. Because this version of the church's tradition conflicted with the newly discovered internal evidence that Mark had united Matthew and Luke, it soon appeared to represent a view of Mark that was very much out of date. As such, it only served to justify scholars under the influence of the Enlightenment in their low estimate of church tradition as a whole.

If the great Augustine could be mistaken, whom could you trust? This may explain in part why these eighteenth-century scholars appeared to have placed no weight on Clement's Testimonium. In any case, an increasing number of scholars became convinced that Mark, quite apart from the Clement Testimonium, had indeed combined his texts of Matthew and Luke. The evidence for this seems first to have been publicly pointed out by the Rev. Dr. Henry Owen, rector of St. Olave in Hart Street, London, and Fellow of the Royal Society.

In his book, *Observations on the Four Gospels; Tending Chiefly to Ascertain the Time of Their Publication; and to Illustrate the Form and Manner of Their Composition*, published in London in 1764, Owen wrote:

> In compiling this narrative (the Gospel of Mark), he had little more to do, it seems, than to abridge the Gospels which lay before him—varying some expressions, and inserting additions, as occasion required. That St. Mark followed this plan, no one can doubt, who compares his Gospel with those of the two former evangelists. He copies largely from both; and takes either the one or the other almost perpetually for his guide. The order indeed is his own, and is very close and well connected. In his account of facts he is also clear, exact, and critical; and the more so perhaps, as he wrote it for the perusal of a learned and critical people. For he seems to proceed with great caution, and to be solicitous that his Gospel should stand clear of all objections (51–52).

Later, Owen wrote:

> It is apparent that St. Mark makes quick and frequent transitions from one evangelist to the other; and blends their accounts, I mean their words, in such a manner as is utterly inexplicable upon any other footing, than by supposing he had both these Gospels before him (74).

This understanding of Mark was subsequently made famous by Johann Jacob Griesbach of Jena University, whose name became associated with this hypothesis. It was widely held by many competent New Testament critics, representing widely diverse approaches, including Friedrich Bleek and Friedrich Schleiermacher in Berlin, and F. C. Baur, Eduard Zeller, and David Friedrich Strauss in Tübingen. It was brought to its most critically defensible form in the highly esteemed work of W.M.L. De Wette of Basel.

Third: The first step in proposing any solution to the synoptic problem is to recognize the literary fact that Matthew, Mark, and Luke all agree significantly with one another to varying degrees in content and order of episodes. It is fundamental to any valid solution to the synoptic problem that the content and order of the three synoptic Gospels be perceived together. It cannot be emphasized too strongly that the fundamental fact of the synoptic problem is precisely this set of agreements and disagreements between Matthew, Mark, and Luke.

The Two-Gospel Theory explains the phenomena of the order of literary units in the synoptic Gospels as follows:

1. Matthew has organized the narrative framework of his Gospel in accordance with a fulfillment of prophecy motif from Isa. 9:1–2. First, those

sitting in darkness in Galilee proper are to see the great light of God's saving work. Then those across the Jordan shall see this light. After this fulfillment of prophecy, Jesus and his disciples will go to Jerusalem where he will be delivered up in accordance with a thrice-repeated prediction of his own passion and resurrection. Into this narrative framework the evangelist has introduced several lengthy discourses, most of which are homogeneous collections of Jesus tradition, like the Sermon on the Mount (Matt. 5—7) and the woes against the scribes and Pharisees (Matt. 23).

2. Luke has in general followed the basic narrative outline of Matthew's Gospel; first, a ministry in Galilee and then the passion narrative in Jerusalem. But Luke has considerably rearranged the narrative framework. All of the lengthy Matthean discourses are represented in Luke, and, except for one reversal, Luke's parallels to Matthew's discourses are all in the same relative sequence—a clear sign of a close compositional relationship between Luke and Matthew. Moreover, when Luke comes to one of Matthew's lengthy discourses, he generally takes only a few sayings, yet he always makes his selection from the opening sayings in Matthew's respective discourses. This is another clear sign of a close literary relationship between Matthew and Luke.[4]

In between the ministry in Galilee and the passion narrative, Luke includes a great central section of sayings material, much of it from other sources. However, Luke has also introduced into this central section many sayings taken from the Matthean discourses. Luke follows understandable literary procedures in his use of material taken from Matthew. In some instances after moving forward in Matthew to bring into his text a story or a saying of Jesus pertinent to his own composition, Luke will copy into his text the passage from Matthew immediately preceding the passage he has just copied. This is further evidence that Luke is compositionally dependent on the sequential arrangement of the Matthean narratives.

3. Mark, writing third, has a power, denied the other two, of controlling how the text of his Gospel will be related to the text of both his predecessors.

Matthew, writing first, had no control over how his Gospel was to be related to either Luke or Mark. Luke could control how his Gospel was to be related to Matthew, but not to Mark. Mark alone could control the relationship of his text to that of both the other synoptists. It is a distinct merit of the Two-Gospel Hypothesis that it can explain the unique synoptic phenomenon of order of episodes (Matthew and Luke almost never agree against Mark, or Mark almost always maintains the common order of Matthew and Luke) by appeal to authorial intent. The hypothesis does not resort to the less satisfactory argument of literary accident due to random chance (random chance is how, on the Two-Source Hypothesis, one must explain that, when Matthew departs from the order of episodes in Mark, Luke supports Mark's order, and vice versa).

Mark had before him two works about Jesus. Often they agreed on the sequence of episodes in Jesus' ministry. Often they disagreed. Seeking to produce a Gospel free of obvious contradictions with the Christian community's other great teaching instruments, Mark generally followed the common order of his sources. Where they disagree, he evenhandedly follows now the order of one and now the order of the other. Mark almost always supports the narrative order of at least one of his predecessors, and where possible, the order of both. The one major exception, the cleansing of the temple, is the exception that proves the rule. Mark places this episode after the first day Jesus was in Jerusalem; both Luke and Matthew place it during the first day.

4. The Q material is simply writings that Luke copied from Matthew but that Mark did not incorporate into his work. This partly explains why it is so difficult to identify the extent or purpose of Q. That Q could have produced an intelligible theology is explained by the fact that Luke selected from Matthew only material that was useful for his Gentile readers. This explains the appeal of Q to some modern theologians. It is generally free of Jewish *Tendenz*. But in omitting Matthean Jesus tradition that was particularly Jewish, Luke's selection becomes historically unrepresentative, and in important respects quite unbalanced. Any reconstruction of the so-called theology of the Q community will thus be correspondingly unrepresentative of the Jesus tradition and historically skewed.

This is a point of the greatest importance for contemporary theology. Q is more representative of Luke's version of the Jesus tradition than it is of Jesus himself.

5. The minor agreements of Matthew and Luke against Mark are to be explained as follows: (a) In composing his Gospel, Luke frequently copied the text of Matthew verbatim. (b) In composing his Gospel, Mark frequently copied the text of Matthew or Luke where Luke had copied Matthew closely. In these instances, Mark could be said to have followed the text to which Matthew and Luke bore concurrent testimony. In any case, whether by copying Matthew or Luke, Mark often copied into his work a text that was nearly identical in both his sources. Even if Mark compared the texts of both his sources at all times, he could hardly have succeeded in incorporating every instance of verbatim agreement between Matthew and Luke without becoming quite pedantic. It is clear that Mark was not that kind of author. Thus, where a small stylistic change can be made without affecting the sense of the text, Mark will frequently introduce it into his version of the Gospel. It is not likely that this was done consciously. In all probability, Mark simply preferred to use the historic present, and because its use did not alter the sense of the scripture, he was prepared to use the historic present even when both sources used a simple past tense. In this way, a "minor agreement between Matthew and Luke against Mark" would materialize. A so-called minor agreement in

omission would occur when Mark has added a word or phrase to a text from Matthew or Luke, or both, where Luke had copied Matthew closely.

Fourth: There is a correlation between agreement in order and agreement in wording among the synoptic Gospels that is most readily explained by the hypothesis that Mark was written after Matthew and Luke and that Mark utilized both Matthew and Luke.

If Mark were third, it would have been natural for him to have given some preference to the text of Matthew when he had deliberately chosen to follow Matthew's order instead of Luke's, and, conversely, it would have been natural for him to have given some preference to the text of Luke when he had chosen to follow Luke's order over that of Matthew. One would not expect Mark to follow such a procedure inflexibly. Indeed, he does not.

Fifth: In 1843, Eduard Zeller, a classicist, published the results of an important study of certain linguistic phenomena within the synoptic Gospels.[5] In the article, Zeller compiled lists of words and phrases shared by any two evangelists. He then refined these lists by limiting his attention to shared expressions that appeared in the text of one evangelist *only* in literary contexts parallel to another evangelist while those same expressions appeared in the text of that other evangelist *not only* in parallel literary contexts but also elsewhere in his Gospel.

Zeller reasoned that an evangelist who used an expression *only* in parallel literary contexts was most likely dependent upon that evangelist who used the same expression not only in parallel literary contexts but also elsewhere.

Neither Heinrich Holtzmann, the nineteenth-century German theologian who is credited with having established the Two-Source Hypothesis, nor his contemporary defender, C. M. Tuckett, recognizes the fine point in Zeller's method of argumentation represented by the words "only" and "not only" emphasized above. Therefore, their responses to Zeller are inadequate. To date, Zeller's position in favor of the Griesbach hypothesis stands as the most adequate linguistic argument for solving the synoptic problem. Zeller concluded that his results on balance support the view that Luke used Matthew, and Mark used both Matthew and Luke.

Sixth: Mark retells the story of the flesh and blood martyrdom of the Son of God in terms remarkably faithful to the common language and story line of Matthew and Luke. It was because Luke had made extensive use of Matthew that the possibility of this literary achievement existed for Mark.

Mark was a very creative and skillful author whose Gospel represents the popular, praise-evoking type of work featuring the story of Jesus that is familiar to readers of either Matthew or Luke, in terms that significantly cohere with both.[6]

Seventh: Luke and Matthew at many points differ in such a way that they appear to contradict each other. This is clear proof that they were not originally intended for the same church readers or audience. Or, at least it suggests that some readers for whom Luke was written did not accept the first as altogether suitable for use as a public teaching document.

Mark is both internally self-consistent and free from contradictions with Matthew and Luke at every point where they appear to contradict one another. This strongly suggests, if it does not require, that this Gospel was written *after* Matthew and Luke. How else can we explain this particular set of facts?

Despite differences and apparent contradictions between Matthew and Luke, Mark's narrative can be used to demonstrate that these two evangelists tell essentially the same story. Such a functional usefulness would suggest for Mark a theological purpose of witnessing to the true doctrine of the community for which the evangelist was writing. This community's partiality to the Pauline school is strongly suggested by the close parallels (especially in *theologia crucis*) between Paul and Mark.

That this community may have had a Roman provenance is consistent with the fact that it is the more peaceful Paul of Romans that has influenced Mark most of all, not the more confronting Paul of Galatians.

The Purpose of Mark
on the Two-Gospel Hypothesis

The unanimous consensus of early tradition locates the composition of the Gospel of Mark with the church in Rome. Further, it is associated with the oral proclamation of the apostle Peter in Rome. While this association is often questioned, it cannot be dismissed out of hand. This association is attested first by Papias in the early second century, then by Irenaeus in the mid-second century and later by Clement of Alexandria near the end of the second century. The manner in which this association between Peter and Mark is attested cannot be adequately explained by the hypothesis that the later testimonies of Irenaeus and Clement simply go back to the testimony of Papias. Some important connection between the preaching of Peter and the composition of the Gospel of Mark is clearly indicated by early church tradition. No scholarly consensus exists on what that connection was, however.

For us to understand Mark more fully, we must first observe the two Gospels on either side of it. The Gospel of Matthew represented the continuing vital interests of those who stood in the apostolic tradition of the Jerusalem apostles. Luke, in its own way, represented the vital interests of the Gentile-oriented churches founded by Paul. Mark, by blending these two traditions, made it possible for local churches to retain and cherish both Matthew and Luke and to do so within the context of a theological tradition which united the martyrological witness of both Peter and Paul.

In bringing this about, Mark underlined the need for more than one perspective on the tradition. In this "more-than-one-Gospel canon," no single written account of the church's Gospel was or ever will provide an adequate textual basis for Christian doctrine or practice. At the same time, the evangelist Mark, under the auspices of the Pauline gospel, unified within the collective consciousness of the church the diverse and sometimes diverging accounts of Matthew and Luke. "Whosoever loses his life for my sake *and for the sake of the Gospel* will save it" (Mark 8:35). Only Mark adds "and for the sake of the Gospel."

This fourfold Gospel canon, especially under Mark's influence, served to steel Christians under persecution and unite them in their apostolic *martyria* to leave all for the sake of Christ and for the sake of the Gospel. "Truly, I say to you, there is no one who has left house or brothers or sisters or mother or father or children or lands, for my sake *and for the sake of the Gospel*, who will not receive a hundredfold now in this time, houses and brothers and sisters and mothers and children and lands, with persecutions, and in the age to come eternal life" (Mark 10:29–30, RSV). Only Mark adds, "and for the sake of the Gospel."

Outside of Mark in the New Testament, only the apostle Paul uses "Gospel" absolutely in this same way. It is striking evidence of Mark's close relationship to Paul that he begins his Gospel with the dramatic statement, "Beginning of the Gospel of Jesus Christ." Thus, Mark is the first evangelist to identify his written text with "the Gospel." It would have been Mark's Gospel, perceived as a written account of "the Gospel of Jesus Christ," that first would have been seen as, "The Gospel according to [a particular author]." From this viewpoint, the fourfold Gospel canon can be seen as a second-century construction made under the ongoing influence of Paul, where these four narrative texts were each perceived as separate but authentic written expressions of the one true Gospel for which Christians were to leave all (Mark 10:29–30), and, if necessary, suffer persecution and even death (Mark 8:35). Once one recognizes the preeminent importance the church gave to this Pauline construction and sees how, through these uniform ascriptions, this theological construction gives shape and impetus to the collective influence of the fourfold Gospel canon, then it becomes possible under the Two-Gospel Hypothesis to see that Mark not only unites Matthew and Luke, but also unifies the narrative corpus of the Gospels with the Pauline theology of the cross. Moreover, by making a Pauline Gospel available to those who composed the fourfold canon, Mark has pioneered the way for the church to prevail against Marcion and the Gnostics in its determination to hold the Pauline epistles together with the fourfold Gospel canon, and thus Paul with the Twelve. Mark's Gospel helped provide the church with some essential unifying principles for its canon.

CHAPTER 3

The Two-Gospel Hypothesis Illustrated by Texts

The Preface of the Gospel according to Luke

[1]Inasmuch as many have undertaken to compile a narrative of the things which have been accomplished among us,
[2]just as they were delivered to us by those who from the beginning were eyewitnesses and ministers of the word,
[3]it seemed good to me also, having followed all things closely for some time past, to write an orderly account for you, most excellent Theophilus,
[4]that you may know the truth concerning the things of which you have been informed. —*Luke 1:1–4 (RSV)*

This famous opening sentence to the Gospel according to Luke comprehensively yet concisely states the purpose of the evangelist in writing his orderly account of the things accomplished among the members of the community to which the author and Theophilus belonged. This new narrative will faithfully record the events just as they have been handed down by eyewitnesses and ministers of the word. And all this has as its purpose the enabling of Theophilus to know the truth concerning matters on which he is already informed.

It is not stated how Theophilus had been previously informed about these matters. But the presumption is that at least some of his information may have come from a narrative (or possibly more than one narrative) that had been circulating in the community of which Theophilus and the evangelist were members.

In any case, this preface clearly implies that the author of Luke knew at least one narrative, which was possibly known to Theophilus as well. Is there any way to identify what that narrative may have been? According to the Two-Gospel Hypothesis, the most important narrative available to Luke was a book otherwise known as the Gospel of Matthew.[1] What evidence supports the view that Luke not only knew of such a narrative, but also made specific use of it? What evidence exists that Luke made direct use of Matthew?

Evidence for a Direct Literary Relationship between Matthew and Luke

²ᵇThe word of God came to John the son of Zechariah <u>in the wilderness</u>;
³and he went into all the region about <u>the Jordan, preaching</u> a baptism of repentance for the forgiveness of sins.
⁴As <u>it is written</u> in the book of the words of <u>Isaiah the prophet,</u>
    "<u>The voice of one crying out in the wilderness:</u>
    <u>Prepare ye the way of the Lord,</u>
    <u>make his paths straight.</u>
    ⁵Every valley shall be filled,
    and every mountain and hill shall be brought low,
    and the crooked shall be made straight,
    and the rough ways shall be made smooth;
    ⁶and all flesh shall see the salvation of God."
⁷He said therefore to the multitudes that came out to be baptized <u>by him</u>, "<u>You brood of vipers! Who warned you to flee from the wrath to come?</u>
⁸<u>Bear fruits that befit repentance, and do not begin to say to yourselves, 'We have Abraham as our father'; for I tell you, God is able from these stones to raise up children to Abraham.</u>
⁹Even <u>now the axe is laid to the root of the trees; every tree therefore that does not bear good fruit is cut down and thrown into the fire.</u>"   —*Luke 3:2b–9* (RSV)

Assuming the validity of the Two-Gospel Hypothesis, the underlined words in this portion of Luke's Gospel indicate the extent to which the evangelist has copied the text of the Gospel of Matthew. Each underlined word stands for a Greek word in the text of the Gospel of Luke that is exactly the same as the Greek text in the Gospel of Matthew. Where the underlining extends through the space between the words, the same Greek words are also in the same word order in both Gospels. At one point the exact agreement in grammar and word order extends through twenty-four consecutive words in the Greek texts of these two Gospels. This is evidence of copying.

To further illustrate the extensive evidence suggesting that the evangelist Luke may have copied the Gospel of Matthew, we may consider the story of Jesus' healing of the centurion's servant.

¹And after he had ended all his sayings in the hearing of the people <u>he entered Capernaum.</u>
²Now a centurion had a servant who was dear to him, who was sick and at the point of death.
³When he heard of Jesus, he sent to him elders of the Jews, asking him <u>to come</u> and heal his servant.
⁴And when they came to Jesus, they besought him earnestly, saying, "He is worthy to have you do this for him,
⁵for he loves our nation, and he built us our synagogue."

⁶And Jesus went with them. When he was not far from the house, the centurion sent friends to him, saying to him, "Lord, do not trouble yourself, for I am not worthy to have you come under my roof;
⁷therefore I did not presume to come to you. But say the word, and let my servant be healed
⁸For I am a man set under authority, with soldiers under me: and I say to one, 'Go,' and he goes; and to another, 'Come,' and he comes; and to my servant, 'Do this,' and he does it."
⁹When Jesus heard this he marveled at him, and turned and said to the multitude that followed him, "I tell you, not even in Israel have I found such faith."
¹⁰And when those who had been sent returned to the house, they found the servant well. —*Luke 7:1–10*

Underlined words are exactly the same in the parallel Greek text of Matt. 8:5–13. Dotted underlining indicates the same word, but in a different grammatical form. In Luke 7:8, the verbatim agreement in the Greek, including agreement in word order, extends through twenty-five consecutive words. This is further evidence of copying.

To clarify why adherents of the Two-Gospel Hypothesis find no reason to doubt that Luke had the opportunity to copy the Gospel of Matthew, we will give a third example.

¹⁸The disciples of John told him all of these things.
¹⁹And John, calling to him two of his disciples, sent them to the Lord, saying "Are you he who is to come, or shall we look for another?"
²⁰ And when the men had come to him, they said, "John the Baptist has sent us to you, saying, 'Are you he who is to come, or shall we look for another?' "
²¹In that hour he cured many of diseases and plagues and evil spirits, and on many that were blind he bestowed sight.
²²And he answered them, "Go and tell John what you have seen and heard: the blind receive their sight, the lame walk, lepers are cleansed, and the deaf hear, the dead are raised up, the poor have good news preached to them.
²³And blessed is he who takes no offense at me."
²⁴When the messengers of John had gone, he began to speak to the crowds concerning John: "What did you go out into the wilderness to behold? A reed shaken by the wind?
²⁵What then did you go out to see? A man clothed in soft clothing? Behold, those who are gorgeously appareled and live in luxury are in kings' courts.
²⁶What then did you go out to see? A prophet? Yes, I tell you, and more than a prophet.
²⁷This is he of whom it is written,
> 'Behold, I send my messenger
>> before thy face,
> who shall prepare thy way
>> before thee.'

[28]I tell you, among those born of women none is greater than John; yet he who is least in the kingdom of God is greater than he."
[29](When they heard this all the people and the tax collectors justified God, having been baptized with the baptism of John;
[30]but the Pharisees and the lawyers rejected the purpose of God for themselves, not having been baptized by him.)
[31]"To what then shall I compare the men of this generation and what are they like?
[32]They are like children sitting in the market place and calling to one another,

> 'We piped to you, and you did not dance;
> we wailed, and you did not weep.'

[33]For John the Baptist has come eating no bread and drinking no wine; and you say, 'He has a demon.'
[34]The Son of man has come eating and drinking; and you say, 'Behold, a glutton and a drunkard, a friend of tax collectors and sinners!'
[35]Yet wisdom is justified by all her children."   —*Luke 7:18–35 (RSV)*

Of 264 words in the Greek text of the parallel passage in Matt. 11:2–19, fully 168 are verbatim in Luke 7:18–35. Sixty-three percent of this extended text of Matthew is verbatim in Luke. The material is also in exactly the same order. This is compelling evidence for copying.

In answering the question "What is the Two-Gospel Hypothesis?" the first point is that, according to this hypothesis, extensive evidence of copying suggests *a direct literary relationship between Matthew and Luke.*[2]

A Major Difficulty for the Theory of Q

Based on the Two-Source Hypothesis, one can argue that Luke has copied most of this material from Q. But this explanation has difficulties. First, this is a narrative passage beginning with the situation where John the Baptist, hearing in prison about Jesus, sends his disciples to find out whether he is the one who is coming, or whether they should look for another. In good narrative fashion, Luke had John's disciples go to Jesus and ask the question. Luke further expands Matthew's narrative by adding that in that hour Jesus healed many persons of their illnesses. This sets up the response of Jesus, who instructs John's disciples to go tell John what they saw and heard. Then after the disciples of John leave, Jesus addresses the crowds about John. Is this not a narrative? This is certainly something different from what one would expect from a collection of the sayings of Jesus like *Thomas*, which is the type of document that Q is said to be by those who believe that it once existed. *Thomas* is an actual noncanonical document. It exists. It is made up of sayings of Jesus, as is Q. But Q does not exist. The content and arrangement of the sayings in each is very different. This argues against the Q hypothesis. For if Q ever existed we would expect some evidence for this in the content and arrangement of the sayings in *Thomas*. The Q hypothesis fails this test.

As we have seen, the story of the healing of the centurion's servant is also narrative in style and does not fit the literary category to which Q is said to belong (see chap. 12). Similarly, the first example about the Baptist's preaching in the wilderness is in narrative form. One wonders how adherents of the Q hypothesis can expect readers to accept their hypothesis in the face of this kind of literary agreement between Luke and Matthew in narrative passages where dependence on Mark cannot explain the data.

In answering the question "What is the Two-Gospel Hypothesis?" the second point to note is that its adherents think that *the theory of Q is not only unnecessary, it is also intrinsically implausible.*[3]

Mark Is Capable of Combining His Sources

In this last passage (Luke 7:18–35), the only verse in Luke also found in Mark is Luke 7:27. This verse is a unique conflation of Mal. 3:1 and Ex. 23:20. Because this unique combination of these two Old Testament passages is found in three synoptic Gospels, it is instructive to compare them carefully and in detail.

Behold, I will send my messenger before your face,
     who shall prepare your way before you.   *—Matt. 11:10*

Behold, [I] will send my messenger before your face,
     who shall prepare your way before you.   *—Luke 7:27*

Behold, [I] will send my messenger before your face,
     who shall prepare your way.   *—Mark 1:2*

This unique conflation of the texts of Mal. 3:1 and Ex. 23:20 is exactly the same in all three Gospels with two exceptions. First, there is no pronoun in the Greek text of Luke and Mark standing behind the English pronoun "I" in the above translation, while there is in Matthew. This pronoun is unnecessary in Greek, since the ending of the Greek verb *apostello* ("I will send") informs the reader that the subject is the first person singular. The English pronoun "I" has been placed in brackets in Luke and Mark to indicate this difference between their texts in Greek and the Greek text of Matthew. The second exception is the absence of the phrase "before you" in the text of Mark. If Matthew and Luke have independently copied Mark, how can one account for the presence of the phrase "before you" in both Matthew and Luke because this phrase is not present in the text of Mark? This is one of the famous agreements of Matthew and Luke against Mark. It clearly stands in the way of accepting the view that Matthew and Luke had independently copied Mark.

Based on the Two-Source Hypothesis, one might first think that Matthew and Luke have independently copied Mark, despite the difficulty of this agreement against Mark. But this agreement against Mark is not the only difficulty. It seems unlikely, even without this difficulty, that Matthew and Luke, *independently*, would *both* take this verse from the beginning of Mark's Gospel and independently place it into a text from their respective copies of Q where it fit perfectly like the missing piece of a jigsaw puzzle.

It would seem less implausible to argue that these words were already in the text of Q and that Mark and Q overlap at this point. But even this explanation will hardly work because of the unusual character of this verse. How could we explain that the unique blending of Mal. 3:1 and Ex. 23:20 present in Q has been so closely preserved in Mark? This close agreement is better explained by a theory that permits a direct literary relationship among these three Gospels.

Assuming the validity of the Two-Source Hypothesis, no satisfactory evidence explains how Mark's text could be so close to the nearly identical texts of Matt. 11:10 and Luke 7:27 without positing that the evangelist Mark himself has gone to his copy of the Q source and abstracted this particular conflated text of Malachi and Exodus and joined it to a citation from Isa. 40:3 in another story concerning John the Baptist. It follows that *Mark, based on the Two-Source Hypothesis, is definitely capable of combining material from different sources.*

It is not unreasonable to think that in composing a text about John the Baptist where he follows a tradition that identifies John in relation to a text from Isaiah, Mark—if he knew a Q source where John is again identified in relation to Old Testament prophecy—would have decided to bring this second citation of scripture together with the text from Isaiah. In so-called Q the source of this conflated text is identified simply as coming from scripture without specifying its author. Because most Christian prophecies are attributed to Isaiah, Mark can be forgiven for including this unidentified prophecy from the same prophet Isaiah. This is the best way to explain the mistake Mark has made in attributing this citation from Malachi-Exodus to the prophet Isaiah.

In answering the question "What is the Two-Gospel Hypothesis?" the third point to note is that adherents of this hypothesis have no difficulty in accepting evidence that *Mark is capable of combining his sources.* In fact, they are prepared to regard this point as crucial for understanding the synoptic problem.[4]

The Critical Advantage
of the Two-Gospel Hypothesis

Based on the Two-Gospel Hypothesis, the explanation of the passages being discussed is as follows: Luke copied Matt. 11:2–19 on the whole rather closely, expanding his account a bit in Luke 7:18–21, and following Matthew more loosely in Luke 7:29–32. Luke 7:18–35 is a version of Matt. 11:2–19, in which Luke copied the unique Matthean conflated version of Malachi and Exodus exactly as he found it, except for the omission of the unnecessary first person singular pronoun. Because Mark's version of this unique form of the Malachi-Exodus text also omits the redundant pronoun, it is clear that Mark in this instance has followed Luke rather than Matthew.

Note that, based on the Two-Gospel Hypothesis, Mark has made a compositional decision very similar to the one he is generally presumed to have made under the Two-Source Hypothesis. He has taken this Malachi-Exodus citation used by Jesus to identify John in Luke 7:18–35 and joined it with a citation of Isaiah 40:3 in Matt. 3:36 | | Luke 3:46, which also helps the reader to identify John. Based on either of these hypotheses, the evangelist *Mark shows himself to be a resourceful author who is capable of bringing together related material from different texts.*

But in this instance, as in many others, the Two-Gospel Hypothesis enjoys the critical advantage of explaining these closely related texts of Matthew, Mark, and Luke without dependence on any hypothetical source. The Two-Source Theory in this instance is in deep trouble. Without conjecturing a dubious and in any case unsatisfactory overlap between Mark and Q, or Mark's use of the hypothetical Q source, the advocate of this hypothesis would be unable to explain the presence in Mark's text of the same unique conflated version of Mal. 3:1 and Ex. 23:20. The Two-*Source* Hypothesis must have a hypothetical Q to explain the data in this case, whereas the Two-*Gospel* Hypothesis can explain the data without appeal to a hypothetical source.

In answering the question "What is the Two-Gospel Hypothesis?" the fourth point to note is that this hypothesis *offers the best solution for evidence that Mark has combined his sources.*

Luke Is Secondary to Matthew

We have given three examples of narrative passages where, based on the Two-Gospel Hypothesis, a direct literary relationship between Matthew and Luke is quite clear. Let us return briefly to the matter of consecutive verbatim agreement, including agreement in word order. In summary, we can say that we find consecutive agreement extending to twenty-four words not only in Luke 3:8–9, but also in 9:58; 11:10; and 11:34. In Luke 7:8 and 12:46 it extends to twenty-five consecutive words. In Luke 16:13 it extends to twenty-six consecutive words. And in Luke 10:21–22 it totals twenty-seven consecutive words. We find evidence for copying in chapters 3, 7, 9, 10, 11, 12, and 16. If we add these examples, which are most simply explained as direct copying between Matthew and Luke, to the three narrative passages already discussed, the case for a direct literary relationship between Luke and Matthew is difficult to refute.[5] Nothing suggests that Matthew has copied Luke. Luke's preface, if it implies anything, suggests that the literary relationship was the other way around, that Luke copied Matthew. Do we have any compelling evidence that Luke is secondary to Matthew? Yes, this evidence exists in abundance.

The highest degree of verbatim agreement between Matthew and Luke in grammar and word order generally occurs with sayings material. In Luke 3:8 it is a saying of John the Baptist. In Luke 7:8 it is a saying of the centurion. In most cases it is a saying of Jesus. Luke, however, does not hesitate to alter radically a saying of Jesus if he finds its original Jewish context problematic or unintelligible to his Gentile readers. This practice of altering the sayings of Jesus to make them more intelligible to Gentile readers gives us a clue to the direction of dependence between Matthew and Luke. Here is an example:

[2] "The scribes and Pharisees sit on Moses' seat;
[3] so practice and observe whatever they tell you, but do not what they do; for they preach, but do not practice.
[4] They bind heavy burdens, hard to bear, and lay them on men's shoulders; but they themselves will not move them with their finger.
[5] They do all their deeds to be seen by men; for they make their phylacteries broad and their fringes long,
[6] and they love the place of honor at feasts and the best seats in the synagogues,
[7] and salutations in the market places, and being called rabbi by men."

—*Matt. 23:2–7 (RSV)*

[46] "Beware of the scribes, who like to go about in long robes, and love salutations in the market places and the best seats in the synagogues and the places of honor at feasts,
[47] who devour widows' houses and for a pretense make long prayers. They will receive the greater condemnation."   —*Luke 20:46–47 (RSV)*

All scholars agree that Matthew has preserved the more original form of this teaching about those who love recognition and places of honor. Although the verbatim agreement is not as extensive as elsewhere, the underlined words in Luke 20:46 are sufficient to indicate some measure of literary dependence. Dotted underlining indicates use of the same root, but a different grammatical form.

Luke's readers could not be expected to know very much about Pharisees who "make their phylacteries broad," a religious practice followed only by those who lived in strict accordance with Ex. 13:9 and Deut. 6:8. These passages led pious Jews in Jesus' day to wear tiny rolled-up texts of the Law on their person. These diminutive rolled-up scrolls were inserted into small leather capsules that were bound by leather bands around the head and on the arm to signify that persons wearing these phylacteries (as the capsules were called) pondered on the Law and kept it. To make these phylacteries (or the bands binding them to the body) broad had the effect of drawing attention to one's observance. Jesus disapproved of such ostentatious religious practices. Making the "fringes" on the prayer shawl long was a similar practice of which Jesus expressed disapproval.

These Jewish practices were not sufficiently well known outside Palestine for Luke to make a possibly confusing reference to them. This presumably would have happened had he followed Matthew's text closely. Instead, Luke made use of a well-understood example (out of the everyday life of his readers) of ostentatious dress, namely, the wearing of long stoles by scribes in the law courts. Luke then substituted this Gentile practice for the Jewish practice that Jesus had mentioned. Some of the irony of religious ostentatiousness is lost in Luke's more secular version of Jesus' teaching. This teaching against ostentatious dress is applied in a much wider social context, and Luke's text goes on to include other offenses not included in Matthew's text.

In answering the question "What is the Two-Gospel Hypothesis?" the fifth point is that adherents of this hypothesis recognize extensive evidence that *Luke is secondary to Matthew* (and probably has copied Matthew).

The Secondary Character of Mark

Assuming the validity of the Two-Gospel Hypothesis, Mark had access to both Matthew and Luke. In the case of the scribes who loved salutations in the marketplaces, Mark preserved the less Jewish version of Luke, including the additional offenses mentioned by Luke. He preserved Luke's account presumably because it was more understandable to his Gentile readers.

> Watch out <u>for the scribes, who want to go about in long robes and</u> (who want) <u>salutations in the market places and the best seats in the synagogues and the</u> <u>places of honor at feasts,</u> who devour <u>widows' houses and for a pretense make</u> <u>long prayers. They will receive the greater condemnation.</u>   —*Mark 12:38–40*

Verbatim agreement between Mark and Luke is indicated by underlining. Luke's text had been accommodated for western Gentile readers not well acquainted with Jewish religious and cultural practices. Luke's text in this case was apparently well enough suited for Mark's intended readers that he could copy it almost word for word.

It may be asked, "Were Mark's readers that unacquainted with Jewish customs?" The answer is, "It appears that they were." In any case, independent evidence exists that Mark's intended readers were unacquainted with the religious practices of Pharisees. We have a well-known case in Mark's text where we are offered an extended explanation of certain Jewish customs. This explanation is not found in the parallel passage in Matthew.

> [1] Then Pharisees and scribes came to Jesus from Jerusalem and said,
> [2] "Why do your disciples transgress the tradition of the elders? For they do not wash their hands when they eat."   —*Matt. 15:1–2 (RSV)*

> [1] Now when the Pharisees gathered together to him, with some of the scribes, who had come from Jerusalem,
> [2] they saw that some of his disciples ate with hands defiled, that is, unwashed.
> [3] [For the Pharisees, and all the Jews, do not eat unless they wash their hands, observing the tradition of the elders;
> [4] and when they come from the market place, they do not eat unless they purify themselves; and there are many other traditions which they observe, the washing of cups and pots and vessels of bronze.]   —*Mark 7:1–4 (RSV)*

The bracketed words in Mark's text are regarded as a later explanatory addition by some scholars who believe Mark to be the earliest Gospel. But no textual evidence supports this conjecture. Based on the view that Mark is secondary to Matthew, these sentences could conceivably have been copied first in the margin of a copy of the Gospel of Matthew that Mark was using. Such an explanatory gloss (or addition) would serve as a comment on the text of Matthew, to make it more understandable for Gentile readers of Matthew who needed such clarifying information. It would be natural for a copy of Matthew circulating as far west as Italy to be glossed in this way. Theoretically, Mark could have seen the advantage of copying such an explanatory gloss into the text of his Gospel for the benefit of his intended readers.

This is one possible explanation of how this gloss could have come into the Markan text. It could have happened in any number of other ways. It is even possible that the evangelist Mark could himself have added these explanatory words. In any case, all copies of Mark have these words of explanation, and all scholars agree that they represent a later and more developed form of the Gospel tradition. This kind of expansion, not present in Matthew, is easily explained if Mark wrote after Matthew.

Weighing against the explanation of some Markan-priority advocates that this gloss was a later addition is the fact that this is the way Mark reads in *all* Greek texts that have survived the ravages of time, as well as in all later versions of Mark in Latin, Syriac, Armenian, and Coptic, among others. The presence of this explanatory addition in all known texts of Mark constitutes a serious problem for those who think of Mark as the earliest Gospel. Why would the evangelist Matthew omit such helpful information? We know that elsewhere in his Gospel, Matthew explained the meaning of Jewish terms that his readers needed to have interpreted. For example, in Matt. 1:23, the evangelist explains that the Hebrew word "Emmanuel" means "God with us," and again in Matt. 27:33, he explains that the place called "Golgotha" means "the place of a skull."

All of the passages are most easily explained based on a hypothesis that the Gospels were composed in the sequence: Matthew, Luke, Mark. We should be quick to note, however, that not all the textual evidence in the Gospels fits so exclusively this one hypothesis. Some passage can be explained equally well based on other hypotheses. But the adherents of the Two-Gospel Hypothesis find a comprehensive network of evidence to support their view, which is stronger than any corresponding network for alternate hypotheses. This is partly because, while some passages can be equally well explained under other hypotheses, no passages are known to exist that cannot be equally well explained based on the Two-Gospel Hypothesis. It is important to emphasize that many passages like those cited thus far cannot be explained equally well under the Two-Source Hypothesis. E. P. Sanders has identified thirty-eight passages spread throughout fourteen chapters of Mark where he has found scholars who hold to Markan priority who have nonetheless come to see that the text of Mark is secondary to that of Matthew or Luke, or both, in at least one or more places.[6]

In answering the question "What is the Two-Gospel Hypothesis?" the sixth point is that according to this hypothesis, *Mark clearly has a secondary character*.[7]

Early Jesus Tradition

Once Matthew, Mark, and Luke are read and studied as documents that have been composed in that sequence, no other written sources are needed to explain *their* agreements and disagreements. Whether Matthew and Luke made use of earlier non-Q collections of sayings of Jesus is a separable question. Most adherents of the Two-Gospel Hypothesis would accept the evidence that they did. But this evidence does not require a hypothetical Q source or any other hypothetical source to explain the extensive amount of agreement and disagreement in closely parallel texts in Matthew and Luke but absent from Mark. It is important to emphasize that it is precisely these written texts and no others that Professor Robinson and his associates are studying in their attempt to reconstruct the Q source. If the evangelist Luke had access to the Gospel of Matthew, his copying and modifying the text of

Matthew is the best way to account for the presence in his Gospel of all of the Lukan material that is closely parallel to Matthew.

It is important to note that this does not include all of the loose parallels like the parable of the lost sheep. The verbatim agreement in some of the parallel material in Matthew and Luke is so slight that it is sometimes reasonable to think that Luke has copied some source other than Matthew, especially when the Lukan form is more original.

Adherents of Q sometimes cite this recognition by Two-Gospel Hypothesis adherents of earlier source material in Luke as an implicit admission of Q's existence. But this would be the case only where Q is used to mean the equivalent of "early Jesus tradition." That is not the classical meaning of Q, nor is that the meaning of Q as understood by the International Q Project. The text of Q being reconstructed by these scholars is a hypothetical source written in Greek. If we had it in our hands, this text would help us understand the agreements and disagreements in the Greek texts of Matthew and Luke where Mark contains no parallel text.

Passages like the parable of the lost sheep are not well explained based on the Q hypothesis because the verbal agreements and disagreements do not indicate that these two versions have been copied from the same source. The evidence suggests rather that these forms have no common literary history and go back to two independent forms of the same parable. In these instances, sometimes Matthew and sometimes Luke may preserve a form of the tradition more original than the other. Some scholars hold that the Lukan form of the parable of the lost sheep is more original than Matthew's.

In answer to the question "What is the Two-Gospel Hypothesis?" the seventh point to note is that according to this hypothesis, *full room must be allowed for early Jesus traditions, both oral and written, but there is no need for Q.*

Why Call This Theory the Two-Gospel Hypothesis?

What should we call the hypothesis that posits that the compositional sequence of the Gospels was Matthew, Luke, and Mark? There are two reasons for naming this view the Two-Gospel Hypothesis. First, this title is designed to contrast the Two-*Gospel* Hypothesis in relation to the Two-*Source* Hypothesis, which requires its adherents to defend the existence of a hypothetical Q source and in some cases a hypothetical Ur-Markus as well. Any minister who asks from the pulpit for a congregation to look in their pew Bibles to read a text from Q will be in difficulty. Q adherents recognize this difficulty, and some are working diligently to reconstruct a Q text that can then be translated for use in the pews. The Q seminar aims to reproduce this hypothetical document. But even if made available for use in churches, Q will not be a part of the Bible. It will be something off to the side.

The Two-Gospel Hypothesis replaces Mark (or Proto- or Deutero-Mark) and a nonexistent Q source with two well-known Gospels of the church, Matthew and Luke. It is worth repeating that the Two-Gospel Hypothesis can explain all of the close agreements and disagreements in parallel passages in the Gospels without positing the existence of any hypothetical documents that may never have existed.

A second reason for the choice of the name "Two-Gospel Hypothesis" is that through the early church historian Eusebius we learn that Clement of Alexandria, a well-traveled second-century scholar, reported an early tradition in which the Gospels with genealogies (Matthew and Luke) were composed before the Gospels without genealogies (Mark, John, and such apocryphal works as the *Gospel of Peter* and *Thomas*). In this sense, advocates of the Two-Gospel Hypothesis want to call attention to the testimony from Clement that Matthew and Luke were written before Mark and all other Gospels without genealogies.[8]

The Two-*Source* Hypothesis has been the reigning hypothesis for more than one hundred years. Its name simply refers to the fact that at the beginning of the Gospel-making process, the main sources were the Gospel of Mark and the hypothetical Q. By contrast, the name of the Two-*Gospel* Hypothesis refers to the fact that, at the earliest stage of Gospel composing, the main sources were the two Gospels of Matthew and Luke. Whichever hypothesis one adopts, behind the Gospels and earlier than all of them there was the Jesus tradition. It is generally agreed that this tradition, beginning with Jesus and his disciples, was handed on to the evangelists in various forms, both oral and written. There is disagreement, however, over whether there was a Q source that embodies most of the sayings of Jesus found in Matthew and Luke but not in Mark.

Summary Statement

In summary, it can be said in answer to the question, "What is the Two-Gospel Hypothesis?" that adherents of this hypothesis recognize (1) that a direct and extensive literary relationship between Matthew and Luke exists; (2) that the theory of Q (to explain this relationship) is not only unnecessary but intrinsically implausible; (3) that Mark is capable of combining his sources; (4) that the Two-Gospel Hypothesis offers the best explanation for the evidence that Mark has combined his sources; (5) that Luke is secondary to Matthew (and probably has copied Matthew); (6) that Mark has a secondary character; (7) that full room should be allowed for early Jesus traditions, both oral and written, but that there is no need for Q. And in answer to the question "Why call this theory the Two-Gospel Hypothesis?" this seems to be the best way to focus attention on the contention that the two Gospels Matthew and Luke (rather than Mark and Q) are the two earliest Gospels of the church. This hypothesis calls for replacing Mark and Q with the two Gospels Matthew and Luke as the earliest and most reliable sources for understanding Christian origins.

What Difference Does It Make?

The reader is entitled to ask: What difference does it make which hypothesis one adopts? Part 3 of this book is devoted to the illustration as well as the documentation of the difference it does make under six headings: The Lord's Prayer; The Lord's Supper; Justification by Faith; The Faithful Witness of Women; God's Special Commitment to the Poor; and the Keys of the Kingdom.

These examples are by no means exhaustive. But each is well documented, and together they make a compelling case for the conclusion that it makes a great deal of difference to those who take the scriptures seriously, whether one continues to invest one's confidence in the Two-Source Hypothesis and turns a deaf ear to new developments in Gospel studies, or whether one takes an interest in the discussion to follow and decides to join with others in asking questions.

PART 3

What Difference Does It Make
for Worship, Theology, and Ethics?

CHAPTER 4

The Lord's Prayer

The Lord's Prayer in Matthew

> Our Father who art in heaven,
> Hallowed be thy name.
> Thy kingdom come,
> Thy will be done,
> On earth as it is in heaven.
> Give us this day our daily bread;
> And forgive us our debts,
> As we also have forgiven our debtors;
> And lead us not into temptation,
> But deliver us from evil.
> [For thine is the kingdom
> And the power
> And the glory
> Forever. Amen.]
> —*Matt. 6:9–13*

The scriptural heart and theological framework of this prayer is found in the prophetic oracles of Isaiah. For example, in the oracle preserved in chapter 64, the prophet, afflicted by remorse for the sins of God's people, looks up to heaven and cries out:

> [1]Oh that thou wouldst rend the heavens and come down,
>   that the mountains might quake at thy presence. . . .
> [5]Thou meetest him that joyfully works righteousness,
>   those that remember thee in thy ways.
> Behold, thou wast angry, and we sinned;
>   in our sins we have been a long time,
>   and shall we be saved?
> [6]We have all become like one who is unclean,
>   and all our righteous deeds are like filthy rags.
> We all fade like a leaf,
>   and our iniquities, like the wind, take us away. . . .
> [7]Thou hast hid thy face from us,
>   and hast delivered us into the hands of our iniquities.

[8]Yet, O Lord, thou art our Father;
    we are the clay, and thou art our potter;
    we are all the work of thy hand.
[9]Be not exceedingly angry, O Lord,
    and remember not our iniquity for ever.
                   —Isa. 64:1–9a

In another oracle, the prophet, distraught over his rejection by Israel and over Israel's rejection of God's righteous remnant for whom the prophet speaks, looks up and cries out to God:

[15]Look down from heaven and see,
    from thy holy and glorious habitation.
Where are thy zeal and thy might?
    The yearning of thy heart and thy compassion
      are withheld from me.
[16]For thou art our Father,
    though Abraham does not know us
    and Israel does not acknowledge us;
thou, O Lord, art our Father,
    our Redeemer from of old
      is thy name.
                —Isa. 63:15–16 (RSV)

When did Jesus first learn to pray "our Father, who art in heaven . . ."? When, but at his mother's knee? Or at table when Joseph offered up thanks to God? In any case, Jesus, nourished on the scriptures, addressed God as "our Father, who art in heaven . . ." And it was in keeping with the scriptures for him to teach his disciples to address God in this way. The beginning of the Lord's Prayer, as it is preserved in the Gospel of Matthew, fits the life situation of Jesus as recorded in all the Gospels. Jesus was a Jew who read and heard others read the Law and the Prophets, including the book of the prophet Isaiah.

The form of the Lord's Prayer that has been passed down in the church until today is, with some variation, the form of the Lord's Prayer that is preserved in the Sermon on the Mount in the Gospel of Matthew. And except for the use of the word "debts" for "trespasses," the wording of the Lord's Prayer in Matthew, as translated above, is the wording most familiar to the greatest number of English-speaking Christians in all parts of the world.

In an early (100–400 C.E.) collection of Christian teachings called the *Teaching of the Twelve Apostles*, referred to by scholars as the *Didache*, which means "teaching" in Greek, readers are instructed to pray as follows:

Our Father who art in heaven,
Hallowed be thy name.
Thy kingdom come,

Thy will be done,
On earth as it is in heaven.
Give us this day our daily bread
And forgive us our debt,
As we also forgive our debtors.
And lead us not into temptation,
But deliver us from evil.
For thine is the power
And the glory
Forever.

Scholars generally agree that when the author of the *Didache* (hereafter referred to as the *Teaching*) prefaces this prayer with the instruction to pray as the Lord commanded "in his Gospel," he has in mind the Gospel of Matthew. The evidence for this rests largely on the very close verbatim agreement between the Greek text of this prayer in the Gospel of Matthew and that in the *Teaching*.

The differences between the two texts are relatively minor. The first difference is completely obscured in translation. In the opening line of the prayer in Matthew, the Greek word translated "heaven" is in the plural and could literally have been translated "heavens." In the Jewish scriptures, God dwells not in "heaven," but in the "heavens." Later in the prayer, both texts read "on earth as it is in heaven" (singular). The second difference is between Matthew's plural "debts" and the *Teaching*'s singular "debt." The third difference is between "as we have forgiven," in Matthew and "as we forgive" in the *Teaching*. And finally in the doxology at the end of the prayer, Matthew reads "thine is the *kingdom*, the power and the glory," and the *Teaching* has only "thine is the power and the glory." Otherwise, the two versions are identical.

Assuming the validity of the Two-Gospel Hypothesis, the simplest way to explain the very close agreement between Matthew and the *Teaching* is to conjecture that the author of the *Teaching* has copied it from the Gospel of Matthew, or from some Greek source that preserved closely Matthew's text. While this latter conjecture is possible, it is also unnecessary.

The form of the Lord's Prayer found in the *Teaching* is far closer to the text in Matthew than it is to the form of that prayer in the Gospel of Luke.

The Lord's Prayer in Luke

Father,
Hallowed be thy name.
Thy kingdom come.
Give us our daily bread day by day;
And forgive us our sins,

> For we ourselves forgive everyone who is indebted to us;
> And lead us not into temptation.
>
> —*Luke 11:2–4*

Assuming the validity of the Two-Gospel Hypothesis, there is little difficulty in explaining this version of the Lord's Prayer. Under this hypothesis, the Gospel of Luke was composed after Matthew, and the evangelist Luke frequently copied the text of Matthew, making changes to suit his literary and theological purposes. All of the important differences between the texts of Luke and Matthew can be explained in terms of Luke's literary and theological purpose.

To begin with, we should note that the form of the Lord's Prayer in Matthew has a certain poetic character that is very well preserved in the *Teaching*. One effect of this poetic character is that it makes the prayer easier to learn, remember, and recite. The most evident characteristic of this poetic form is the art of repetition, a notable feature of orality, where the same idea is repeated using different words. For example, "thy kingdom come, thy will be done." Both these petitions are to the same effect: the one is equivalent to the other. This feature of Hebrew poetry is referred to as a "balance of ideas." Hebrew poetry does not rest so much on rhyme as on this "balance of ideas." Thus, prayers structured in this way lose relatively little of their poetic power in translation. The widespread use of the Psalms in all languages is clear evidence that, while it is relatively difficult to retain rhyme in translation, it is relatively simple to retain poetic form based on a balance of ideas.

Sometimes, the balance of ideas is antithetical: "lead us not into temptation, but deliver us from evil." Here still is a balance of ideas, but this balance is expressed not as essential equivalency, but as contrasting equivalency.

Once these poetic features of the Lord's Prayer are pointed out, it is clear that the Lord's Prayer as preserved in Luke is virtually devoid of balance of ideas. There is, however, still a trace of balance of ideas in the line, "forgive us our sins, for we ourselves forgive everyone who is indebted to us." Even here, while the progression in thought in the original "Forgive us our debts, as we also have forgiven our debtors" has been retained by Luke, the balance of ideas is not as well maintained as in Matthew and the *Teaching*. Poetry has become prose.

Luke's form of the prayer would be more difficult to commit to memory. Absent the balance of ideas, it would lack that sense of rhythm that facilitates oral recital. Nothing of substance, however, has been lost by the omission of the repetitious second half of the lines beginning "thy kingdom come [thy will be done]" and "lead us not into temptation [but deliver us from evil]." In fact, as a list of topics on which to meditate in prayer, the Lukan form may be pedagogically superior. Luke achieves a certain economy of language by omitting phrases that could be construed as redundant. But, because it has not retained the oral character given to it by Jesus, even modern churches with strong educational programs and an interest in shortening traditional liturgies have shown little interest in adopting it. The form of the Lord's Prayer universally used in the church from the beginning has always been the more original oral form of Matthew rather than the prose form of Luke.

Further supporting the conclusion that the Lukan form of the Lord's Prayer is later than Matthew's is the telling point that some differences in the Lukan form are clearly due to the evangelist Luke's editorial work.

The best example of this is found in the Lukan petition, "Give us our daily bread *day by day*," as compared to the petition found in Matthew's and the *Teaching*'s form of the prayer, "Give us this day our daily bread." To note more precisely the exact difference between Luke's form of the petition and that found in Matthew and the *Teaching*, it is necessary to translate the Greek in a very literal manner, preserving the basic word order of the original texts:

> Matthew and the *Teaching:* "Our daily bread give us *today*";
> Luke: "Our daily bread give us *day by day*."

It is the phrase *kath' hemeran*, translated "day by day," on which we need to focus. This phrase is not unique to Luke. We find it, for example, once in 1 Cor. 15:31, once in 2 Cor. 11:28, and twice in Heb. 7:27 and 10:11. However, it is clearly a favorite expression of Luke. Matthew uses it only once (26:55), in a passage that is also present in the parallel texts of Luke (22:53) and Mark (14:49). Mark and Matthew never use this phrase a second time. Luke, however, uses this phrase elsewhere, not only in his version of the Lord's Prayer, but also in 9:23; 16:19; 19:47; and four times in the Acts of the Apostles, 2:46; 2:47; 16:5; and 17:11.

We can consider the following text as an example of the way the evangelist Luke was prepared to use this phrase in editing the words of Jesus. We suggest that Luke has added "day by day" to accommodate Jesus' teaching to the intended readers of his Gospel.

> If anyone wishes to come after me,
> Let him deny himself,
> And take up his cross
> And follow me.
> —*Matt. 16:24*

The parallel text in Luke reads:

> If anyone wishes to come after me,
> Let him deny himself,
> And take up his cross *day by day*
> And follow me.
> —*Luke 9:23*

Virtually all scholars agree that the evangelist Luke has added his favorite phrase "day by day" to the more original form of the saying preserved in the text of Matthew. The form of the saying in Matthew fits the life situation of Jesus, who was teaching his disciples to pray for the imminent yet still future coming of the kingdom. His disciples were being asked to take up the same cross of self-denial and self-offering that he is taking up in his own ministry.

By editing the saying very slightly, Luke has managed to accommodate it to the situation of Christians in the early church who are no longer simply looking forward to the coming of God's kingdom. Through the redemptive death and resurrection of Jesus, those disciples who live on this side of the cross and resurrection are members of a church in which much of what was promised by the Prophets is already being fulfilled (Acts 2). So the evangelist Luke's intended readers are urged to take up their cross "day by day" and to pray for their daily bread "day by day" while they await a still future post-resurrection, postascension, post-Pentecost coming of the Lord in the fullness of his power and glory.

One further difference between the form of the Lord's Prayer in Matthew (and the *Teaching*) and its form in Luke deserves mention. Luke's simple "Father" in the opening line of the prayer is an abbreviated form of the more original "our Father who art in heaven." We have an abbreviation of a similar phrase, "your heavenly Father" found in Matt. 5:48 and 6:32, in the Lukan "your Father" found in Luke 6:36 and 12:30. As further examples of Luke's tendency to avoid the use of "heaven" and "heavenly" in reference to God, we may note the use of "sons of the most high" (Luke 6:35) for "sons of your Father who is in heaven" (Matt. 5:45), and the use of "God" (Luke 12:24) in place of "your heavenly father" (Matt. 6:26). There is one case where Matthew's "your Father who is in heaven" (Matt. 7:11) becomes Luke's "the Father who is out of heaven" (Luke 11:13). This curious and unparalleled usage in the Greek is obscured in English translations by use of the paraphrase "the heavenly Father."

In general, Luke prefers not to ask his intended readers to think of God as associated with heaven or the heavens. The one time he uses "heaven" with reference to God, Luke is careful to note that he is "the Father who is *out of* heaven," whatever that may mean.

Where Matthew has the petition, "Forgive us our *debts*," the *Teaching* has, "Forgive us our *debt* (singular)" but Luke has "Forgive us our *sins*." The use of the singular "debt" in the *Teaching* is a minor difference with Matthew. But Luke's use of "sin" is significant. It is explained by the fact that the use of "debt" for "sin" was a Jewish usage. The origin of this usage resides in the Jewish idea that, as we sin against God, we become indebted to him. We owe him recompense. This usage seems to have been little understood outside Jewish circles. Although "debt" for "sin" was probably used by Jesus, it was presumably not well understood by Luke's intended Gentile readers. The evangelist has accommodated the text for his readers by substituting the readily understood word "sin" for the less well understood word "debt." We find it used in this sense also by Luke in another saying of Jesus:

> Do you think that
>> these Galileans were worse <u>sinners</u>
>>> than all the other Galileans,
>>>> because they suffered thus?
> I tell you, no;
>> but unless you repent,
>>> you will all likewise perish.
>> Or those eighteen
>>> on whom the Tower of Siloam fell
>>> and killed them.
> Do you think that
>> they were worse <u>debtors</u>
>>> than all the others
>>>> who dwelt in Jerusalem?
> I tell you, no;
>> but unless you repent
>>> you will all likewise perish.
>>>> —*Luke 13:1–5*

The rhetorical question-and-answer structure of Jesus' twofold saying is probably original. It is likely that in preserving the same language in the first part, to maintain as much balance as possible with the second part, that "debt" was originally used in the first part as well. If Luke has substituted "sins" for "debts" in his use of Matthew's form of the Lord's Prayer, it would suggest that he also has substituted "sinners" for "debtors" here, and for the same reasons. The practice of leaving the original word "debtors" in the second half of this saying would be in accord with what Luke did with "debtors" in this Lord's Prayer. In this way, we see Luke as basically a conservative author transmitting the words of Jesus to his readers with only those changes he thinks necessary to assist them understand the text.

Finally, we come to Luke's omission of the phrase, "on earth as it is in heaven." Because Luke has already abbreviated the opening line of the prayer by omitting any reference to God being in heaven, the omission of a phrase that presupposes what has been omitted, namely, that God dwells in heaven, should come as no surprise. In any case, the words "on earth as it is in heaven" are present in both Matthew and the *Didache* where they are integral to the prayer.

With Jesus' first disciples we can imagine that the petitioner stands with the people of God and looks up to heaven, the dwelling place of God. He joins others in a very intimate address to God: "Our Father." Yet, he immediately acknowledges God's transcendent character: "Thou who art in the heavens" (high above the earth), "Highest praise to your holiness." He then goes directly to the heart of the matter and implores God: "Let your kingdom come, let your will be done." Where? Here on earth, where God's people dwell. Where else? As God's sovereign will now rules in heaven let it speedily rule here on earth, where, in its absence, God's people suffer oppression, hunger, and injustice—all summed up in the terse phrase: "As in heaven, also upon earth." The essential structure of the prayer requires this petitionary movement from earth up to heaven, and back to earth. So the prayer as we find it in Matthew would have been prayed.

We have now offered an explanation of all the major differences between the Lord's Prayer in Luke and in Matthew. Matthew's form is virtually unaltered in the *Teaching* and is used with appropriate liturgical freedom by all Christian churches of all times and all places. Assuming the validity of the Two-Gospel Hypothesis, we have encountered no difficulty in explaining the texts. The Lord's Prayer as we find it in Matthew fits what we can know about Jesus' life situation. It is attributed to Jesus in all known sources. No doubt, it is a prayer Jesus taught his disciples; they probably learned it by heart and prayed it together often. It is virtually certain that when two or three disciples gathered in his name following his death and resurrection, they prayed this prayer together. It is a universally unifying experience for Christians to pray this prayer as Jesus taught them to pray.

The Lord's Prayer and the Two-Source Hypothesis

The Two-Source Hypothesis presupposes that Matthew and Luke are independent of one another. To explain the extensive evidence of verbatim agreement between Matthew and Luke, it is assumed that behind all the canonical Gospels, and earlier than any one of them, lies a reliable source. It was the great German theologian of civil religion and popularizer of the Two-Document Hypothesis (that is, the Two-Source Hypothesis), Heinrich Holtzmann, who in 1863 designated this source as an apostolic *Grundschrift*. Holtzmann divided this *Grundschrift* into two main sources, which he named *Alpha* and *Lambda*. *Alpha* was a primitive narrative source, and *Lambda* was an early collection of the sayings of Jesus.

The Two-Source Hypothesis therefore points to two early apostolic sources, the first (*Alpha*) mainly made up of narrative material, and the second (*Lambda*) mainly consisting of sayings. After World War I, especially at the hands of the British scholar B. H. Streeter (1924), the idea of a primitive narrative source gave way to the idea that the Gospel of Mark was the real *Alpha*, the real apostolic narrative source. In the same period, the letter Q, as the first letter in the German word *Quelle* (meaning "source"), firmly replaced the use of L for *Logia*, standing for the source of sayings. Streeter and his followers, unlike Holtzmann (who, interestingly enough, put the Sermon on the Mount in *Alpha*), include the Lord's Prayer in Q.

Some scholars, like Joachim Jeremias, have argued that Q existed only in oral form. This theory would explain why there seems to be so much difficulty in reconstructing a literary text of Q. However, the main argument against a completely oral Q is the extensive verbal agreement between the Greek texts of Matthew and Luke in the so-called Q passages.

Scholars find compelling evidence for a written Q in the Sermon on the Mount, particularly in the Lord's Prayer. One Greek word in the Lord's Prayer appears to require some direct literary relationship between the texts of Matthew and Luke. This is the virtually untranslatable word *epiousion*, generally rendered "daily." Since the Two-Source Hypothesis regards Matthew and Luke as independent of one another, Matthew and Luke must have copied some source written in Greek that contained this very rare Greek word. Assuming the Two-Source Hypothesis, this serves to prove the existence of Q as a source written in Greek. How else could one explain the presence of this most unusual Greek work in both Matthew's and Luke's versions of the Lord's Prayer? *Epiousion* never appears in the surviving Greek literature before we find it in the Lord's Prayer in Matthew and Luke.

In the case of the Q sayings of Jesus, it is generally conjectured that behind the sayings in the Greek texts of Q were Hebrew or more probably Aramaic originals. In their new International Critical Commentary on *Matthew*, W. D. Davies and Dale C. Allison tentatively reconstruct what they conjecture may have been the Greek translation of a Hebrew or Aramaic original of the Lord's Prayer (vol. 1, p. 591). Their reconstruction of the text of the Lord's Prayer in Greek may be translated as follows:

> Father,
> Hallowed be your name.
> Thy kingdom come.
> Give us this day our daily bread.
> And forgive us our debts,
> For also we ourselves have forgiven the ones indebted to us.
> And do not lead us into temptation.[1]

One can achieve very nearly the same results reached by Davies and Allison by assuming that Luke's shorter form of the Lord's Prayer is more original, and that the phrases of the prayer in Matthew but not in Luke have been added to the original and should be omitted in reconstructing the original.

In support of the view that the shorter form of Luke's prayer is more original is the fact that important Greek manuscripts of Matthew do not include the words at the close of the prayer "for thine is the kingdom, the power, and the glory forever. Amen." For that reason, these words were bracketed in the form of the Lord's Prayer set forth at the beginning of this chapter. Most scholars today have concluded that the Greek manuscripts which include these words are not accurate, and that these words were added by the early church.

If one were to proceed on the assumption that Luke's shorter form is closer to the original, it would be possible to assume, as Davies and Allison do not, that if Luke's shorter form of the prayer is closer to the original, possibly Luke's text is also closer to the original text. This line of reasoning would justify regarding Luke's "day by day" as a part of the original text of the prayer. One could then conjecture that Luke has taken a liking to this phrase significantly used by Jesus in what Luke regards as an important and normative prayer, and made it one of his favorite expressions.

If one concludes that "day by day" was a part of this prayer as originally prayed in the church, this could be taken as evidence that the prayer itself, as we have it in Luke, originated not in the life situation of Jesus, but in a postresurrection Gentile church for the reasons already discussed. One would then be constrained to explain the later form of the prayer in Matthew as due to its having been edited to fit the needs of some Jewish-Christian community that retained the more original outlook of Jesus and his first disciples.

This general line of reasoning could be cited in support of the conclusion reached by the Jesus Seminar in the 1980s that Jesus probably did not teach his disciples the Lord's Prayer, that this prayer originated in the Gentile church, and that the more Jewish form of the prayer in Matthew was written later and represents editorial changes made for the sake of churches with a Jewish-Christian background.

The Two-Document Hypothesis does not require the conclusion that Jesus did not teach his disciples the Lord's Prayer. Davies and Allison, for example, do not reach that conclusion. However, their reconstruction of the more original form of this prayer, assuming as they do the existence of Q, has led them to propose a history of the Lord's Prayer that in certain essential respects is the same as that proposed by the Jesus Seminar. Both the New International Critical Commentary on *Matthew* and the Jesus Seminar agree that the Lord's Prayer as preserved in Matthew is a product of the church, greatly expanded in comparison to its earlier form preserved in the Gospel of Luke.

If Q existed, the Davies-Allison reconstruction of the Lord's Prayer has merit as a scholarly approximation of the original. That it is a literary travesty of a prayer that is loved and cherished in the church would not be a reason to reject it, or to disregard its scientific value. But if Q did not exist, and Luke had access to Matthew and copied Matthew, one would pay little attention to the Davies-Allison reconstruction of this prayer, other than to point to it as a curiosity of Q scholarship. And if Q never existed, one would pay even less attention to the conclusion of the Jesus Seminar, except to point to it as an atypical but not uncritical fruit of Q scholarship. On the other hand, if Luke copied Matthew, one would focus on the Matthean form of the prayer, study carefully the differences between Luke's text and Matthew's text, and note how Christian teaching developed at this earliest stage in its development. One then would turn to the *Didache* and note the relationship of its Lord's Prayer to the two earlier forms. This way, it would be possible to note that the liturgical use of the Matthean form of the prayer began very early in the Christian church, and the form of the prayer in Luke belongs less to the liturgical history of the prayer than to the history of the development of Christian doctrine.

What difference does it make? It makes a great deal of difference to any person seriously interested in understanding Christian origins, both historically and theologically. And above all, it is important for the church's liturgists, who must make the difficult decisions of how to pass on to coming generations the faith and practice of their mothers and fathers. What difference does it make? Look again at the Davies-Allison reconstruction of the Q form of the Lord's Prayer. Try to pray that prayer. Try to teach it to your children. Try to commit it to memory. Try to recite it orally.

CHAPTER 5

The Lord's Supper

The Lord's Supper in Matthew

> [26]And while they were eating, Jesus, after taking bread, and after blessing it, broke it, and gave it to the disciples and said, "Take, eat; this is my body."
> [27]And after taking a cup, and after giving thanks, he gave it to them, saying: "All of you, drink of it;
> [28]For this is my blood of the covenant, which is being poured out for many for the forgiveness of sins.
> [29]I say to you: I shall not drink again of this fruit of the vine until that day when I drink it new with you in my Father's kingdom."   —*Matt. 26:26–29*

To understand the Lord's Supper, we must position ourselves within the context of Jesus' disciples in the upper room. That context was the life of Israel in their day, but it was more particularly the collective life they shared with their teacher, about to become the redeemer. We have seen in the Lord's Prayer how Jesus taught his disciples to petition God for the forgiveness of sins, and we have noted how this was in accordance with the scriptures by which Jesus and his disciples were spiritually formed:

> . . . in our sins we have been for a long time,
>   and shall we be saved?
> We have all become like one who is unclean,
>   and all our righteous deeds are like filthy rags. . . .
> Be not exceedingly angry, O Lord,
>   and remember not our iniquity forever.
>   —*Isa. 64:5–9*

The reference in the Lord's Supper to Jesus' blood being "poured out" for "many" for the forgiveness of sins is a clear reference to the redemptive act of the Suffering Servant in Isa. 53:12, where the Servant "*poured out* his soul unto death," and "bore the sin of *many*." The connection is both conceptional and linguistic. Scholars working carefully with the Hebrew text of Isaiah and its Aramaic translation have demonstrated that the Greek words translated "poured out" and "many" in this context of Matthew's passion narrative have clear linguistic ties to the text of Isaiah 53. In making their demonstrations credible, scholars bring certain passages from Paul's letters into their discussions.[1] One of the most compelling of these Pauline texts is found in the very early pre-Pauline tradition that the apostle passes on to his readers in 1 Corinthians:

[1]Now I would remind you, brethren, in what terms I preached to you the gospel, which you received, in which you stand,
[2]by which you are saved, if you hold it fast—unless you believed in vain.
[3]For I delivered to you as of first importance what I also received, that Christ died for our sins in accordance with the scriptures.   —*1 Cor. 15:1–3 (RSV)*

Most scholars cite Isa. 53:5–12 in identifying the scriptures referred to in 1 Cor. 15:3.

A Subtext for the Lord's Supper

[5]He was wounded for our transgressions. He was bruised for our iniquities; upon him was the chastisement that made us whole, and with his stripes we are healed.
[6]All we like sheep have gone astray; we have turned everyone to his own way; and the Lord has laid on him the iniquity of us all.
[7]He was oppressed and he was afflicted, yet he opened not his mouth; like a lamb that is led to the slaughter, and like a sheep that before its shearers is dumb, so he opened not his mouth.
[8]By oppression and judgment he was taken away; and as for his generation, who considered that he was cut off out of the land of the living, stricken for the transgression of my people?
[9]And they made his grave with the wicked and with a rich man in his death, although he had done no violence, and there was no deceit in his mouth.
[10]Yet it was the will of the Lord to bruise him; he has put him to grief; when he makes himself an offering for sin, he shall see his offspring, he shall prolong his days; the will of the Lord shall prosper in his hand;
[11]he shall see the fruit of the travail of his soul and be satisfied; by his knowledge shall the righteous one, my servant, make many to be accounted righteous; and he shall bear their iniquities.
[12]Therefore I will divide him a portion with the great, and he shall divide the spoil with the strong; because he poured out his soul to death, and was numbered with the transgressors; yet he bore the sin of many and made intercessions for the transgressors.   —*Isa. 53:5–12 (RSV)*

In literary criticism, a subtext is one so well known that it is banal to cite it explicitly. In a world of discourse where the subtext is taken for granted, it can be presupposed and is most powerfully present when it is only alluded to, providing the allusion is appropriate. Such is the case here.

According to Matthew's text of the Lord's Supper, Jesus, after taking a cup and offering thanks, gave it to his disciples and said, "All of you drink of it." When he went on to say, "For this is my blood of the covenant, which is being *poured out for many for the forgiveness of sins*," he was clarifying the meaning of the "breaking of the bread," referring to his death. He wanted his disciples to understand that he was freely offering up himself, pouring out his soul to death for the sins of many, in accordance with the scriptures.

The church has always understood the Lord's Supper in this sense. While the wording of the church's eucharistic liturgies may vary from time to time and from place to place, one constant runs through them all: the blood of Christ is shed for the forgiveness of sins. This has been and remains at the very heart of this central act of worship in all Christian churches of all times.[2]

The apostle Paul, in his magisterial letter to Christians in Rome, clarifies this doctrine of Jesus' redemptive death on a decisive point, whether its benefits extend to all who believe, Jew and Gentile alike:

> [21]The righteousness of God has been manifested apart from law, although the law and the prophets bear witness to it,
> [22]the righteousness of God through faith in Christ Jesus for all who believe. For there is no distinction;
> [23]since all have sinned and fall short of the glory of God,
> [24]they are justified by his grace as a gift, through the redemption which is in Jesus Christ,
> [25]whom God put forward as an expiation by his blood, to be received by faith. This was to show God's righteousness, because in his divine forbearance he has passed over former sins;
> [26]it was to prove at the present time that he himself is righteous and that he justified him who has faith in Jesus.   —*Rom. 3:21–26 (RSV)*

These verses tell us, very simply, that when the Christian participates in the Lord's Supper, she is invited to have faith in "our Lord Jesus Christ, who gave himself for our sins" (Gal. 1:3b–4a). The communicant is invited to believe that "God showed God's love for us in that while we were yet sinners, Christ died for us" (Rom. 5:8). In the Lord's Supper, the Christian is invited to believe that God and Christ are in such perfect union that God can show God's love for us in Jesus' giving of himself, offering himself for the remission of our sins, dying for us. "No one has greater love than this, to lay down one's life for one's friends" (John 15:13, NRSV). All of these thoughts and countless others may fittingly come into the mind of the person who faithfully takes part in Holy Communion at the Lord's table.

The Lord's Supper in Luke

> [14]And when the hour came, he sat at table, and the apostles with him.
> [15]And he said to them, "I have earnestly desired to eat this Passover with you before I suffer;

[16]for I tell you I shall not eat it again until it is fulfilled <u>in the kingdom</u> of God."
[17]And he took a cup, and when he had given thanks he said, "Take this, and divide it among yourselves;
[18]for <u>I tell you</u> that from now on <u>I shall not drink of the fruit of the vine until</u> the kingdom of God comes."
[19]After taking <u>bread</u>, and <u>after giving thanks, he broke it and</u> gave it to them, saying, "<u>This is my body</u>"   *—Luke 22:14–19a*

Some manuscripts add, with variations in wording and arrangement:

[19b] "which is given for you; do this as a memorial of me."
[20]In the same way he took the <u>cup</u> after supper, and said, "<u>This</u> cup, <u>poured out</u> for you, is the new covenant sealed by <u>my</u> blood."   *—Luke 22:19a–20*

The verbatim agreement between Luke's text of the Lord's Supper and Matthew's has been indicated by the underlined words. They are exactly the same in the corresponding Greek text of Matthew's Gospel.

Based on the Two-Gospel Hypothesis, one can say that Luke has made some use of the text of Matt. 26:26–29, but by no means can it be said that Luke has taken his account of the Lord's Supper from Matthew. In fact, the similarities between Luke's account and the pre-Pauline tradition in 1 Cor. 11:23–26 are more notable than the similarities between the accounts of Matthew and Luke. It is important to note that Matt. 26:28: "For this is my blood of the covenant, which is being poured out for many for the forgiveness of sins" is not present at all in the main body of Luke's account of the Lord's Supper, and appears only in a fragmentary form in the addition that is found in some ancient manuscripts.

The Lord's Supper in 1 Corinthians

[23]For I received from the Lord what I also delivered to you, that the Lord Jesus on the night when he was handed over took bread,
[24]and when he had given thanks, he broke it, and said: "This is my body which is [broken] for you. Do this in remembrance of me."
[25]In the same way also he took the cup, after supper, saying, "This cup is the new covenant in my blood. Do this, as often as you drink it, in remembrance of me."
[26]For as often as you eat this bread and drink this cup, you proclaim the Lord's death until he comes.   *—1 Cor. 11:23–26 (RSV)*

To this may be added the following observations of Paul:

[16]The cup of blessing which we bless, is it not a participation in the blood of Christ? The bread which we break, is it not a participation in the body of Christ?

¹⁷Because there is one bread, we who are many are one body, for we all partake
of the one bread.   —*1 Cor. 10:16–17 (RSV)*

A similarity between this very early pre-Pauline tradition and Matthew's
text of the Lord's Supper is worth noting. Both have a similar formal
structure: In both, Jesus takes bread and after a blessing or thanksgiving, he
breaks it and says: "This is my body." In both, Jesus takes a cup and in a
similar way gives a (blessing or thanksgiving?) and then identifies his blood
with the covenant. Both accounts close on an eschatological note, each in a
quite different manner.

While little or no formal structural similarity exists between 1 Corinthians
11 and the Lord's Prayer in Luke, the verbatim agreement between Paul and
Luke is greater than that between Luke and Matthew. Luke 22:19b–20 is very
closely related to 1 Cor. 11:24b–25. Finally, while the tradition passed on by
Paul refers to the new covenant in Jesus' blood, it contains no explicit
reference to that blood "being poured out for many for the remission of sins."

The Lord's Supper in Mark

²²And while they were eating, [Jesus], after taking bread [and] after blessing it,
broke it and gave to them and said: "Take; this is my body."
²³And after taking a cup [and] after giving thanks, he gave it to them, and they all
drank of it.
²⁴And he said to them: "This is my blood of the covenant, which is being poured
out in behalf of many.
²⁵Truly I say to you: I shall never drink of the fruit of the vine until that day
when I drink it new in the kingdom of God."   —*Mark 14:22–25*

Based on the Two-Gospel Hypothesis, it is clear that Mark closely
followed Matthew's text of the Lord's Supper. In a few places, the style or
grammar of Mark reflects the text of Luke; however, on the whole, Mark's
text is a faithful version of the Lord's Supper as preserved in Matthew.
With very few exceptions, Mark has preserved all the language common to
Luke and Matthew. Of the thirty-three words Luke and Matthew share in
common, Mark has skillfully managed to preserve thirty-one. While seven
(mostly separated) words of Mark's text are closer to Luke than to
Matthew, only in one case—Mark's preference for Luke's expression
"kingdom of God" over Matthew's "kingdom of my Father"—is Mark's
agreement with Luke substantial. Mark's version of the Lord's Supper
totals sixty-nine words; fifty-five of them are copied from Matthew
verbatim, very often maintaining the same word order. In Mark 14:25
alone are eleven successive words exactly the same as the Matthew text,

including in the same word order. This confirms a close literary relationship between Mark and Matthew. Assuming the validity of the Two-Gospel Hypothesis, Mark has carefully followed the text of Matthew in producing his text of the Lord's Supper, preserving both the blessing of the bread and thanks over the cup, in that order, while at the same time preserving Luke's text where Luke has preserved the language of Matthew.

Mark preserves that part of Matthew related linguistically to Isaiah 53, including both the expression "poured out," as well as the term "many," although he agrees with Luke in omitting the decisive doctrinal phrase "for the forgiveness of sins."

Although Luke's account preserves none of these explicit linguistic connections with Isaiah 53, it is nonetheless clear that he recognized the importance of Jesus' suffering and presumably saw that suffering in relation to Isaiah 53. In Luke 22:15 we read, "I have earnestly desired to eat this Passover with you before I suffer," referring to his death, and in 22:37 we read, "For I tell you that this scripture must be fulfilled in me, 'And he was reckoned with transgressors'; for what is written about me has its fulfillment." This is an explicit reference to Isa. 53:12. Isaiah's importance to Luke in understanding Jesus is made clear in the account of the opening of Jesus' public ministry in Nazareth.

> [16]And he came to Nazareth, where he had been brought up; and he went to the synagogue, as his custom was on the Sabbath day. And he stood up to read;
> [17]and there was given to him the book of the prophet Isaiah. He opened the book and found the place where it was written,
> [18]"The spirit of the Lord is upon me because he has anointed me; he has sent me to announce good news to the poor; to proclaim release for prisoners and recovery of sight for the blind; to let the broken victims go free;
> [19]to proclaim the acceptable year of the Lord."
> [20]And he closed the book, and gave it back to the attendant, and sat down; and the eyes of all in the synagogue were fixed on him.
> [21]And he began to say to them, "Today this scripture has been fulfilled in your hearing." —*Luke 4:16–21*

From the closing chapter of Luke's Gospel, it is clear he recognized that the suffering death of Jesus was redemptive and was a fulfillment of scripture. On the road to Emmaus, Jesus, unrecognized by two disciples, asks a question, and in reply one of them answers:

> [20]". . . our chief priests and rulers delivered him up to be condemned to death, and crucified him.
> [21]But we had hoped that he was the one to redeem Israel. . . ."
> —*Luke 24:20–21 (RSV)*

And Jesus replied:

> [25]"Oh foolish men, and slow of heart to believe all that the prophets have
> spoken!
> [26]Was it not necessary that the Christ should suffer these things and enter into
> his glory?"
> [27]And beginning with Moses and all the prophets, he interpreted to them in all
> the scriptures the things concerning himself.   *—Luke 24:25–27 (RSV)*

Later, when Jesus stood among the eleven in Jerusalem, "he opened their
minds to understand the scriptures, and he said to them, 'Thus it is written,
that the Christ should suffer, and on the third day rise from the dead' " (Luke
24:46). This is a clear reference to the very early pre-Pauline tradition in
1 Corinthians:

> [3]For I delivered to you as of first importance what I also received, that Christ
> died for our sins in accordance with the scriptures,
> [4]that he was buried, and that he was raised on the third day according to the
> scriptures.   *—1 Cor. 15:3–4*

As already noted, the reference to Christ having died for our sins in
accordance with the scriptures can only refer to Isaiah 53. The Lukan phrase
"the Christ should suffer" also clearly refers to the suffering death of the
servant in Isaiah 53.

Thus, based on the Two-Gospel Hypothesis, the importance of Isaiah and
especially Isaiah 53, which is clear in the Gospel of Matthew, is also clear in
the Gospel of Luke—although the evidence for this importance is distinc-
tively different in each. From the historian's point of view, assuming the
validity of the Two-Gospel Hypothesis, we have very strong independent
evidence from Matthew converging with strong independent evidence from
Luke, that Isaiah—especially chapter 53—was of importance for the early
church. If the text of the Lord's Supper in Matthew is to be trusted, the
unquestioned importance of Isaiah 53 for the church can be traced back to
Jesus himself. That is the clear implication of Jesus' words: "This is my blood
of the covenant, which is being poured out for many for the forgiveness of
sins" (Matt. 26:28). It is also the clear implication of the words of the risen
Christ in Luke's Gospel (24:25–27, 44–48).

On the road to Emmaus, Jesus, in response to the disciples' failure to
believe all that the prophets had spoken, asked: "Was it not necessary that the
Christ should suffer these things (referring to the testimony they have just
given concerning his condemnation and death)?" The oracle about the
Suffering Servant in Isa. 52:13—53:12 is the central subtext to be taken for
granted in the unspecified words "that the prophets had spoken."

The Christological Hymn in Philippians

⁵Have this mind among yourselves, which you have in Christ Jesus
⁶who, though he was in the form of God, did not count equality with God a thing to be grasped,
⁷but emptied himself, taking the form of a servant, being born in the likeness of men.
⁸And found in human form humbled himself and became obedient unto death, even death on a cross.
⁹Therefore God has highly exalted him and bestowed on him the name which is above every name,
¹⁰that at the name of Jesus every knee should bow, in heaven and on earth and under the earth, and every tongue confess that Jesus Christ is Lord, to the glory of God the Father.   —*Phil. 2:5–10*

This early christological hymn clearly witnesses to the primitive church's belief in Jesus as the servant who humbles himself and is obedient unto death before being exalted in accordance with Isa. 52:13.

The Suffering of Christ in 1 Peter, Acts of the Apostles, and Hebrews

²¹For to this [suffering] you have been called, because Christ also suffered for you, leaving you an example that you should follow in his steps.
²²He committed no sin; no guile was found on his lips.
²³When he was reviled, he did not revile in return; when he suffered, he did not threaten; but he trusted to him who judges justly.
²⁴He himself bore our sins in his body on the tree, that we might die to sin and live to righteousness. By his wounds you have been healed.
                                              —*1 Peter 2:21–24*

We find in this scripture the teaching that our suffering is to be understood in reference to the example of Christ. The concluding sentence "By his wounds you have been healed" is an allusion to Isaiah 53:

> He was wounded for our transgressions;
> he was bruised for our iniquities;
> upon him was the chastisement that made us whole,
> and with his stripes we are healed.
>   —*Isa. 53:5*

The whole of 1 Peter 2:21–24 has its origin in the early church's practice of finding the deepest source of its faith and practice in its belief that "Christ died for our sins, according to the scriptures" (1 Cor. 15:3). Based on the Two-Gospel Hypothesis, the whole of the New Testament coheres with this understanding of Christian faith. What is normative in the Bible is the concordance and harmony between Moses and the prophets and the covenant of Jesus Christ witnessed to, by and in the books of the New Testament. The Eucharist and the eucharistic texts of the New Testament provide the hermeneutical key to understanding the Christian Bible, and the faith of the church.

Further evidence of Isaiah 53's importance for the faith of the church is found in the following passages:

[25]Now when they [Peter and John] had testified and spoken the word of the Lord, they returned to Jerusalem, preaching the gospel to many villages of the Samaritans.
[26]But an angel of the Lord said to Philip, "Rise and go toward the south to the road that goes down from Jerusalem to Gaza." This is a desert road.
[27]And he rose and went. And behold, an Ethiopian, a eunuch, a minister of the Candace, queen of the Ethiopians, in charge of all her treasure, had come to Jerusalem to worship
[28]and was returning; seated in his chariot, he was reading the prophet Isaiah.
[29]And the Spirit said to Philip, "Go up and join this chariot."
[30]So Philip ran to him, and heard him reading Isaiah the prophet, and asked, "Do you understand what you are reading?"
[31]And he said, "How can I, unless some one guides me?" And he invited Philip to come up and sit with him.
[32]Now the passage of the scripture which he was reading was this:
"As a sheep led to the slaughter
or a lamb before its shearer is dumb,
so he opens not his mouth.
[33]In his humiliation justice was denied him.
Who can describe his generation?
For his life is taken up from the earth."
[34]And the eunuch said to Philip, "About whom, pray, does the prophet say this, about himself or about some one else?"
[35]Then Philip opened his mouth, and beginning with the scriptures he told him the good news of Jesus.   *—Acts 8:25–35 (RSV)*

[1]Therefore, since we are surrounded by so great a cloud of witnesses, let us also lay aside every weight, and sin which clings so closely, and let us run with perseverance the race that is set before us,
[2]looking to Jesus the pioneer and perfecter of our faith, who for the joy that was set before him endured the cross, despising the shame, and is seated at the right hand of the throne of God.
[3]Consider him who endured from sinners such hostility against himself, so that you may not grow weary or fainthearted.

⁴In your struggle against sin you have not yet resisted to the point of shedding your blood.
⁵And have you forgotten the exhortation which addresses you as sons?
"My son, do not regard lightly the discipline of the Lord,
nor lose courage when you are punished by him.
⁶For the Lord disciplines him whom he loves,
and chastizes every son whom he receives."
⁷It is for discipline that you have to endure. God is treating you as sons; for what son is there whom his father does not discipline?   —*Heb. 12:1–7*

From the above analysis, it is clear that, based on the Two-Gospel Hypothesis, Luke's omission of the covenant words, "for this is my blood of the covenant, which is being poured out for many for the forgiveness of sins," from his version of the Lord's Supper cannot be construed to mean that Luke placed no importance on the suffering of Christ in relation to the words spoken by the prophets, particularly Isaiah.

Similarly, based on the Two-Gospel Hypothesis, Mark's omission of the concluding expression of these covenantal words, "for the forgiveness of sins," cannot be construed to mean that Mark placed no importance on the close connection between Jesus and Isaiah 53. Indeed, Mark's version preserves the greater part of Jesus' covenantal words, including the telltale linguistic ties to the text of Isaiah: "For this is my blood of the covenant, which is being *poured out* for *many*."

Moreover, based on the Two-Gospel Hypothesis, Mark's retention of the teaching: "The Son of Man came not to be served, but to serve, and give his life as ransom for many" (Matt. 20:28 and Mark 10:45), provides evidence that Mark accepted the doctrine of the redemptive character of Jesus' self-offering. Most scholars would agree with Herbert G. May and Bruce M. Metzger that the thought of Jesus' words in this passage "seems to be based on Isaiah chapter 53."

The Lord's Supper and the Two-Source Hypothesis

Based on the Two-Source Hypothesis, Matthew and Luke have independently copied Mark. But in this case, the agreements and disagreements between Mark and Luke are best explained if Luke had access not only to Mark, but also to one or more additional sources. The tradition preserved in Luke 22:19b–20 appears to be based upon 1 Cor. 11:24b–25, or some text closely related to it.

Matthew, on the other hand, based on the Two-Source Hypothesis, has followed the text of Mark rather closely. The major difference between the two accounts is Matthew's words, "for the forgiveness of sins." These words are not found in Mark. Has Matthew added these words, or did he take them from some other source? A great deal hangs on how we answer this question. If, assuming the validity of the Two-Source Hypothesis, the evangelist Matthew is the author of these words, they represent the way the text of the Lord's Supper developed in the early church, this time at the hands of an evangelist writing for his own church. On the other hand, if the evangelist Matthew had access not only to Mark but also to a second source closely parallel to Mark, it is possible that the words "for the forgiveness of sins" were copied from this other source and may go back to Jesus himself. If these words go back to Jesus, they serve to strengthen faith in a Christ who "gave himself for our sins" (Gal. 1:4). Conversely, if these words do not go back to Jesus, the connection between Jesus' covenantal statement: "This is my blood of the covenant, which is being poured out for [or: in behalf of] many for the forgiveness of sins," and Isaiah 53 is somewhat weakened. In any case, the allusion to Isa. 53:10–12 in Mark's text of the Lord's Supper is not as strong as the allusion to that subtext in Matthew's Gospel.

In fact, based on the Two-Source Hypothesis, one can argue that because the words "for the forgiveness of sins" are absent from Mark, their presence in Matthew can most easily be explained by assuming that they have been added to the more original form of the tradition by the evangelist Matthew himself.

If this seems credible, while continuing to assume the validity of the Two-Source Hypothesis, one could go further and argue that the absence of the covenantal words, "this is my blood of the covenant, which is being poured out in behalf of many," both in Paul's account of the Lord's Supper and from the texts concerning this supper in Luke's Gospel, suggests that these words may also have been added to the more original form of the tradition, possibly by the evangelist Mark.

In support of this line of reasoning, one could observe that, again assuming the validity of the Two-Source Hypothesis, the two later Gospels of Matthew and Luke, in comparison to the earlier Gospel of Mark, show an increasing interest in Isaiah, especially Isaiah 53. One could explain much if not all of the data according to a theory that Jesus himself showed no demonstrable interest in Isaiah 53, but the early church showed an increasing interest in explaining to itself the shameful execution of Jesus by appeal to Isaiah 53.

Many, if not most, adherents of the Two-Source Hypothesis reject this conclusion, dismissing it as unnecessarily skeptical. Some have sought to refute it by a careful use of the contrary evidence from Paul's letters. But few have taken the full measure of the critical case that the Cambridge University New Testament scholar Morna Hooker has made in favor of this hypothesis in her book *Jesus and the Servant*.[3] In fact, assuming the validity of the Two-Source Hypothesis, as Professor Hooker does, it is difficult to refute her conclusions. Based on the Two-Source Hypothesis, the way members of the church have experienced and continue to experience the forgiveness of sins in and through the church's eucharistic services can be construed as resting on a relatively naive acceptance of a Lord's Supper tradition that has become critically questionable because it appears to assume certain historical claims that have been rendered dubious.

As an example of scholarship leading to skepticism, we may take the work of Rudolf Bultmann, who, in his book *History of the Synoptic Tradition*,[4] following Johann Gottfried Eichhorn and Wilhelm Heitmüller, dismisses the historical value of the synoptic tradition concerning the Lord's Supper. All three of these German scholars assume the validity of the Two-Source Hypothesis.

Assuming the validity of the Two-Gospel Hypothesis, however, the eucharistic texts, seen in a different compositional configuration, serve to support—rather than cast doubt upon—the universal faith and practice of Christians in their worship at the table of the Lord.[5]

CHAPTER 6

Justification by Faith

The Parable of the Two Men
Who Went Up to the Temple to Pray

[10]"Two men went up into the temple to pray, one a Pharisee and the other a tax collector.

[11]The Pharisee stood and prayed thus with himself, 'God, I thank thee that I am not like other men, extortioners, unjust, adulterers, and even like this tax collector.

[12]I fast twice a week, I give tithes of all that I get.'

[13]But the tax collector, standing far off, would not even lift up his eyes to heaven, but beat his breast, saying, 'God, be merciful to me a sinner!'

[14a]I tell you, this man went down to his house justified rather than the other."

—Luke 18:9–14a (RSV)

As in the Lord's Prayer and the Lord's Supper, so in this parable[1] Jesus once again addresses forgiveness of sins. The sinner is to place his trust in the mercy of God. In that way, he will enter into a right relationship with God. Jesus' hearers would have expected the man who avoided injustice of all kinds and did all and more than the law required to go down to his house justified, in a right relationship with God. To have this man who was righteous according to the law (tithing, for instance) be the one who did not go down to his house "justified" would have caused no little surprise. And to have Jesus say that it was the sinner (transgressor of God's law) who was justified in the sight of God must have startled Jesus' hearers. On what basis could Jesus have made this striking and unexpected assertion? The answer is that the man who was righteous according to the law displeased God by placing his trust in his own righteousness and by thanking God that he was not like those who were unrighteous. The sinner, on the other hand, standing before God condemned by the law, simply cast himself upon God's mercy, beating his breast in remorse for his sins and crying out, "God, be merciful to me a sinner."

The phrase "justification by faith" became the watchword of the sixteenth-century reformers of the medieval church, and although at the Council of Trent (1545–1563) it was agreed that the Catholic Church teaches justification by faith, this doctrine remains a divisive factor today and is very unclear in the minds of many Christians.

The apostle Paul is the New Testament author who has the most to say about justification by faith, especially in Romans (3:20–30) and Galatians (2:16–17). This parable of Jesus, however, provides the best explanation of what it means to be justified by faith. In fact, the church has always used this parable to explain how one can be justified by faith apart from the law. The sinner in this parable had no righteousness according to the law, and yet he was justified. How? By his faith, obviously. How else could he have cried out "God, be merciful to me a sinner"? He had to believe that God was willing to forgive his sins upon turning to God in remorse and asking for mercy. In this way, the sinner put himself in a position to receive and benefit from divine forgiveness. In this context, faith is the trust this man had in the mercy of God. When Jesus says that this sinner went down to his house in a right relationship with God, he is teaching that God wants something more than mere mechanical obedience to the law. God wants our trust in the goodness and the forgiving love God is prepared to bestow on us.

It is a sign of comprehensive misunderstanding and lack of authentic trust in God when the righteous person, out of confidence in his righteousness, stands aloof from and looks down upon the sinner (Luke 18:19). It has been said that Paul may have been using this parable of Jesus when he developed his teaching on how Gentiles are to be justified apart from the law. Paul, as a former Pharisee, may have had the boasting Pharisee of this parable in mind when he wrote to the Romans:

> [27]Then what becomes of our boasting? It is excluded. On what principle? On the principle of works? No, but on the principle of faith.
> [28]For we hold that a man is justified by faith apart from works of law.[2]
> [29]Or is God the God of Jews only? Yes, of Gentiles also,
> [30]since God is one; and he will justify the circumcised on the ground of their faith and the uncircumcised through their faith.   —*Rom. 3:27–30*

Paul possibly discussed this parable with Peter during the fifteen days he spent with him in Jerusalem some three years after his conversion (Gal. 1:18–20). In any case, these two apostles must have come to a fundamental agreement on justification by faith because otherwise we cannot make sense of what Paul said on the occasion of Peter's withdrawal from table fellowship with the Gentiles in Antioch.

> [14]"If you, though a Jew, live like a Gentile [as you have been doing, eating with the Gentiles here in Antioch] and not like a Jew, how can you pressure the Gentiles to live like Jews [which is the effect of your present withdrawal from eating with them]?"
> [15]We ourselves, who are Jews . . .
> [16]. . . know that a man is not justified by works of law, but through faith in Jesus Christ. . . .   —*Gal. 2:14–16*

Paul's whole argument is premised on this crucial agreement with Peter on the fundamental basis for a right relationship with God—we are justified on the basis of faith. Nowhere is this vital point in theology more clearly made than in this parable.

The Two-Gospel Hypothesis offers no impediment to recognizing this parable of Jesus as an important source for understanding justification by faith. Paul could call Peter to account on this matter precisely because he knew that Peter would comprehend Paul's theological point. Peter was not walking in a straightforward manner with reference to the truth of the Gospel. In other words, Paul's appeal to Peter for consistency between his "walk" and his "talk" proceeds from the premise that he and Peter agreed on the cardinal doctrine, which Peter was perceived to be violating. There appears to be no other satisfactory way to explain Gal. 2:11–21.

Until the coming of the Two-Source Hypothesis, no one in the church ever questioned this parable's authenticity. But in recent decades, many committed to this hypothesis have refused to use this parable in their reconstructions of Jesus' message. And in our own day, some scholars belonging to the Jesus Seminar questioned whether this parable should be attributed to Jesus.

Do we have a reliable criterion when considering whether this parable should be attributed to Jesus? Yes, the criterion of coherence. If this parable is an authentic parable of Jesus, it ought to fit together in language, conceptuality, and interest with other sayings whose attribution to Jesus are virtually certain or at least highly probable. Such a saying is the parable in Luke 15:11–32, concerning the man who had two sons.

The Parable of the Man Who Had Two Sons

[11]"There was a man who had two sons;

[12]and the younger of them said to his father, 'Father, give me the share of property that falls to me.' And he divided his living between them.

[13]Not many days later, the younger son gathered all he had and took his journey into a far country, and there he squandered his property in loose living.

[14]And when he had spent everything, a great famine arose in that country, and he began to be in want.

[15]So he went and joined himself to one of the citizens of that country, who sent him into his fields to feed swine.

[16]And he would gladly have fed on the pods that the swine ate; and no one gave him anything.

[17]But when he came to himself, he said, 'How many of my father's hired servants have bread enough and to spare, but I perish here with hunger!

[18]I will arise and go to my father, and I will say to him, "Father, I have sinned against heaven and before you;

¹⁹I am no longer worthy to be called your son; treat me as one of your hired servants.'' '

²⁰And he arose and came to his father. But while he was yet at a distance, his father saw him and had compassion, and ran and embraced him and kissed him.

²¹And the son said to him, 'Father, I have sinned against heaven and before you; I am no longer worthy to be called your son,'

²²But the father said to his servants, 'Bring quickly the best robe, and put it on him; and put a ring on his hand, and shoes on his feet;

²³and bring the fatted calf and kill it, and let us eat and make merry;

²⁴for this my son was dead, and is alive again; he was lost, and is found.' And they began to make merry.

²⁵Now his elder son was in the field; and as he came and drew near to the house, he heard the music and dancing.

²⁶And he called one of the servants and asked what this meant.

²⁷And he said to him, 'Your brother has come, and your father has killed the fatted calf, because he has received him safe and sound.'

²⁸But he was angry and refused to go in. His father came out and entreated him,

²⁹but he answered his father, 'Lo, these many years I have served you, and I never disobeyed your command; yet you never gave me a kid, that I might make merry with my friends.

³⁰But when this son of yours came, who has devoured your living with harlots, you killed for him the fatted calf!'

³¹And he said to him, 'Son, you are always with me, and all that is mine is yours.

³²It was fitting to make merry and be glad,

for this your brother was dead, and is alive;

he was lost, and is found.' ''

—*Luke 15:11–32 (RSV)*

Certainly, what is said about the sinner in the temple who cast himself on the mercy of God coheres with what is said about the younger son in this parable. Neither is righteous according to the law. The younger son could not say that he had never gone against his father's commandments. On the contrary, he confessed that he was a sinner; he had sinned not only against his father but also against God.

The sinners in both parables show signs of remorse: the one, by beating his breast, the other, by crying out, "I am not worthy." The righteous persons in both parables commit the sin of self-righteousness, which leads one to look down on others less righteous than he, and the other to stand aloof from a celebration of his sinful brother's repentance. Both the Pharisee in the temple and the elder brother are righteous according to the law. Neither has neglected what was expected of him. Both were caught up in a comprehensive misunderstanding of the one thing that is necessary, trust in the sovereign love of a God who is not waiting for God's children to become perfect before in compassion reaching out to them and embracing them precisely in their sinful condition. That is, of course, providing they have turned from their wicked ways and, full of remorse for their sins, are by faith now casting themselves upon God's mercy. Christian preachers move from one of these parables to the other very easily; one serves to complement and supplement the other. They work together and cohere so convincingly that it is perfectly natural to receive them as coming from a single mind (without evidence to the contrary, presumably the mind of the one to whom these parables are attributed) seeking to illustrate by different stories how the grace of God works for those who repent and trust in divine mercy. They both converge in showing how inappropriate it is to place trust in one's own righteousness and to engage in invidious comparisons at the expense of sinners.

Justification by Faith and the Two-Source Hypothesis

The Two-Source Hypothesis serves to sever the connection between the teaching of Jesus and the theology of Paul. How this severance takes place in the case of the New Testament teaching on justification by faith is instructive.

Assuming the validity of the Two-Source Hypothesis, the first point to note is that nowhere in either of the two earliest and most reliable sources, the Gospel of Mark and the important apostolic collection of the sayings of Jesus called Q, is there any teaching of Jesus in which the verb "to justify" is used in the sense that Paul uses it. The only place where that happens is in the parable of the two men who went up to the temple in Jerusalem to pray. And because this parable is in neither Mark nor Q, assuming the Two-Source Hypothesis, a reasonable doubt can be raised concerning its authenticity. It would be wrong, however, to say that no teaching of Jesus' in either Mark or Q coheres with this parable. One such saying is found in Mark 2:17, where Jesus states that he came "not to call the righteous, but sinners." While this is not an instance in which the verb "to justify" is used, the word translated "righteous" in this saying has the same linguistic root as the verb "to justify." And while the verb "to justify" is not used in Mark, this saying clearly coheres with the interests in the parable of the two men who went up to the temple to pray; for one of these men was "righteous" according to the law, and the other was a "sinner." And in both teachings, Jesus shows a favorable concern for "sinners." With this possible exception, however, it can be said that Mark and Q offer very little, if any, support for significant continuity between Jesus and Paul on the doctrine of justification by faith.

How is the origin of this parable generally accounted for by the advocates of the Two-Source Hypothesis? While some Two-Source advocates accept this parable as authentic, many do not. Those who do not generally contend that Luke or someone else under Pauline influence wrote it. After all, the teaching of this parable is very close to the theology of Paul, and Luke traditionally has been identified as Paul's traveling companion.

This same conjecture, which is itself very problematic, technically could be offered by adherents of the Two-Gospel Hypothesis. But based on this hypothesis, such a conjecture is unnecessary. We have no evidence that Paul or anyone else in the early church created parables like those attributed to Jesus in the Gospels. We have other parables that are similar in form to the parables of Jesus; however, these are found not in Christian literature, but rather in rabbinic literature.

What difference does it make? Based on the Two-Source Hypothesis, this parable is found in neither the Gospel of Mark nor Q. It is only found in the later Gospel of Luke, where its presence is often explained away as due to Paul's influence on Luke. Based on this hypothesis, it would be precarious to attempt to argue for continuity between Jesus and Paul on the doctrine of justification by faith.

On the other hand, assuming the validity of the Two-Gospel Hypothesis, this parable is found in one of the two earlier Gospels. There it serves as a pivotal text, offering scriptural evidence that the doctrine of justification by faith, as it was developed and applied in the early church to defend admission of Gentiles on the basis of faith, rests securely upon the originating event of Jesus Christ in whom, according to the apostle, "God was reconciling the world to himself" (2 Cor. 5:19).

Some adherents of the Two-Source Hypothesis will claim the right to reach this same conclusion, still adhering to this hypothesis; other adherents of this hypothesis will strongly dispute this. The latter argue that such a "conservative" interpretation of the evidence, assuming the validity of the Two-Source Hypothesis, is "uncritical." This is the difference it makes. Based on one hypothesis, this is a thoroughly acceptable conclusion, in accord with all the evidence. Based on the other hypothesis, it may be questioned whether this conclusion rests on sound scholarship.

Epilogue

Adherents of the Two-Source Hypothesis are not required to reject all parables attributed to Jesus in the Gospel of Luke that cohere with Paul's theology. Few, if any, go that far. Most accept the Lukan parables as authentic parables of Jesus. The Jesus Seminar has voted that the parable of the man who had two sons, popularly known as the parable of the prodigal son, is probably an authentic parable of Jesus. And the theology of this parable certainly coheres closely with the theology of Paul.

However, adherents of the Two-Source Hypothesis can justly entertain the opinion that if, in writing about Jesus, they give weight to these parables of grace in the Gospel of Luke that cohere so closely to the thought of Paul, they could be involved in a great interpretative circle where they are reading the mind of Paul back into the mind of Jesus. The reasoning goes like this: because it is possible, even if not probable, that these Lukan parables (not found in Mark or Q) have been composed by the evangelist Luke or some other Paulinist, we cannot with confidence build on these materials, central though they are in the preaching of the church. Bultmann so reasoned.

This haunting skepticism is rooted in the fact that the theology of these Lukan parables coheres more closely to the theology of Paul than to the teaching of Jesus in Mark and Q. So long as the Two-Source Hypothesis continues to hold sway in the minds of New Testament scholars and theologians who follow these scholars, so long will the church be denied the fruits of Gospel research and theology that, in an unreserved manner, regards these Lukan parables as authentic parables of Jesus. As such, these parables disclose to us the mind of Jesus as clearly as, if not more clearly than, Paul's letters disclose the mind of the apostle.

Approaching the texts of the New Testament in this way enables us to make more sense out of the apostolic witness as a whole, so that when the apostle speaks of the mind of Christ, we do not limit ourselves to what he himself says in his authentic letters about the mind of Christ. We allow what he says to resonate with what is disclosed to us about the mind of Jesus Christ in the Gospels, including the mind of Christ disclosed in the parable upon which our attention is focused in this chapter.[3] Let us read an important text in Philippians with this principle in mind.

[1]So if there is any encouragement in Christ, any incentive of love, any participation in the Spirit, any affection and sympathy,
[2]complete my joy by being of the same mind, having the same love, being in full accord and of one mind.
[3]Do nothing from selfishness or conceit, but in humility count others better than yourselves.
[4]Let each of you look not only to his own interests, but also to the interests of others.
[5]Have this mind among yourselves, which is yours in Christ Jesus,
[6]who, though he was in the form of God, did not count equality with God a thing to be grasped,
[7]but emptied himself, taking the form of a servant, being born in the likeness of men.
[8]And being found in human form he humbled himself and became obedient unto death, even death on a cross.   —*Phil. 2:1–8 (RSV)*

As you read the following verses, think of the Pharisee in the temple who was righteous according to the law but who went down to his house in a wrong relationship to God:

> [4b] If any other person thinks he has reason for confidence in the flesh, I have more:
> [5] circumcised on the eighth day, of the people of Israel, of the tribe of Benjamin, a Hebrew born of the Hebrews; as to the law a Pharisee,
> [6] as to zeal a persecutor of the church, as to righteousness under the law blameless.
> [7] But whatever gain I had, I counted as loss for the sake of Christ.
> [8] Indeed I count everything as loss because of the surpassing worth of knowing Christ Jesus my Lord. For his sake I have suffered the loss of all things, and count them as refuse, in order that I may gain Christ
> [9] and be found in him, not having a righteousness of my own, based on law, but that which is through faith in Christ, the righteousness from God that depends on faith;
> [10] that I may know him and the power of his resurrection, and may share his sufferings, becoming like him in his death,
> [11] that if possible I may attain the resurrection from the dead.
>
> —*Phil. 3:4b–11 (RSV)*

Paul does not want us to boast but to be humble, like the sinner in the temple whose justification was based on faith. Paul wants us to lay aside all our grounds for confidence in the flesh; that we are baptized in the name of the Father, the Son, and the Holy Spirit; that we are members of some denomination, whether Catholics, Protestants, or Orthodox; that we are born-again Christians; that we are vigilant in our zeal for the purity of the faith; or that we are perfect in love. The one thing that counts above all else is our faith, our trust in the sovereign and redemptive love of God. It is our gratitude for God's mercy to us that is the true fount of all good works— without which our faith is worthless and makes a mockery of God's grace. This does not mean that being a member of the body of Christ is not decisive. Rather, membership is rooted in and sustained by an apostolic faith in God who in Christ is reconciling the world unto God.

Justification by faith, as it developed in the mind of Paul, was inseparably bound up with the redemptive consequences of the death of Christ. The grace of God is not cheap.

> [1] Therefore, since we are justified by faith, we have peace with God through our Lord Jesus Christ.
> [2] Through him we have obtained access to this grace in which we stand, and we rejoice in our hope of sharing the glory of God. . . .

[8]But God shows his love for us in that while we were yet sinners Christ died for us.

[9]Since, therefore, we are now justified by his blood, much more shall we be saved by him from the wrath of God.

[10]For if while we were enemies we were reconciled to God by the death of his Son, much more, now that we are reconciled, shall we be saved by his life.

—Rom. 5:1–2, 8–10

We should not expect this developed form of the doctrine of justification by faith, which is in the mind of the apostle, to be found on the lips of the flesh-and-blood Jesus. Where that appears to happen in the Gospels, we have a right to think that the Gospel texts have been influenced by the theological and christological reflection of the postresurrection community. But the parable in question is quite free of all such later doctrinal development. Here we see the doctrine of justification by faith in its pristine form, conveyed in the most powerful way possible—in imaginative and captivating story form. Jesus paints a verbal picture for us. This has made an indelible impression on our minds. We can never be the same after hearing this parable. Nor, apparently, could Saul of Tarsus. Yes, it is likely that Paul knew this parable. Why should he not? It is likely that this parable, like Isaiah 53, was one of the great subtexts of Paul's faith.

No teaching of Jesus, no matter how powerfully presented, could by itself have turned a persecutor of the church into a proclaimer of "the faith he once tried to destroy" (Gal. 2:23). That required Jesus Christ to be "publicly portrayed as crucified" (Gal. 3:1). It required the receiving of the Spirit by "hearing with faith" (Gal. 3:2–5).

This faith, this trust in the sovereign redemptive love of God, inspired Jesus. We see this clearly once we realize who Jesus was (and is). He was the one who spoke these parables. And he walked his talk—all the way to the cross, thereby breaking down "the dividing wall of hostility, by abolishing in his flesh the law of commandments and ordinances, that he might create in himself one new man in place of the two, . . . and might reconcile us both to God in one body" (Eph. 2:14–16).

This is how we can in good conscience read the evidence once we are no longer fettered by the constraints, still felt by many, of looking at these matters through the lens of the Two-Source Hypothesis. This is the difference it makes. Individual adherents of the Two-Source Hypothesis may attribute the Lukan parables to Jesus. But few give Luke 18:9–14a the importance it receives on the Two-Gospel Hypothesis (see Appendix).

CHAPTER 7

The Faithful Witness of Women

The Faithful Witness of Women in Matthew

^{27:55}There were also many women there, looking on from afar, who had followed Jesus from Galilee, ministering to him;

⁵⁶among whom were Mary Magdalene, and Mary the mother of James and Joseph, and the mother of the sons of Zebedee.

⁵⁷When it was evening, there came a rich man from Arimathea, named Joseph, who was also a disciple of Jesus.

⁵⁸He went to Pilate and asked for the body of Jesus. Then Pilate ordered it to be given to him.

⁵⁹And Joseph took the body, and wrapped it in a clean linen shroud,

⁶⁰and laid it in his own new tomb, which he had hewn in the rock; and he rolled a great stone to the door of the tomb, and departed.

⁶¹Mary Magdalene and the other Mary were there, sitting opposite the sepulchre.

^{28:1}Now after the Sabbath, toward the dawn of the first day of the week, Mary Magdalene and the other Mary went to see the sepulchre.

²And behold, there was a great earthquake; for an angel of the Lord descended from heaven and came and rolled back the stone, and sat upon it.

³His appearance was like lightning, and his raiment white as snow.

⁴And for fear of him the guards trembled and became like dead men.

⁵But the angel said to the women, "Do not be afraid; for I know that you seek Jesus who was crucified.

⁶He is not here; for he has risen, as he said. Come, see the place where he lay.

⁷Then go quickly and tell his disciples that he has risen from the dead, and behold, he is going before you to Galilee; there you will see him. Lo, I have told you."

⁸So they departed quickly from the tomb with fear and great joy, and ran to tell his disciples.

⁹And behold, Jesus met them and said, "Hail!" And they came up and took hold of his feet and worshiped him.

¹⁰Then Jesus said to them, "Do not be afraid; go and tell my brethren to go to Galilee, and there they will see me."

¹⁶Now the eleven disciples went to Galilee, to the mountain to which Jesus directed them.

¹⁷And when they saw him, they worshiped him; but some doubted.

¹⁸And Jesus came and said to them, "All authority in heaven and on earth has been given to me.

¹⁹Go therefore and make disciples of all nations, baptizing them in the name of the Father and of the Son and of the Holy Spirit,

²⁰teaching them to observe all that I have commanded you; and lo, I am with you always, to the close of the age."

—Matt. 27:55–61; 28:1–10, 16–20 (RSV)

Based on the Two-Gospel Hypothesis, the earliest Gospel—Matthew—gives a central and essential role to the faithful witness of certain women who knew Jesus well, who had heard his parables, who had traveled with him from Galilee on his way to Jerusalem, who had ministered to him, and who had been ministered to by him. This crucially important role for women in Christian life and faith, however, is not restricted to being the chief witnesses to the cardinal events of the crucifixion, burial, and resurrection of Jesus. Women play an important role in the story of Jesus throughout this Gospel.

References to Women in Matthew 1:1—26:35

The Matthean Genealogy

At the very beginning of Matthew's Gospel, the basic pattern of Jesus' genealogy is interrupted four times, and in each instance a woman takes her place in the history of Israel as a stunning reminder of the covenant relationship between God and his people. As such, these women are perceived as offering legal precedents for change, precedents so important to the early church in its struggle to break old patterns and to become the new creation for which Christ died.

Jesus' genealogy in Matthew, beginning with Abraham, the prototype of the uncircumcised Gentile member of the covenant, has been drawn up with the express purpose of teaching that Gentiles can be full members of the covenant. Thus all four interruptions of the genealogy (in each instance some ancestor is identified by a relationship to a collateral figure in the history of Israel) relate to the question of how the law of Moses bears on the question of covenantal membership. First, Tamar, who was accused of playing the harlot, was an Israelite sinner who was justified by the patriarch Judah: "She is more righteous than I" (Gen. 38:6–30). Second, Rahab was a harlot in Jericho who was incorporated with her family into the covenant of Israel—simply because of an act of "covenantal love," not because of obedience to the law of Moses (Josh. 2). Third, Ruth was a Gentile who was brought into close relationship with Israel when she married an Israelite. Later, she left her people, and, in the company of Naomi, placed her trust in the God of Israel, and went to live in the land of promise, becoming a full member of the covenant community and one of King David's ancestors (Ruth). Fourth, Bathsheba was a sinner in her relationship with David, and, because she was the wife of Uriah the Hittite, she also represented the Israelite who had formerly been married to a Gentile (2 Sam. 11:1—12:24). For these reasons and because she was the mother of King Solomon, Bathsheba would have been important for those concerned with the problem of admitting Gentiles into the church.

All four of these women would have been marginal figures in the program of Ezra and Nehemiah. Although the strict marriage laws enforced by Ezra and Nehemiah were temporarily salvific for a small, tight-knit postexilic Jewish community bent on reestablishing Israel as a viable nation, the greater saving story of the covenantal relationship always surpasses the law. And with the good news that God was now fulfilling his promise to save the nations through the death, burial, and resurrection of Jesus Christ, the situation for Israel changed radically. Gentiles being admitted into the covenant in increasing numbers shook the law to its foundations. For the most part, Gentiles admitted to the covenant did not adhere to the law, especially the laws prescribing circumcision and proscribing the eating of certain foods.

Out of this crisis was born the church. Women, as portrayed in the Gospel of Matthew, play an essential role. They are living testimonies to the triumph of the covenant over the law, giving birth over and over again to the Word made flesh, Emmanuel, God with us.

Mary

The first sentence following the genealogy reads: "Now the birth of Jesus Christ took place in this way: when as his mother Mary was espoused to Joseph, before they came together, she was found with child of the Holy Ghost" (Matt. 1:18). Then follows the account of Jesus' birth. It is not unimportant for Matthew's readers that this birth was irregular, while being seen as taking place in fulfillment of scripture: "Behold a virgin shall conceive and bear a son, and his name shall be called Emmanuel" (Matt. 1:23; cf. Isa. 7:14).

When the wise men entered "into the house, they saw the child with Mary his mother, and they fell down and worshiped him" (Matt. 2:11). An angel of the Lord warns Joseph to flee by night to Egypt with Mary and Jesus, forewarning them of Herod's attempts to kill the Christ child. There, they live as refugees until the tyrant dies. When they return, they eventually resettle in Galilee (Matt. 2:13–23).

Women in Jesus' Public Ministry

When Jesus began his public ministry, both men and women presumably were present in the crowds that were astonished at his teaching. At the opening of Jesus' healing ministry, Matthew is careful to mention the healing of Peter's mother-in-law as well as a leper and the servant of the centurion (Matt. 8:1–15). Jesus healed "all who were sick" to fulfill the inclusive words spoken by the prophet Isaiah: "He took our infirmities and bore our diseases" (Isa. 53:3; Matt. 8:17). Later, after healing the paralytic, Jesus also healed both the daughter of the ruler and the woman who had suffered from a hemorrhage for twelve years (Matt. 9:1–8, 18–28).

Men and women are treated equally in the teaching of Jesus:

> "Think not that I have come to bring peace on earth;
> I have not come to bring peace, but a sword.
> For I have come to set a man against his father,
> and a daughter against her mother,
> and a daughter-in-law against her mother-in-law."
> —*Matt. 10:34–36*

When in chapter 12 the evangelist writes that many followed Jesus, presumably that encompasses both women and men. Thus, when Jesus healed them all, he healed both men and women. This is to be borne in mind when the evangelist relates that Jesus ordered those whom he had healed "not to make him known," and then tells the reader that "this was to fulfill what was spoken by the prophet Isaiah":

> "Behold, my servant whom I have chosen,
> my beloved with whom my soul is well pleased.
> I will put my Spirit upon him,
> and he shall proclaim justice to the Gentiles.
> He will not wrangle or cry aloud,
> nor will any one hear his voice in the streets;
> he will not break a bruised reed
> or quench a smoldering wick,
> till he brings justice to victory;
> and in his name will the Nations hope."
> —*Matt. 12:18–21; Isa. 42:1–4*

Because both women and men followed Jesus, when he could effectively do so, he would deftly illustrate his teaching with dual examples:

> "The men of Nineveh
> will arise at the judgment
> with this generation
> and condemn it;
> for they repented at the preaching of Jonah
> and behold, something greater than Jonah is here.
> The queen of the South
> will arise at the judgment
> with this generation

and condemn it;
For she came from the ends of the earth
to hear the wisdom of Solomon,
and behold, something greater than Solomon is here."
—*Matt. 12:41–42 (RSV)*

Again in chapter 13, we read:

"The kingdom of heaven is like a grain of mustard seed
which a man took and sowed in his field;
it is the smallest of all seeds,
but when it has grown it is the greatest of shrubs. . . ."
"The kingdom of heaven is like leaven
which a woman took and hid in three measures of meal,
till it was all leavened."
—*Matt. 13:31–33 (RSV)*

When Jesus needed to express his teaching in its most radical terms, he was especially constrained to be inclusive in his language. We see this in his reply when he was interrupted in his teaching and told that his mother and brothers stood outside asking to speak to him:

"Who is my mother, and who are my brothers?"
—*Matt. 12:48*

Matthew's text continues:

Stretching out his hand toward his disciples,
Jesus said:
"Here are my mother and my brothers!
For whoever does the will of my Father in heaven
is my brother, and sister, and mother."   —*Matt. 12:49–50*

The evenhanded and inclusive language with which Moses commanded the Israelites to honor their fathers *and* their mothers (Ex. 20:12; Deut. 5:16) is used by Jesus when condemning the Pharisees and scribes for their hypocrisy in voiding the commandment of God by their tradition (Matt. 15:1–9).

When a Canaanite woman from the district of Tyre and Sidon cried out, "Have mercy on me. O Lord, son of David, my daughter is severely possessed by a demon," Jesus, recognizing the danger of his situation, did not respond. His disciples urged him to send her away, and Jesus replied by stating that he was sent only to the "lost sheep of the house of Israel." But the woman persisted in appealing for Jesus' help. He then replied in the hardest terms: "It is not fair to take the children's bread and throw it to the dogs." Matching the full measure of his irony, she responded, "Yes, Lord, yet even the dogs eat the crumbs that fall from the master's table." Then, giving public recognition to the hollow mockery of what he had just said, Jesus with compassion responded: "Oh woman, great is your faith!" The evangelist adds: "And her daughter was healed instantly" (Matt. 15:21–28).

It is significant that in the Gospel of Matthew, the one episode in Gentile territory—in Tyre and Sidon—again illustrates the covenantal love of God for all believers through a dialogue between Jesus and a woman, this time a Canaanite. She takes on the Son of God in her determination to have his assistance in healing her daughter. By the persistence grounded in her great faith, this woman prophetically calls forth from the Lord a public announcement on a decisive issue facing Israel—the basis for membership in the covenant.

Her great faith in the mercy of God constrained Jesus to fulfill his mission and his destiny, to advance the Gospel at whatever cost. Few scenes in the Bible are as dramatic as this. Jesus, according to Matthew, realized the far-reaching consequences of this radical departure from conventional practice. In chapter 15, after Peter correctly confessed Jesus to be the Christ, the Son of the living God, the evangelist tells us that Jesus began to prepare his disciples for the necessity of his going to Jerusalem to suffer and be killed.

The Women Compared with the Disciples

Peter began to rebuke Jesus for predicting his passion, saying: "God forbid, Lord! This shall never happen to you." But Jesus said: "Get out of my sight, Satan! You are a hindrance to me; for you are not on the side of God, but of men" (Matt. 16:13–23). This prediction of his passion is repeated in Matt. 17:22–23; and again in Matt. 21:17–19.

In chapter 19, the Pharisees ask Jesus: "Is it lawful to divorce one's wife for any cause?" Jesus answered: "Have you not read that he who made them from the beginning made them male and female and said, 'For this reason a man shall leave his father and mother and be joined to his wife, and the two shall become one flesh.' What God hath joined together, let no man put asunder" (Matt. 19:3–6). After further dialogue with the Pharisees, Jesus concludes: "Whoever divorces his wife, except for unchastity, and marries another, commits adultery" (v. 9). One wonders how many women who followed Jesus and supported his ministry did so out of the conviction that the kingdom he was preaching would mitigate their marginalization by divorce and other oppressive consequences of living in a male-dominated society. The attraction of an intimate faithful relationship with God is a source of great comfort to the marginalized and oppressed women of all times. Did these women then live in hope? If so, would the end that Peter said "shall never happen" bring them to despair or to a deeper faith? If, as Matthew relates in chapter 28, the women were the first to go to the tomb at the close of the Sabbath, could it be because they would not give up their faith?

On his way to Jerusalem, Jesus stopped by the house of Simon the leper, another marginalized person according to the law of Moses. There in Bethany, a woman who realized what the end was to be came with an alabaster jar of very expensive ointment and poured it on Jesus' head as he sat at table. The disciples, still not realizing the cost of the ransom that must be paid for the redemption they expected, protested the waste and observed that the ointment might have been sold for a large sum and the money given to the poor. Jesus said to them: "Why do you trouble the woman? For she has done a beautiful thing to me. The poor you have with you always, but you will not always have me. When she poured this oil on my body, it was her way of preparing me for burial." Then came Jesus' memorable words: "I tell you this: whenever in all the world this gospel is proclaimed, what she has done will be told in memory of her" (Matt. 26:6–13).

One night shortly thereafter, in an upper room in Jerusalem, Jesus took bread and broke it and blessed it and gave it to the twelve disciples and said: "Take, eat; this is my body." After this reference to the breaking of his body, he took a cup and after making it clear that he wanted all twelve—including the one who was to betray him—to drink of the cup, Jesus said: "This is my blood of the covenant, which is poured out for many for the forgiveness of sins" (Matt. 26:20–29).

When they had sung a hymn, Jesus and his disciples went out to the Mount of Olives. There Jesus tells them that they will all fall away. Peter said: "Even if I must die with you, I will not deny you." The evangelist adds: "And so said all the disciples" (Matt. 26:30–35).

In this chapter, the evangelist Matthew juxtaposes and highlights the denial and unbelief of the twelve disciples with the faithfulness of women who traveled with Jesus from Galilee and ministered to him.

The Faithful Witness of Women in Matthean Perspective

At the crucifixion, the disciples are notable by their absence. All presumably had fallen away, as Jesus had said they would. But not so the women, many of whom were there, including "Mary Magdalene, and Mary the mother of James and Joseph, and the mother of the sons of Zebedee" (Matt. 27:56). Intending to highlight the faithfulness of certain women, Matthew represents these particular women as being the sole witnesses (among those who followed Jesus) to his death. Two of these women remained until the evening to witness the burial of Jesus (Matt. 27:61). After the end of the Sabbath, they returned to the tomb. There, an "angel of the Lord" instructed them to "go quickly and tell his disciples that he has risen from the dead, and behold, he is going before you to Galilee; there you will see him" (Matt. 28:7).

On their way to carry out this mission, Jesus meets them and, telling them to have courage, reiterates the instructions. It is to be assumed, according to Matthew's dramatic account, that these women carried out their mission. The eleven went to Galilee, where they saw Jesus and worshiped him. "But some doubted" (Matt. 28:17), which, according to Matthew's account, none of the women is said to have done.

By the standards of Matthew's first readers, women fare well in his account, very well indeed. Although no women are among the Twelve, they do not suffer by comparison as faithful disciples of Jesus. They share in his ministry as the chief, if not sole, faithful witnesses to his death and burial, and the first to see and worship the risen Lord. The faith and witness of these women is substantial and constitutive of the church's self-identity. These women as witnesses and messengers, ministers and visionaries, lovers and believers, were a necessary cause of the church.

The Faithful Witness of Women in Luke

23:49And all his acquaintances and the <u>women</u> who had followed him <u>from Galilee</u> stood <u>at a distance</u> and saw these things.

50Now there was a man named <u>Joseph</u> from the Jewish town of <u>Arimathea</u>. He was a member of the council, a good and righteous man,

51who had not consented to their purpose and deed, and he was looking for the kingdom of God.

52<u>This man</u> went <u>to Pilate and asked for the body of Jesus</u>.

53Then he took it down and <u>wrapped it in a linen shroud, and laid</u> him in a rock-hewn tomb, where no one had ever yet been laid.

54It was the day of Preparation, and the sabbath was beginning.

55The women who had come with him from Galilee followed, and saw the tomb, and how his body was laid;

56then they returned, and prepared spices and ointments. On the sabbath they rested according to the commandment.

24:1But on the first day <u>of the week,</u> early at dawn, they went to the tomb, taking the spices which they had prepared.

2And they found <u>the stone</u> rolled away from the tomb,

3but when they went in they did not find the body.

4While they were perplexed about this, behold, two men stood by them in dazzling apparel;

5and as they were frightened and bowed their faces to the ground, the men said to them, "Why <u>do you seek</u> the living among <u>the dead</u>?"

6Remember how he told <u>you</u>, while he was still in Galilee,

[7]that the Son of Man must be delivered into the hands of sinful men, and be crucified, and on the third day rise."
[8]And they remembered his words,
[9]and returning <u>from the tomb,</u> they told all this to the eleven and to all the rest.
[10]Now it was Mary <u>Magdalene</u> and Joanna <u>and Mary</u> the mother of James and the other women with them who told this to the apostles;
[11]but these words seemed to them an idle tale, and they did not believe them. . . .
[24:22]"Moreover, some women of our company amazed us. They were at the tomb early in the morning
[23]and did not find his body; and they came back saying that they had seen a vision of angels, who said that he was alive.
[24]Some of those who were with us went to the tomb, and found it just as the women had said; but him they did not see. . . ."
[33]And they arose that same hour and returned to Jerusalem; and they found the eleven gathered together and those who were with them,
[34]who said, "The Lord has risen indeed, and has appeared to Simon!"
—*Luke 23:49—24:11; 24:22-24, 33-34 (RSV)*

Luke's version of the women's witness to the death, burial, and resurrection of Jesus follows loosely the account given in Matt. 27:55—28:17. The degree of verbatim agreement, indicated by the underlined words in the above translation, comports with the view of the Two-Gospel Hypothesis that Luke knows Matthew and often follows the story line and sometimes the wording. Nonetheless, Luke can retell that story very freely, sometimes drawing upon independent tradition. The story of the two disciples on the road to Emmaus is widely accepted as an independent postresurrection story utilized by Luke.

If this were an independent story, it would be clear that some earlier editor, if not Luke himself, had woven together the story line in Matthew with the Emmaus story to allow the women a very positive role in the passion narrative while conforming it to the pre-Pauline tradition where the risen Christ appears first to Peter, then to a series of other men (1 Cor. 15:5), without reference to a conflicting first "appearance" to the women (Matt. 28:9-10), and for that matter, without reference to any appearance to women at any time. This point of agreement between Paul and Luke deserves emphasis. In Luke, the risen Christ appears to the two disciples on the road to Emmaus; when they returned to Jerusalem, they learned from the eleven that "the Lord has risen indeed, and has appeared to Simon!" But not, so far as we are told, to Mary Magdalene or to any other women. Did the appearance to Simon precede the appearance to the two disciples on the road to Emmaus? Luke is silent on this question. His account does not conflict with Paul's. Given the very different accounts in Matthew and Paul, Luke utilizes the independent Emmaus story and brings together all his sources with remarkable literary and theological skill.

Luke does not weaken the role of women in witnessing to the earlier death and burial of Jesus. Indeed, where Matthew's account does not mention the women until the scene of Jesus' death, Luke places them not only there, but earlier in the story as well.

[26]And as they led him away, they seized on Simon of Cyrene, who was coming in from the country, and laid on him the cross, to carry it behind Jesus.

[27]And there followed him a great multitude of the people, and of women who bewailed and lamented him.

[28]But Jesus, turning to them said, "Daughters of Jerusalem, do not weep for me, but weep for yourselves and for your children.

[29]For behold, the days are coming when they will say, 'Blessed are the barren, and the wombs that never bore, and the breasts that never gave suck!'

[30]Then they will begin to say to the mountains, 'Fall on us'; and to the hills, 'Cover us.'

[31]For if they do this when the wood is green, what will happen when it is dry?"

—Luke 23:26–31 (RSV)

And what is true in Luke's passion narrative is true even more so in Luke's story of Jesus as a whole. The story about Elizabeth, which is woven with the story of the annunciation and visitation of Mary flows through the opening chapter of Luke, highlighted by the Magnificat (Luke 1:49–55). Chapter 2 features women in the story of the birth of Jesus by Mary (1–20); his presentation in the temple by Mary and Joseph (22–35); the story of the prophetess Anna, who spoke in the temple of Jesus "to all who were looking for the redemption of Jerusalem," as well as the story of Mary and Joseph when Jesus tarried behind in Jerusalem (41–52).

Luke does not skip over Matthew's story of Jesus healing Peter's mother-in-law (4:38–39). However, the story of healing the son of the widow of Nain is unique to Luke (7:11–17), as is the story of the woman who anointed Jesus in the house of a Pharisee (7:36–50), as well as the tradition about Mary Magdalene and other women who provided for the Twelve including "Joanna, the wife of Chuza, Herod's steward, and Susanna, and many others" (8:1–3). Luke includes Matthew's stories (1) of Jesus' response when informed that his mother and his brothers wanted to see him but could not because of the crowd (8:19–21); (2) of the woman who had a flow of blood for twelve years, which as in Matthew is encapsulated inside the story of healing of Jairus's daughter (8:40–48); and (3) of the raising from the dead of the synagogue ruler's daughter (8:49–56).

Luke also features women prominently in the story of Mary and Martha (10:38–42). This story is unique to Luke's Gospel, as is the story of the woman in the crowd who cried out to Jesus, "Blessed is the womb that bore you, and the breasts that you sucked!" and to whom he replied, "Blessed rather are those who hear the word of God and keep it!" (11:27–28).

Matthew's saying about Jonah and the queen of the south is retained by Luke (11:29–32) with typical Lukan alteration of the original poetic form of the saying; also retained is the saying about giving peace on earth. Here the inclusive language utilized by Jesus in his illustrations is very loosely revised by Luke (12:45–53).

The story of Jesus' healing of the bent-over woman on the Sabbath is unique to Luke (13:10–17). Luke retains Matthew's form of the twin saying about the grain of a mustard seed sowed by a man and the leaven hid in three measures of meal by a woman (13:18–21). He copies almost verbatim the lament in Matthew, where Jesus likens his concern for the children of Jerusalem to that of a mother hen who gathers her brood under her wings (13:34–35).

The twin sayings (15:3–10) about the man who seeks and finds a lost sheep, and the woman who seeks and finds a lost coin have been drawn by Luke from an early collection of Jesus' parables. The presence of such a twin teaching in this collection confirms that Jesus in his teaching sometimes illustrated his point by drawing comparable examples from the life situations of both men and women.

The parable about the unrighteous judge and the widow who would not cease from crying out for justice is unique to Luke (18:1–8). It is not unusual for Luke to substitute parables from his special source material for parables or stories in Matthew that convey a very similar teaching. One case in point is Luke's substitution of the parable of the elder brother (Luke 15:11–32) for that of the laborers in the vineyard (Matt. 20:1–15). In both cases, Jesus rebukes the self-righteous attitude of those who resent God's mercy.

The story about the importunate or persistent widow conveys in parable form a teaching found in Matthew's story of the Canaanite woman. In both cases, a marginal person—a Gentile woman in one case, and in the other a woman without a male relative to plead her case in court—models Jesus' teaching. Under duress, the oppressed are to insist on their right to access the ultimate power that sanctions oppressive or repressive societal structures. To these women and all deprived people, Jesus says:

> "Ask and it will be given to you;
> Seek and you will find;
> Knock and it will be opened to you.
> For everyone who asks receives,
> And the one who seeks finds,
> And to the one who knocks it will be opened."
> —*Matt. 7:7–8; Luke 11:9–10*

The Greek original of this saying contains twenty-four words. Based on the Two-Gospel Hypothesis, Luke has chosen to copy the text of Matthew exactly, maintaining the same word order in every instance. These words of

Jesus, preserved in Matthew in their original poetic form and transmitted unchanged by Luke, lie behind and ground the teaching found in the stories of the Gentile woman and the persistent widow. God has revealed his will in these prescient words of Jesus. The concise truth of this teaching may then be reinforced by parable or story.

Luke introduced the story of the widow's mite (Luke 21:1–4) from some source other than Matthew. This woman is a model of faith and righteousness in the eyes of Jesus. The red thread of sacrifice from which the rich turn away holds her life together and gives it meaning for others.

Based on the Two-Gospel Hypothesis, the impact of Jesus' teaching in the church is reinforced by materials in one or both of these two earlier Gospels that complement and supplement one another. From these two Gospels, we learn the most about the importance of women in the Gospel story and the importance of their witness to some of the cardinal events of the church's message.

Assuming the validity of the Two-Gospel Hypothesis, a comparison of Luke's account of the witness of the women with Matthew's discloses to the careful reader how the Gospel tradition developed in response to the church's need for accounts that were less vulnerable to the debunking attacks of those who were skeptical of Jesus' resurrection.

In contrast to Matthew, Luke specifies that the women not only witnessed his crucifixion but also "followed closely" when Jesus' body was taken to the tomb. They "saw the tomb, and how his body was laid" (Luke 23:55). Luke also provides the women with a motive for leaving the tomb: they desire to see Jesus' body more properly prepared for burial, thus requiring that they leave to acquire spices and aromatic ointments (Luke 23:56a). Further, their failure to return that evening or the next morning could be understood as observance of the Sabbath (Luke 23:56b). However, the delay until Sunday morning for their return to the tomb, in view of their freedom to return at the end of the Sabbath, after sunset the preceding evening, is best understood in terms of the need to set their inspection of the tomb in the light of the dawning day with Peter's subsequent inspection of the tomb coming in broad daylight.

The omission of the appearance of Jesus to the women makes it possible for Luke's readers to perceive that the earliest witnesses to Jesus as the resurrected Lord were not two "frightened and confused women," but two hard-headed disciples (Luke 24:25) who had the opportunity to recognize Jesus and establish his identity under almost ideal circumstances (Luke 24:12–32). This testimony was also corroborated by an independent appearance to Simon Peter (Luke 24:34), who before seeing Jesus had gone to the tomb to verify what the women had reported (Luke 24:12).

There is a particular interest in the Lukan version of what happened after the death of Jesus, which comes to expression during Jesus' later appearance to the disciples in Jerusalem. Jesus asks the disciples to touch him to see that he is no spirit, but has "flesh and bones" (Luke 24:39). He demonstrates this by consuming food in their presence (Luke 24:41–43). In these ways Luke's narrative reassures the faithful in whose minds doubt concerning the resurrection has been raised by unbelievers who see loopholes in the story. Luke's account helps to deflect attention from some of the problem-causing features of Matthew's account.

The Witness of Women in Mark

15:40There were also women looking on from afar, among whom were Mary Magdalene, and Mary the mother of James the younger and of Joses, and Salome,

41who, when he was in Galilee, followed him, and ministered to him; and also many other women who came up with him to Jerusalem.

42And when evening had come, since it was the day of Preparation, that is, the day before the sabbath,

43Joseph of Arimathea, a respected member of the council, who was also himself looking for the kingdom of God, took courage and went to Pilate, and asked for the body of Jesus.

[44And Pilate wondered if he were already dead; and summoning the centurion, he asked him whether he was already dead.

45And when he learned from the centurion that he was dead, he granted the body to Joseph.]

46And he bought a linen shroud, and taking him down, wrapped him in the linen shroud, and laid him in a tomb which had been hewn out of the rock; and he rolled a stone against the door of the tomb.

47Mary Magdalene and Mary the mother of Joses saw where he was laid.

16:1And when the sabbath was past, Mary Magdalene, and Mary the mother of James, and Salome, bought spices, so that they might go and anoint him.

2And very early on the first day of the week they went to the tomb when the sun had risen.

3And they were saying to one another, "Who will roll away the stone for us from the door of the tomb?"

[4And looking up, they saw that the stone was rolled back—it was very large.

5And entering the tomb, they saw a young man sitting on the right side, dressed in a white robe; and they were amazed.]

6And he said to them, "Do not be amazed; you seek Jesus of Nazareth, who was crucified.

7But go, tell his disciples and Peter that he is going before you to Galilee; there you will see him, as he told you."

8And they went out and fled from the tomb; for trembling and astonishment had come upon them, and they said nothing to any one, for they were afraid.

[9Now when he rose early on the first day of the week, he appeared first to Mary Magdalene, from whom he had cast out seven demons.

¹⁰She went out and told those who had been with him, as they mourned and wept.

¹¹But when they heard that he was alive and had been seen by her, they would not believe it.

¹²After this he appeared in another form to two of them, as they were walking into the country.

¹³And they went back and told the rest, but they did not believe them.

¹⁴Afterward he appeared to the eleven themselves as they sat at table; and he upbraided them for their unbelief and hardness of heart, because they had not believed those who saw him after he had risen.

¹⁵And he said to them, "Go into all the world and preach the gospel to the whole creation.

¹⁶He who believes and is baptized will be saved; but he who does not believe will be condemned.

¹⁷And these signs will accompany those who believe: in my name they will cast out demons; they will speak in new tongues;

¹⁸they will pick up serpents, and if they drink any deadly thing, it will not hurt them; and they will lay their hands on the sick, and they will recover."

¹⁹So then the Lord Jesus, after he had spoken to them, was taken up into heaven, and sat down at the right hand of God.

²⁰And they went forth and preached everywhere, while the Lord worked with them and confirmed the messages by the signs that attended it. Amen.]

—Mark 15:40—16:8 [or 20] (RSV)

Based on the Two-Gospel Hypothesis, Mark 15:40—16:8, as well as the whole of most of the text of Mark, has been taken from the parallel parts of Matthew or Luke, or both. Brackets are used to show pure Markan expansion of the narrative.

Speaking generally, and assuming the validity of the Two-Gospel Hypothesis, we can say that Mark has followed Matthew and Luke in 15:40 when he places Mary Magdalene and other women at the scene of Jesus' death "looking on from afar." On the other hand, 15:44–45 represents a Markan addition to the story in Matthew and Luke that has an apologetic purpose. It answers the objection that Jesus did not really die on the cross. After his burial, he might have revived and left the tomb. Any subsequent appearance of Jesus to the women or to the disciples would not necessarily have been a resurrection appearance. Mark's account in this way checks any doubt concerning the death and resurrection. One might ask, under the Two-Source Hypothesis, why either Matthew or Luke, let alone both, omitted this apologetic passage in Mark's text.

The conflated character of Mark 16:9–14 is easy to see, and the author's purpose is not hard to detect. He has produced an intelligible account of Jesus' postresurrection appearances that draws upon events in both Matthew and Luke and serves to harmonize them, though not in any mechanical way nor in every detail. The three appearances in verses 9, 12, and 14 correspond to (1) the appearance of Jesus to Mary Magdalene in Matthew; (2) the appearance to the disciples on the road to Emmaus in Luke; and (3) finally the appearance to the Eleven in Jerusalem, also in Luke. All readers would know that the reference to the eleven in verse 14 would include Peter, and Mark emphasizes this by the otherwise gratuitous addition of Peter's name in 16:7.

Most modern translations place 16:9–20 in smaller-size print, noting that not all manuscripts include those verses. The author of these verses, however, almost certainly knew the resurrection stories in Matthew and Luke. Assuming the validity of the Two-Gospel Hypothesis, there is no difficulty in accounting for the conflated character of these verses. Mark would have had reason to give his church a version of Jesus' appearances that included rival and conflicting traditions. Having said that, it must be noted that Mary Magdalene in Mark 16:9 is the person to whom Jesus *first* appeared. So in this regard the text of Mark follows Matthew, not Luke nor the pre-Pauline tradition (where Peter is listed as the first in a series of witnesses to whom the risen Lord had appeared).

The Faithful Witness of Women and the Two-Source Hypothesis

Based on the Two-Source Hypothesis, the church's earliest source concerning Jesus is Q. While the hypothetical Q is mainly a collection of Jesus' sayings, it is not made up of sayings alone. All reconstructions of Q contain at least one miracle story, the healing of the centurion's daughter (Matt. 8:5–10 and Luke 7:1–10). All Q reconstructions also contain the story of Jesus' temptation (Matt. 4:1–11 | | Luke 4:1–13), as well as the story of John the Baptist's disciples coming to Jesus (Matt. 11:2–6).

Most scholars would also place the Beelzebul story in Q because of the very extensive verbatim agreement between Matthew and Luke at points where the story has no parallel in Mark (Matt. 12:22–32 | | Luke 11:14–23; 12:10 | | Mark 3:22–30).

In fact, the Gospels contain several passages where the agreements between Matthew and Luke against the text of Mark are so extensive that, unless one is prepared to acknowledge that Luke has copied Matthew, the simplest explanation on the Two-Source Hypothesis is to posit further overlaps of Mark with Q. The most celebrated of these passages is in the passion narrative where Jesus is mocked (Matt. 26:67–68 | | Luke 22:63–65 | | Mark 14:65). But this would mean Q included a passion narrative.[1] And if Q included a passion narrative as well as the other narrative passages (Matt. 3:1–10 | | Luke 3:2–16 | | Mark 1:2–8; Matt. 8:5–12 | | Luke 7:1–10; Matt. 11:2–19 | | Luke 7:18–35) that scholars posit as being in Q, then this hypothetical document takes on more and more of a Gospel form. In that case, there is no reason in principle why Q should not show some trace of the stories in the other Gospels where women are present at one or more of the cardinal events of Jesus' crucifixion, burial, and resurrection. However, it does not.

If Q existed—and is accepted as the most important Christian document we have, as some Q advocates contend—then its silence on the important witness of women would be a deliminating nail in the coffin of the church aspiring to live out the liberating truth that in Christ there is neither male nor female (Gal. 3:28). This is not because advocates of Q are antifeminist. It is because Q, assuming the validity of the Two-Gospel Hypothesis, is a literary accident. Q is material Luke copied from Matthew but that Mark did not include in his Gospel. Under these circumstances, the absence from such a purely literary construct of any particular teaching or theme cannot be said to be of any importance whatsoever to the understanding of Christian origins. But if Q is the most important Christian document we have, which one can assert under the Two-Source Hypothesis, then the absence from this document of any trace of the importance of a faithful witness of women in the church weighs against the view that women were important in the ministry of Jesus.

In the Gospel of Mark, women are present to witness the crucifixion and burial, and at least one woman, Mary Magdalene, witnesses an appearance of the risen Lord. However, the text in Mark where the words "he appeared first to Mary Magdalene" (16:9) are found is not attested in some important early textual witnesses. The first edition of the Revised Standard Version New Testament, following the advocates of the majority view, included verses 9–20 only as "additions" to Mark, not as belonging to the original text.

Virtually all adherents of the Two-Source Hypothesis reject the authenticity of Mark 16:9–20, the "longer ending of Mark." Important manuscript evidence supports this rejection, mainly from the famous fourth-century manuscripts Codex Vaticanus and Codex Sinaiticus. Both end with 16:8. Moreover, compelling evidence exists that the author of 16:9–20 knew the stories about the appearances of the risen Lord as they are preserved in Matthew and Luke, and this conflationary character of 16:9–20 (assuming the theory of Markan primacy) works against their having been composed by the author of Mark.

Adherents of both the Two-Source and the Two-Gospel Hypothesis generally characterize the resurrection appearances in Mark 16:9–20 as a blending of the appearance stories in the other Gospels. If these verses belong to the original text of Mark, their blended character would create no problem for adherents of the Two-Gospel Hypothesis.[2]

Based on the Two-Source Hypothesis, as has been noted with the hypothetical Q and the unquestioned text of Mark, there is no evidence to support the witness of women to the risen Lord. The later Gospels, Matthew and Luke, both repeat the testimony of Mark that women were present at the crucifixion and burial of Jesus. But on the question of whether they witnessed the appearance of the risen Lord, they offer conflicting evidence. Matthew states that women were present, but Luke does not. In Luke, Jesus appears to Peter, and he also appears to two other disciples on the road to Emmaus and then to the Eleven. Luke contains no appearance of the risen Lord to women.

Assuming the validity of the Two-Source Hypothesis, when we pick up the later more gender-inclusive Gospels of Matthew and Luke, where women receive considerable attention from the beginning to the end of each Gospel, and then proceed backward in time, we find a reduced attention to women in Mark and almost no attention to women at all in Q. Assuming this sequence of our sources, it is not at all unreasonable to conclude that because the later Gospels show an increasing interest in women, it is possible that this reflects the church developing a greater interest in women as time went by. Since the earliest Gospel, Mark, gives less importance to women, and the earliest source Q mentions them hardly at all, it is possible that women were actually of little or no importance in the ministry of Jesus. It is quite possible that the church's assumption of a very meaningful—albeit sometimes subordinate—role of women in Jesus' ministry is based on a pious or uncritical reading of the Gospels, which upon examination turns out to be largely illusory. Based on the Two-Source Hypothesis, it is not unreasonable to conclude that the interest in women in the Gospels, undeniably present, is due not to their importance during the ministry of Jesus but rather to later developments in the early church when, for a time at least, the role of women became increasingly important.

By way of contrast, a critical reading of the texts of the Gospels, assuming the sequence Matthew, Luke, and Mark, leads to very different conclusions. Based on this hypothesis, the two earliest Gospels, each in its own distinctive way, present ample evidence for the view that women were important in, for, and to Jesus' ministry. At the same time, the decreased attention to women in Mark's Gospel, assuming the validity of the Two-Gospel Hypothesis, does not signify Mark's lack of interest in women. It is simply due to Mark's compositional purpose to present the Gospel story in a new and fresh form, drawing largely from the narrative material common to the two earlier Gospels. Mark never intended his Gospel to replace the earlier and more ample Gospel accounts. One of his purposes, based on the Two-Gospel Hypothesis, was to unify Matthew and Luke; to demonstrate that each in its own distinctive way was telling essentially the same story of the flesh-and-blood martyrdom of the Son of God. That explains why Mark added to his passion narrative the information about Pilate making certain that Jesus was dead. This served to check any tendency to argue that Jesus did not really die on the cross but only seemed to die, and was later resuscitated.

The Women's Bible Commentary
and the Source Question

Amy L. Wordelman, in her essay on "Everyday Life: Women in the Period of the New Testament," in *The Women's Bible Commentary*,[3] notes that religious associations, including synagogues and churches, "provided an arena in which women could and did exercise leadership roles." Professor Jane Schaberg, in her commentary on Luke, notes that "Matthew's treatment of leadership as shared (16:19; 18:18) is theoretically more egalitarian than Luke's treatment," and then observes: "Furthermore, the women at the tomb in Matthew not only receive a commission, but as they run to tell the disciples, the risen Christ appears first to them [28:1–10]" (279–80).

Under the heading "Historical Women in the Early Christian Movement," Schaberg provides this thought-provoking paragraph:

> Luke's depiction of women must be placed alongside reconstructions of the early Christian movement, which indicate that the movement was truly egalitarian in its initial stages, with women in positions of leadership and authority (see, e.g., Romans 16). The roots or sources of the experiment in inclusive community remain a historical puzzle, but Jewish egalitarian movements based on apocalyptic and wisdom traditions seem likely keys (280).

Schaberg regards the Gospel of Luke as perhaps the "most dangerous" text in the Bible because Luke contains much material about women that is not found in the other Gospels, and some scholars think that the evangelist is "enhancing or promoting the status of women." This is not the case, contends Schaberg, who sees Luke portraying women in conventional roles as oppressed persons. Although Mary's Magnificat is "precious to women and other oppressed people . . . ," Luke's portrait of Mary is ambiguous and hints at "the restriction of women seen in the rest of the Gospel" (284–85).

In her discussion of the differences between Luke's account of the empty tomb and those in other Gospels, Schaberg writes:

> Most important, in Luke the women are not commissioned to go tell the disciples that they will see the risen Jesus in Galilee. Instead, reference is made to a prediction of the passion and resurrection made by Jesus to them in Galilee. Strangely, however, this prediction does not match any in Luke's Gospel (9:22, 44; 18:32–33) but rather is closest to the non-Markan tradition found in Matthew 20:19 (290).

After listing the risen Lord's appearances and teachings to Peter, to the two disciples going to Emmaus, and to the Eleven and their companions, Schaberg laconically observes: "But in Luke the risen Jesus does not appear to women. Their witness is not essential to the Christian faith" (291).

In a section "Conclusions and Open Questions," Schaberg credits Luke with having been influential "in the creation of Christian assumptions, ideas, and institutions that do not affirm women but instead relegate them to the margins of the community and especially its leadership" (291).

After recognizing the negative side of Luke's ambivalent tradition concerning women, Schaberg wrote, one can then turn "with enthusiasm and even respect" to positive and promising aspects in Luke's Gospel. One can, for example, "bring to light egalitarian traditions preserved in the sources of this Gospel" (291).

None of Schaberg's careful and critical feminist analysis of Luke would be substantially affected were she to abandon the Two-Source Hypothesis, which she has "followed provisionally" (276) in her commentary, and in place of Mark and Q substitute the Gospel of Matthew as a source for Luke. The effect of such a paradigm shift, however, would be dramatic for her hermeneutical project, for then she would have the Gospel that she has noted is theoretically more egalitarian as an earlier source. This would strengthen her grounds for believing that the early Christian movement was, as the evidence she cites from Romans 16 indicates, "truly egalitarian in its initial stages" (280). This would help to solve the "historical puzzle" of the roots and sources of the "experiment in inclusive community" to which Romans 16 witnesses, by suggesting that these "roots and sources" go back to a gender-inclusive ministry of Jesus.

To assume that the Gospel of Matthew was available to Luke would also explain the fact that the reference in Luke 24:7, Jesus' prediction in Galilee of the passion and resurrection, strangely does not match any in Mark's Gospel, but is closest to that in Matt. 20:19. What is indeed strange under the theory that Luke had Mark for a source, is easy to explain if Luke had Matthew as a source.

Professor Amy-Jill Levine's commentary on Matthew in *The Women's Bible Commentary* is essentially favorable to the first evangelist. "The Gospel decries various structures that cause social oppression. . . . The evangelist attempts to eliminate all relationships in which one group exploits or dominates another" (252).

With regard to women specifically, Levine writes:

> Women frequently represent both the ideal of service that Jesus requests of his disciples (20:26–27) and the model of fidelity that the Church requests of its members. But this service is not equated with women's stereotypical duty as servant to spouse or children. Rather, women who appear apart from husband, father, or son assume positive, active roles in the Gospel (253).

Levine notes that the evangelist in his passion narrative has attempted to juxtapose the disciples' lack of true understanding with a depiction of women as "aware, sympathetic, and loyal" (261).

Although they [the women] are not included in the reference to "his disciples" (28:7) or mentioned as present at the Great Commission (28:16–20), the angel's words (28:7) and the meeting with Jesus (28:9–10) indicate their substantive role in the Easter mission. Indeed it is Jesus who first greets them, and they in turn are the first to worship him. Matthew records of the Eleven that "some doubted" (28:17), but of the women only their legitimate fear and their joy are reported. These independent, motivated women are both the first witnesses to the resurrection and the first missionaries of the Church (262).

There is nothing in this careful and critical feminist interpretation of Matthew that would be called into question were we to assume that Matthew was indeed the earliest Gospel. But to see Matthew, which Levine regards as so favorable to women, as the earliest Gospel would put the role of women in the earliest church in a radically different interpretive framework.

Professor Mary Ann Tolbert begins her commentary on Mark with this interesting sentence: "The Gospel of Mark, perhaps the earliest of the canonical Gospels, has received little attention through most of Christian history." It is the choice of the word "perhaps" that calls for comment. Nothing explicitly indicates that Tolbert has any doubt that Mark is our earliest Gospel. And yet, Tolbert says things about this Gospel that suggest she might have once wished that the text of the Gospel of Mark could be read differently.

According to Tolbert's reading of Mark, the women who witnessed both the crucifixion and the burial of Jesus go to the tomb on the morning of the third day, only to find the stone rolled away and a young man in white there to address them. He announces the resurrection and then sends them to tell the disciples, even Peter, that Jesus is going before them into Galilee. The women, however, like the Twelve before them, are fearful. They flee from the tomb in trembling and astonishment, saying nothing to anyone, for they are afraid. As Tolbert reads the text of Mark, she makes the case that

> women who behave conventionally or concern themselves with social status, power, or customary rules have *not* been those whose faith has proved fruitful. The "good news" Jesus has been preaching of a different world on the horizon demands followers who are willing to act outside the constraints of society, religiously and socially (274).

Then comes Tolbert's terse judgment: "The two Marys and Salome, like the twelve men earlier, are evidently not of that quality." To see this negative judgment of these three women in perspective, it is important to note that earlier in her commentary, Tolbert has declared that most of the women characters in Mark belong in that group of persons who "come to Jesus in faith, are healed (or saved) by that faith, and often go out to preach to others (e.g. 1:40–45; 2:1–12; 5:1–20; 5:25–34; 7:25–30; 9:14–29; 10:46–52)." These men and women, mostly anonymous, "illustrate the fertile ground which bears abundant fruit" (266).

Thus, the witness of women at the end of Mark's Gospel stands in stark contrast to that of most of the women in the rest of the Gospel. This is explained by Tolbert in terms of the fact that "ancient writing was intended to *do* things, to make people act or believe or change their behavior" (274).

> The expectations raised and then crushed by the end of the Gospel are intended to move the hearers of the Gospel into action. . . . The ending of Mark intends to arouse the emotions of its hearers on behalf of Jesus and the "good news" he came to preach. It intends to make hearers and readers into faithful disciples and followers, for very little time remains until this present evil world is wiped away and God's fruitful kingdom is established (274).

But if all this is true, what are we to make of Levine's positive judgment about Mary Magdalene and the other Mary? She views these women not as failures, but as "the first witnesses to the resurrection and the first missionaries of the church."

If Mark is the earliest of the canonical Gospels, as Tolbert writes is perhaps the case, then the author of the later Gospel, Matthew, appears to have gone against the witness of his source Mark and created for his Gospel story an ending more favorable to women. On the other hand, if Matthew is the earliest Gospel, then Levine's conclusions would be quite credible, that the first witnesses of the resurrection and the first missionaries of the church probably were women.

In summary, we need to ask: "What light has been thrown by this discussion of the work of Levine, Tolbert and Schaberg on the question: 'What difference does it make?' " Broadly speaking on the question of the role of women, the main difference comes down to how the favorable treatment of women in Matthew's Gospel is to affect our understanding of the role of women in Jesus' ministry. If Matthew is a later Gospel based on Mark and Q, then it is clear that he has taken the basically favorable depiction of women in Mark and changed the end as given in Mark's Gospel to bring it more into line with the basic story line of the rest of that Gospel. On the other hand, if Matthew is the earliest Gospel, the favorable treatment of women in Matthew can be cited as evidence that converges with the independent evidence from Romans 16 to support a hypothesis that the equalitarian character of Paul's church doctrine is consonant with a gender-inclusive ministry of Jesus. This character of Jesus' ministry was presumably rooted in his reading of Moses and the prophets concerning God being no respecter of persons. Thus, it would follow for Paul that in Jesus Christ and his kingdom there can be neither male nor female.[4]

The point is not that everything will change with a shift in our source paradigm, but some, if not many, questions and problems will now be seen in a very different light.

CHAPTER 8

God's Special Commitment to the Poor

Matthew 11:2–6

[2]Now when John heard in prison about the deeds of the Christ, he sent word by his disciples

[3]and said to him, "Are you he who is to come, or shall we look for another?"

[4]And Jesus answered them, "Go and tell John what you hear and see:

[5]the blind receive their sight
and the lame walk,
lepers are cleansed
and the deaf hear,
and the dead are raised up,
and the poor have good news preached to them.

[6]And blessed is he who takes no offense at me."

Based on the Two-Gospel Hypothesis, Matthew was the first evangelist to use this story where Jesus, after being questioned by John's disciples, instructs them to return to John and report what they see and hear—including the fact that the poor are having "good news" preached to them.[1] These instructions are intended to convey to John that the words of the prophet Isaiah are being fulfilled:

[18]In that day the deaf shall hear the words of a book, and out of their gloom and darkness the eyes of the blind shall see.
[19]The meek shall obtain fresh joy in the Lord, and the poor among men shall exult in the Holy One of Israel. —*Isa. 29:18–19 (RSV)*

[1]The Spirit of the Lord is upon me, because the Lord has anointed me to bring "good news" to the poor. . . . —*Isa. 61:1*

Luke 7:18–23

[18]The disciples of <u>John</u> told him of all these things.
[19]And John, calling to him two of <u>his disciples</u>, sent them to the Lord, saying, "<u>Are you he who is to come, or shall we look</u> for another?"

²⁰And when the men had come to him, they said, "John the Baptist has sent us to [you, saying, 'Are you he who is to come, or shall we look for another?' " ²¹In that hour he cured many of diseases and plagues and evil spirits, and on many that were blind he bestowed sight.] ²²And he answered them, "Go and tell John what you have seen and heard:

> the blind receive their sight,
> > the lame walk,
> lepers are cleansed,
> > and the deaf hear,
> the dead are raised up,
> > the poor have good news preached to them.

²³And blessed is he who takes no offense at me."

The evangelist Luke has typically expanded Matthew's terse narrative, by adding the redundant information, enclosed in brackets, that when John's disciples reached Jesus, they told him that John had sent them to ask him, "Are you the one who is to come, or shall we look for another?" He went on to add that Jesus "cured many of diseases and plagues and evil spirits, and on many that were blind he bestowed sight." After that, Luke appears to have followed the text of Matthew closely, as the underlining clearly suggests.

Based on the Two-Gospel Hypothesis, we can say that Luke has taken over this text from Matthew rather faithfully but with some amplification. And it is possible that it was this Matthean passage that first suggested to Luke that he give an important place to the story of Jesus in the synagogue of Nazareth, where this text from Isaiah 61 is cited more fully (Luke 4:16–21).

Jesus in the Synagogue of Nazareth

¹⁶And he came to Nazareth, where he had been brought up; and he went into the synagogue, as his custom was, on the sabbath day. And he stood up to read; ¹⁷and there was given to him the book of the prophet Isaiah. He opened the book and found the place where it was written, ¹⁸"The Spirit of the Lord is upon me,
> because he has anointed me
> > to preach good news to the poor.
> He has sent me
> > to proclaim release to the captives
> > and recovering of sight to the blind,
> > to set at liberty those who are oppressed,
> > to proclaim the acceptable year of the Lord."   —*Luke 4:16–18 (RSV)*

The evangelist Luke has given Isa. 61:1–2, where the poor have good news preached to them, a normative place in his Gospel. By placing this passage from Isaiah at the beginning of Jesus' public ministry, it becomes programmatic for the whole of Luke's Gospel. That this theme of God's concern for the poor is programmatic for the Gospel of Luke is underlined by a succession of passages scattered throughout Luke's Gospel. In the following passages, we find mention of God's concern for the poor—God's concern for those who are hurting in any way, and especially for those who are neglected, excluded, or oppressed by the rich.

The Magnificat

[46]"My soul magnifies the Lord,
[47]and my spirit rejoices in God my Savior,
[48]for he has regarded the low estate
    of his handmaiden.
For behold, henceforth all generations
    will call me blessed;
[49]for he who is mighty
has done great things for me,
    and holy is his name.
[50]And his mercy is on those who fear him
    from generation to generation.
[51]He has shown strength with his arm,
    he has scattered the proud
    in the imagination of their hearts,
[52]he has put down the mighty from their thrones,
    and exalted those of low degree;
[53]he has filled the hungry with good things,
    and the rich he has sent empty away.
[54]He has helped his servant Israel,
    in remembrance of his mercy,
[55]as he spoke to our fathers,
    to Abraham, and to his posterity forever."
               —Luke 1:46–55 (RSV)

The Lukan Beatitudes

[20]"Blessed are you poor,
    for yours is the kingdom of God.
[21]"Blessed are you that hunger now,
    for you shall be satisfied.
"Blessed are you that weep now,
    for you shall laugh.
[22]"Blessed are you when men hate you, . . .

^{23}for behold, your reward is great in heaven.
^{24}"But woe to you that are rich,
for you have received your consolation.
^{25}"Woe to you that are full now,
for you shall hunger.
"Woe to you that laugh now,
for you shall mourn and weep.
^{26}"Woe to you, when all men speak well of you,
for so their fathers did to the false prophets."
—Luke 6:20–26 (RSV)

The Parable of the Poor Man Lazarus

^{19}"There was a rich man, who was clothed in purple and fine linen and who feasted sumptuously every day.
^{20}And at his gate lay a poor man named Lazarus, full of sores,
^{21}who desired to be fed with what fell from the rich man's table; moreover the dogs came and licked his sores.
^{22}The poor man died and was carried by the angels to Abraham's bosom. The rich man also died and was buried;
^{23}and in Hades, being in torment, he lifted up his eyes, and saw Abraham far off and Lazarus in his bosom.
^{24}And he called out, 'Father Abraham, have mercy upon me, and send Lazarus to dip the end of his finger in water and cool my tongue; for I am in anguish in this flame.'
^{25}But Abraham said, 'Son, remember that you in your lifetime received your good things, and Lazarus in like manner evil things; but now he is comforted here, and you are in anguish.
^{26}And besides all this, between us and you a great chasm has been fixed, in order that those who would pass from here to you may not be able, and none may cross from there to us.'
^{27}And he said, 'Then I beg you, father, to send him to my father's house,
^{28}for I have five brothers, so that he may warn them, lest they also come into this place of torment.'
^{29}But Abraham said, 'They have Moses and the prophets; let them hear them.'
^{30}And he said, 'No, father Abraham; but if someone goes to them from the dead, they will repent.'
^{31}He said to him, 'If they do not hear Moses and the prophets, neither will they be convinced if someone should rise from the dead.'" *—Luke 16:19–31 (RSV)*

The Parable of the Vindicated Widow

^{2}"In a certain city there was a judge who neither feared God nor regarded man;
^{3}and there was a widow in that city who kept coming to him and saying,

'Vindicate me against my adversary.'

⁴For a while he refused; but afterward he said to himself, 'Though I neither fear God nor regard man,

⁵yet because this widow bothers me, I will vindicate her, or she will wear me out by her continual coming.' "

⁶And the Lord said, "Hear what the unrighteous judge says.

⁷And will not God vindicate his elect, who cry out to him day and night? Will he delay long over them?

⁸I tell you, he will vindicate them speedily."   —*Luke 18:2–8*

The Parable of the Rich Man Zacchaeus

¹He entered Jericho and was passing through.

²And there was a man named Zacchaeus; he was a chief tax collector, and rich.

³And he sought to see who Jesus was, but could not, on account of the crowd, because he was small of stature.

⁴So he ran on ahead and climbed up into a sycamore tree to see him, for he was to pass that way.

⁵And when Jesus came to the place, he looked up and said to him, "Zacchaeus, make haste and come down; for I must stay at your house today."

⁶So he made haste and came down, and received him joyfully,

⁷And when they saw it they all murmured, "He has gone in to be the guest of a sinner."

⁸And Zacchaeus stood and said to the Lord, "Behold, Lord, the half of my goods I give to the poor; and if I have defrauded anyone of anything, I restore it fourfold."

⁹And Jesus said to him, "Today salvation has come to this house. . . ."

—*Luke 19:1–9(RSV)*

We intentionally reserve the most stunning text from Luke for the last.

The Parable of the Good Samaritan

³⁰"A man was going down from Jerusalem to Jericho, and he fell among robbers, who stripped him and beat him, and departed, leaving him half dead.

³¹Now by chance a priest was going down that road; and when he saw him he passed by on the other side.

³²So likewise a Levite, when he came to the place and saw him, passed by on the other side.

³³But a Samaritan, as he journeyed, came to where he was; and when he saw him, he had compassion,

³⁴and went to him and bound up his wounds, pouring on oil and wine; then he set him on his own beast and brought him to an inn, and took care of him.

³⁵And the next day he took out two denarii and gave them to the innkeeper,

saying, 'Take care of him, and whatever more you spend, I will repay you when I come back.' " —*Luke 10:30–35 (RSV)*

This powerful story expresses an ethic that calls for risk-taking on behalf of persons needing a compassionate response by those able to assist them and accompany them to recovery. A corresponding concern for "little ones" is powerfully expressed in Matthew's parable of the last judgment.

The Parable of the Last Judgment

[31]"When the Son of man comes in his glory, and all the angels with him, then he will sit on his glorious throne.

[32]Before him will be gathered all the nations, and he will separate them one from another as a shepherd separates the sheep from the goats,

[33]and he will place the sheep at his right hand, but the goats at the left.

[34]Then the King will say to those at his right hand,

'Come, O blessed of my Father,
inherit the kingdom prepared for you
from the foundation of the world;
[35]for I was hungry and you gave me food,
I was thirsty and you gave me drink,
I was a stranger and you welcomed me,
[36]I was naked and you clothed me,
I was sick and you visited me,
I was in prison and you came to me.'

[37]Then the righteous will answer him,

'Lord, when did we see thee
hungry and feed thee,
or thirsty and give thee drink?
[38]And when did we see thee
a stranger and welcome thee,
or naked and clothe thee?
[39]And when did we see thee
sick or in prison and visit thee?'

[40]And the King will answer them,

'Truly, I say to you,
as you did it to one of the least of these my brethren,
you did it to me.'

[41]Then he will say to those at his left hand,

'Depart from me, you cursed,
into the eternal fire
prepared for the devil and his angels;
[42]for I was hungry
and you gave me no food,
I was thirsty

and you gave me no drink,
⁴³I was a stranger
and you did not welcome me,
naked and you did not clothe me,
sick and in prison and you did not visit me.'
⁴⁴Then they also will answer,
'Lord, when did we see thee
hungry
or thirsty
or a stranger
or naked
or sick
or in prison,
and did not minister to thee?'
⁴⁵Then he will answer them,
'Truly, I say to you,
as you did it not to one of the least of these,
you did it not to me.'
⁴⁶And they will go away into eternal punishment, but the righteous into eternal life."   —*Matt. 25:31–46*

Christ does not differentiate between the worthy and unworthy poor, the innocent or guilty prisoner, the Christian or non-Christian stranger. He identified totally with all the poor, the oppressed, the imprisoned. The person in prison has no freedom to leave the prison. One of the "least" of Christ's brethren, the prisoner is subject to verbal and physical abuse, not only from guards but also from fellow prisoners venting their frustrations by violating each other's bodies, minds, and spirits.

This litany of the hungry, the thirsty, the alienated, the ill-clothed, the sick, and the imprisoned is only representative of the poor. The list could have been extended to include widows and orphans, the lepers, the slaves, and in our own day, indigenous peoples, or any oppressed persons or groups suffering deprivation, exclusion, and indignities at the hands of those who are at ease in Zion, living in their houses of cedar and turning their backs on those left beaten and half-dead along the byways of life.

Good News for the Poor

Those advocating liberation theologies look at the Bible as a whole but pay special attention to scriptures like those above. Following an interpretative procedure of going from the experience of the poor to the texts of scripture and then back to the realities of struggles for justice and liberation, theologians find these and related texts coming alive as "good news" for the poor and full of hope and promise for excluded peoples and nations. They conclude from these teachings that we make the most sense out of the Bible only if we approach it as a book that creates and nurtures a belief in God as the God of the oppressed. Of course, a God concerned with the plight of the excluded and the marginalized in society—the "poor"—will also lay strong claims on the powerful and empowered—the "rich." Israel's bondage to pharaoh in Egypt and liberation under Moses, along with the prophets' call for righteousness, all sparkle with meaning when these "rich-poor" texts are kept in focus. These texts are not generally "good news" for the privileged and powerful. Nor are they "good news" for those in the rising middle classes who aspire to become rich and powerful. In particular, these passages are not "good news" for a society yearning for social stability at the cost of social justice.

This was precisely the reactionary situation in Germany after the failed political revolution of 1848. At the risk of oversimplification, it may be said that, when government-paid scholars at the German universities came up with a "scientific" way to read the Gospels, they "inadvertently" marginalized these potentially dangerous passages of scripture. The rising middle class and especially its educated elite were more than willing to combine patriotism with faith and follow Bismarck under the hidden banner of a new civil religion, dedicated to a strong Germany. This liberal or liberating "scientific" approach to religion immobilized both Protestant and Catholic as well as Jewish orthodoxies, and it gave support to a strong new German state vying for its rightful place alongside rival empires, chiefly the empires of Britain and France.

People in the elite, educated middle class, to which all German professors and pastors belonged, were not alarmed that these socially troublesome passages ended up being discounted because they were not in the earliest Gospel, Mark. In truth, their own class interests were better served by a Gospel free of such socially disturbing passages.

But can it be said that the Gospel of Mark never refers to the poor? No, that is not the point. However, the only references to the poor in Mark serve to support the status quo. The Gospel of Mark was and is a very comforting Gospel for the haves who wish not to be disturbed by the claims of a theology that advances the cause of the have-nots.

The Gospel of Mark contains the hard saying that "it is easier for a camel to go through the eye of a needle than for a rich man to enter the kingdom of God" (Mark 10:25). This teaching is useful for pressuring the "rich" in the church to give. And in conjunction with the story of the rich man who asked Jesus how to inherit eternal life, it can lead to a counsel of perfection, where the rich are advised: "Go sell what you have, and give to the poor, and you will have treasures in heaven; and come follow me" (Mark 10:21). This counsel of perfection was understood to be aimed at those who were already rich and represented no immediate threat to the interests of the middle class. From the period of early monasticism until Luther, and culminating earlier in the religious order of St. Francis of Assisi, the church has long learned to accommodate to individuals and groups following this counsel. It was not at all difficult for conservative middle-class Germans in the second half of the nineteenth century to live with this teaching. After all, it applied to others, not to them. Nor is the story of the poor widow, who put more into the temple treasury than the many rich people who put in large sums (Mark 12:41–44), disturbing to persons in the aspiring middle class. Indeed, they can admire this saintly person and say, "Amen!"

Finally, the story of the women who anointed Jesus for his burial and was rebuked by his undiscerning disciples for wasting the expensive ointment, which "might have been sold for more than three hundred denarii and given to the poor" (Mark 14:3–9), actually serves to cancel out the radical claims on the rich deriving from the story of the rich man who wanted eternal life.

Any one of the four Gospels, if considered as the norm by which all others are to be understood, is subject to serious misunderstanding. This occurred in the nineteenth century when the Gospel of Mark was made the chief historical norm for interpreting the other Gospels in the church's fourfold Gospel canon.

What difference does it make? This can be measured by answering the question, What difference has it made? The simple answer is this: Nineteenth- and twentieth-century theology, focusing on the Gospel of Mark as the earliest and most reliable source for understanding the good news, has left middle-class and upper-class believers spiritually and morally enfeebled. Not having heard the full Gospel message, not having learned the full significance of the liberating theology found in the good news that Christ brought to the poor, we in fact have become the poor in spirit. Not equipped with the truth of the Gospel of the poor, we stand defenseless before a rampant secular mammonism. The church itself, either intentionally or unintentionally blinded, sits at ease in Zion. Without our "loins girt about with truth," both individual believers and the church as a whole are impotent; our sins of racism, classism, elitism, sexism, clericalism, and denominationalism indict us.

One may accept the conclusion that the beautiful Gospel of Mark has little or no good news for the poor, but one must then ask whether Q also is void of such good news. Not necessarily. Matthew and Luke relate the story of John sending his disciples to query Jesus. That passage is not in Mark. So if Q encompasses narrative material in Matthew and Luke that does not appear in Mark, this passage should be attributed to Q, assuming, of course, a modified form of the Q hypothesis. This is significantly other than a simple collection of sayings.

In one additional passage, the poor may be referred to in a Q saying. In Matthew's Sermon on the Mount, we have the Beatitudes in their most familiar form:

3"Blessed are the poor in spirit,
>   for theirs is the kingdom of heaven.
4"Blessed are those who mourn,
>   for they shall be comforted.
5"Blessed are the meek,
>   for they shall inherit the earth.
6"Blessed are those who hunger and thirst for righteousness,
>   for they shall be satisfied.
7"Blessed are the merciful,
>   for they shall obtain mercy.
8"Blessed are the pure in heart,
>   for they shall see God.
9"Blessed are the peacemakers,
>   for they shall be called sons of God.
10"Blessed are those who are persecuted for
>   righteousness' sake,
>   for theirs is the kingdom of heaven."
>   —*Matt. 5:3–10 (RSV)*

The first Beatitude refers to the "poor in spirit." This is not a reference to the "poor" in contrast to the "rich." No evangelist would have ever attributed to Jesus a saying like: "Woe to the rich in spirit." For this reason, unless we conclude that Luke has preserved the more original form of the Beatitudes as they stood in the hypothetical Q document, we are left in doubt whether Q contained a beatitude concerning the "poor." The Matthean form of the Beatitudes may well have originated with Jesus. Assuming Q's existence, this form may have been drawn by Matthew from Q in which case the Lukan Beatitudes may have come to Luke from some other collection of Jesus' sayings. As we have already seen, advocates of the Q hypothesis often complicate their hypothesis by adding extra conjectural conditions. So perhaps in this case, there were two forms of Q, one copied by Matthew and the other copied by Luke. Like many matters concerning Q this one is shrouded in uncertainty.

But even those who are open to the possibility that the Lukan form of the Beatitudes stood in Q face a problem: this reference to the poor is not found in Matthew. Therefore, it is not strongly enough attested to warrant critical confidence in its authenticity as a Q saying. For that reason, those who believe in Q are constrained, at least in some measure, to question the authenticity of this saying. Thus, reconstructions of Jesus' message based on Markan priority and the existence of Q have not given God's preferential love for the poor an important role in understanding Jesus—although this concern is well-attested in the prophetic literature, which presumably would have shaped Jesus' message. Recent lives of Jesus, still presupposing the validity of the Two-Source Hypothesis, can represent Jesus as a wandering Cynic preacher whose teaching is less shaped by Jewish scriptures than by popular Hellenistic philosophical sources.[2]

Vatican Council II

Vatican Council II was important not only for the Roman Catholic Church but also for all Christians. Vatican Council II is increasingly being viewed as a new Pentecost. Absolutely unexpected consequences have flowed from this new outpouring of the Holy Spirit upon Christ's church.

One of these consequences is a newfound determination by the Roman Catholic Church to take more seriously the Christians' obligation to choose the side of the poor in the struggle for justice in societies all around the world. This represents a giant step forward by the Roman Catholic Church, a step not yet effectively matched by any major Protestant body and certainly not by any of the Orthodox churches. However, thousands of individual Protestants and not a few Protestant congregations have joined their Roman Catholic sisters and brothers in working together on local, national, and international justice issues.

When participants and observers gathered from all parts of the world to take part in Vatican Council II, no one anticipated the collective impact of having hundreds of bishops from poor parts of Asia, Africa, and Latin America come together in Rome. The tremendous wealth invested in St. Peter's and all the Vatican buildings stood in such stark contrast with the poverty of most of the faithful Catholics in Asia, Africa, and Latin America that bishops from these parts of the world collectively broke rank and cried out for a change of heart on the part of the church. This cry was heard and has since received magisterial form in statements coming from bishops' conferences that have been held subsequently to find remedies for unjust conditions under which so many of the faithful must live in the underdeveloped countries of the Third World. Most recently, a teaching on God's preferential love for the poor has been included in the Universal Catechism of the Roman Catholic Church.[3]

From the very beginning of this far-reaching development within the Roman Catholic Church, these cardinal passages in the Gospels of Luke and Matthew have served theologically to stiffen the resistance of Latin American bishops and their theological advisers, who have been pressured to abandon or qualify their call for change. Like the importunate widow, these bishops cry out for justice. They know that God will vindicate the poor who cry to him day and night. "He will not delay long over them. He will vindicate them speedily."

This action by the Roman Catholic Church is now leading to a theological revolution among Protestants as well. The very concept of the poor, until recent years, has been practically unknown even in circles ostensibly committed to the so-called social gospel. The poor, for example, were seldom, if ever, mentioned by theologians like Karl Barth, Paul Tillich, Reinhold Niebuhr, or Rudolf Bultmann. Paul Ramsey's reference to "the little ones" in Jesus' teaching as being basic to Christian ethics fell on deaf ears as that discipline moved further and further from its scriptural base.[4]

For this reason, all contemporary theologies that feature the God of the Bible as the God of the poor have had a difficult time getting a hearing in a world of theological scholarship that still tends to adhere to the older nineteenth-century exegetical tradition codified for theologians by Bultmann and his disciples, chiefly in Europe and North America. In the case of Protestants, this older exegetical tradition was critically formed by developments in nineteenth-century Germany where the poor became theologically invisible. Their needs, if they were to be met, would be met structurally by political forces working in large measure independently of the churches. This would be largely true even with regard to such movements as Christian socialism. Notwithstanding the above, individual Christians who were sympathetic to these movements, working within or alongside the church, could also be effective advocates for social justice, for example, Reinhold Niebuhr and John Bennett.

The research schools favored by the state-sponsored universities in Germany were those that served the interests of the state. Professor Adolf Harnack, a servant of German state interests, oversaw the investment of large sums of academic research funds for the Prussian state government. In this role, he defended public support for the History of Religions school on grounds that the state would benefit from having German-trained missionaries who would be more effective at relating to people of other religions than missionaries of rival colonial powers. Thus, there is no serious question about the ideological needs of German society affecting the development of biblical criticism in nineteenth-century Germany.

The more important ideological needs that dominated state interests, however, were accommodation between Catholics and Protestants on the one hand and between Christians and Jews on the other. This points to the topic of chapter 11, "A Social History of Markan Primacy."

CHAPTER 9

The Keys of the Kingdom

Peter's Confession in Matthew

[13]And after Jesus had come into the region of Caesarea Philippi, he asked his disciples saying: "Who do men say the Son of man to be?"
[14]And they said: "Some say John the Baptist, and others Elijah, and still others say Jeremiah or one of the prophets."
[15]He said to them: "And who do you say that I am?"
[16]And Simon Peter answering said: "You are the Christ, the Son of the living God."
[17]And answering Jesus said to him:
>   "Blessed are you, Simon Bar-Jonah,
>   Because flesh and blood
>   have not revealed this to you;
>   Rather my Father who is in the heavens
>   (has revealed this to you).
[18]And I say to you that you are 'Petros,'
>   And on this 'petra' I shall build my church,
>   And the gates of hell will not prevail against it.
[19]And I will give to you the keys of the kingdom of the heavens,
>   And whatever you bind upon the earth shall be bound in the heavens,
>   And whatever you loose upon the earth shall be loosed in the heavens."
[20]Then he warned his disciples that they were to tell no one that he was the Christ.
[21]After that Jesus began to show his disciples that it was necessary for him to go to Jerusalem, and suffer many things at the hands of the elders and high priests and scribes, and to be killed, and on the third day to be raised.
[22]And Peter, after taking him aside, began to warn him, saying:
>   "May God have mercy on you, Lord,
>   May this not happen to you."
[23]And turning he said to Peter:
>   "Get out of my sight, Satan.
>   You are a stumbling block in my path
>   Because you do not have your mind on matters
>   Which are of concern to God.
>   Rather, (you have your mind on)
>   Matters which are of concern to man."

[24]Then Jesus said to his disciples:
>"If anyone wants to come after me,
>>Let him deny himself
>>And take up his cross
>>And follow me.

[25]For whoever wants to save his life will lose it.
>>And whoever would risk his life for my sake will find it.

[26]For what advantage is it to a man
>>If he should gain the whole world at the cost of his soul?
>>Or what will a man give in exchange for his soul?

[27]For the Son of man is about to come
>>in the glory of his Father with his angels,
>>And then he will reward each person according to his deeds.

[28]Truly I say to you
>>That there are some standing here who will not taste death
>>Until they see the Son of man coming in his kingdom."

>>>>>>>>*—Matt. 16:13–28*

This is certainly one of the most interesting and possibly most controversial texts in the Bible. It includes Jesus giving to Peter the keys of the kingdom of heaven. From this text have come ten thousand innocent and amusing stories about Saint Peter at the pearly gates, deciding who is to enter heaven and who is to be turned away. This text was central in the development of the medieval doctrine of Petrine jurisdictional primacy in the church. Because this text has been used to support papal claims, it has become freighted with theological and ecclesiastical meanings that make it difficult to discuss. And yet, this is exactly what we must do. What should people interested in the church know about this text? What difference, if any, does it make whether one reads this text in the light of the Two-Gospel Hypothesis or of the Two-Source Hypothesis?

Recent scholarship serves to defuse the potentially explosive character of this text. In *Peter and Paul in the Church of Rome: The Ecumenical Potential of a Forgotten Perspective*,[1] it is suggested that the historical importance of the bishop of Rome rests basically on an early development in church history that was commented on by Irenaeus. Irenaeus makes no use of this passage in Matthew to argue for any connection between Peter and the bishop of Rome. Rather, Irenaeus focuses on the witness unto death of the two chief apostles, Peter and Paul, during the persecution of the church under Nero.

These two apostles, Irenaeus contended, founded the church of Rome. And they founded it not only through their preaching but above all through their martyrdom. From this perspective, the church that received Paul's letter to the Romans had no more importance than the church in Corinth to which Paul also wrote. It was only after (and in consequence of) the martyrdom of both Peter and Paul in Rome that the church in that city began to assume for bishops like Irenaeus a special importance for all other churches.

Even more recently, attention has been focused on the work of Edouard Massaux, who documents the Gospel of Matthew's influence on the Christian literature before Irenaeus. Incredible as it might seem, this Peter passage in Matthew, which has played such an important role in medieval and modern church history, according to Massaux's work, exerted very little if any influence in the early church. [2]

Although Massaux shows that Matthew was indeed the foundational gospel of the early church, no evidence exists that this text was ever used in the pre-Irenaeus church to make a case for the bishop of Rome as Peter's successor. This conclusion enables ecumenically minded Christians to approach this text in a new light.

Based on the Two-Gospel Hypothesis, the first stage in the development of Christian doctrine begins with the changes that the evangelist Luke made in the text of the Gospel of Matthew. We turn now to Luke's text with great interest. What has Luke done with this text? We will underline all the words that Luke has taken verbatim from Matthew.

Peter's Confession in Luke

[18]And it happened that while he was praying alone, his disciples being with him, he asked saying: "Who do the crowds say me to be?

[19]And answering they said: "John the Baptist, and others Elijah, and others that a certain prophet from of old has arisen."

[20]And he said to them: "And who do you say that I am?" And Peter answering said: "The Christ of God."

[21]And after warning them, he told them to tell this to no one,

[22]saying that it was necessary for the Son of man to suffer many things and to be rejected by the elders and high priests and scribes, and to be killed, and on the third day to be raised.

[23]And he was saying to all:

"If any one wants to come after me,
     Let him deny himself
          And take up his cross day by day,
               And follow me.

[24]For whoever wants to save his soul will lose it.
     And whoever would risk his soul for my sake, this man will save it.

[25]For what advantage is it to a man
     If he should gain the whole world
     But lose or forfeit himself?

[26]For whoever is ashamed of me and my words,
          Of this person will the Son of man be ashamed,
               When he comes in his glory

And (the glory) of the Father
And the holy angels.
²⁷And I say to you truly,
There are some standing here who will not taste death
Until they see the kingdom of God."
—Luke 9:18–27

This is a skillful reduction of the text in Matthew. However, we note right away the addition of the characteristic Lukan expression "day by day." In place of the words, "Let him deny himself and take up his cross" as recorded in Matthew, the Gospel of Luke has "Let him deny himself and take up his cross *day by day*." We find Luke following Matthew rather closely, often word for word. But just as often, Luke freely recasts Matthew's thoughts in terms he regards as more natural to his own way of expression or better phrased for his intended readers. Much of the poetic character of Jesus' words in Matthew has been lost in Luke's use of a more literate Greek prose. But the basic teaching of Jesus is retained, even while being transposed.

The major addition that Luke has made to the text of Matthew is found in 9:26: "For whoever is ashamed of me and my words, of this person will the Son of man be ashamed, when he comes in his glory and (the glory) of the Father."

Otherwise Luke 9:18–27 is a fairly straightforward Lukan version of Matt. 16:13–28, with two major exceptions, both exceptions being omissions. Why has Luke omitted the words of Jesus:

"Blessed are you, Simon Bar-Jonah,
Because flesh and blood
have not revealed this to you.
Rather my Father who is in the heavens
(has revealed this to you).
And I say to you
That you are 'Petros,'
And on this 'petra' I will build my church,
And the gates of hell will not prevail against it.
And I will give to you the keys of the kingdom of the heavens,
And whatever you bind upon the earth shall be bound in the heavens,
And whatever you loose upon the earth shall be loosed in the heavens."

Is Luke anti-Petrine? Is this why he omitted from his Gospel the text where Jesus gives to Peter the keys of the kingdom? Not necessarily. Before we can answer such questions, we must consider that Matthew contains a parallel text where Jesus gives the keys of the kingdom of heaven to his disciples in general, not to Peter specifically.

"Amen I say to you,
whatever you bind upon this earth shall be bound in heaven,
And whatever you loose upon the earth shall be loosed on heaven."
—Matt. 18:18

The verbal agreement of Matt. 18:18 with Matt. 16:19b is very close but not exact. Clearly the teaching is the same, but the grammatical variations indicate that this doublet in Matthew 18 has had a separate history of transmission in the early Greek-speaking church from the parallel text in chapter 16. The plural form, "in the heavens," is used in Matt. 16:19, but we find the singular "in heaven" in Matt. 18:18. This suggests that the evangelist is copying faithfully Jesus' tradition as written in Greek in separate Greek texts, each with its own history of transmission. There is little reason to think that the evangelist Matthew would introduce on his own this kind of grammatical variation into Greek texts he is using (or for that matter into his own composition).

However, the situation is quite different for Luke, who is using the text of Matthew. It is clear from Luke's literary procedure that he is prepared to modify Matthew's text freely. So, why did he not incorporate Matt. 16:17–19 into his version of Matt. 16:13–28 with whatever modifications he thought fit? The answer may be found in Luke's treatment of doublets.

There are many examples where Matthew has the same or nearly the same text in two different parts of his Gospel. Here Luke omits both. But Luke is also free to take one and leave the other, or even to take both. When he takes both, he almost always paraphrases one member of the doublet to avoid being criticized as redundant or unaware of using the same source more than once.

Luke would have recognized that, at one point in Matthew's Gospel, Jesus gives the authority to bind and to loose to the single disciple Peter, and at another point Jesus gives the same authority to his disciples in general. Whatever Luke thought about this difference, based on the Two-Gospel Hypothesis, he omitted both doublets. However, it seems unlikely that he intentionally omitted these verses so favorable to Peter because of any anti-Petrine tendency. If he had had such a tendency, he presumably would have included the anti-Petrine tradition in which Jesus rebukes Peter with the devastating words:

> "Get out of my sight, Satan.
>   You are a stumbling block in my path
>   Because you do not have your mind on
>   Matters which are of concern to God.
>   Rather, (you have your mind on)
>   Matters which are of concern to man."

Luke presumably omitted these sharp words for some reason. Matthew's text invites the reader to think that at one moment Jesus was bestowing on Peter some great and far-reaching blessing (vv. 17–19) while at the next moment he was turning against Peter, rebuking him as Satan and a "stumbling block" (vv. 22–23). Luke probably did not want to represent Jesus as being so volatile. In any case, by omitting these contrasting and conflicting portions of Matthew, Luke has succeeded in producing a more consistent and less conflictive account of Jesus' relationship with Peter. In the Acts of the Apostles and throughout his Gospel, Luke presents Peter as the leader among the disciples (cf. Luke 22:31–32 and Acts 1:15).

> [31]And the Lord said:
> "Simon, Simon!
> Indeed Satan has asked for you
> that he may sift you as wheat.
> [32]But I have prayed for you
> that your faith should not fail;
> and when you have returned to me,
> strengthen your brethren."
> —*Luke 22:31–32*

These words to Peter are set by Luke "within the framework of the institution of the Eucharist."[3] Thus, in Luke's Gospel they occupy a place equal in importance to, if not greater than, the prominent place given to the famous Peter Passage in Matthew. In both cases, Jesus addresses Peter in the highest terms while recognizing the importance of Satan's influence over him.

In Luke, Jesus envisions both Peter's betrayal and his repentance. Peter is commanded to strengthen his brethren, once he has returned to his Lord. At the same time, Jesus informs Peter that he has prayed for him that his "faith should not fail."

This evidence should answer the question of whether Luke is anti-Petrine. Certainly not in the last analysis. Jesus is not uncritical of Peter, but Luke, no less than Matthew, recognizes Peter's leadership role among the Twelve.

This leadership role is recognized throughout the first half of Acts, where it is balanced by an equal prominence given to Paul in the second half. Luke is not anti-Petrine, and he singles out Peter from among the Twelve to pair off with Paul as one of the two chief apostles of the apostolic period.

Peter's Confession in Mark

> [8:27]And Jesus and his disciples went out into the villages of Caesarea Philippi, and on the way he questioned his disciples saying to them: "Who do men say that I am?"
> [28]And they spoke to him saying that (you are) John the Baptist, and others say Elijah, and others that (you are) one of the prophets.
> [29]And he questioned them: "And who do you say that I am?" Peter answering says to him: "You are the Christ."
> [30]And he warned them that they should tell no one about him.
> [31]And he began to teach them that it was necessary for the Son of man to suffer many things and to be rejected by the elders and the high priests and the scribes and to be killed and after three days to be raised.

³²<u>And he was speaking the word in public.</u> And Peter, after taking him (Jesus) aside began to warn him.

³³And he, after turning and seeing his disciples, rebuked Peter saying:
> "Get out of my sight, Satan,
>> Because you do not have your mind on
>>> Matters which are of concern to God.
>>> Rather, (you have your mind on)
>>>> Matters which are of concern to man."

³⁴<u>And after calling together the crowd</u> with his disciples, he said to them:
> "If any one wants to come after me,
>> Let him deny himself
>> And take up his cross
>> And follow me.

³⁵For whoever wants to save his soul will lose it.
> And whoever would risk his soul for my sake
> <u>And for (the sake of) the Gospel</u> will save it.

³⁶For what advantage is it to a man
> if he should gain the whole world and forfeit his soul?

³⁷For what will a man give in exchange for his soul?

³⁸For whoever is ashamed of me and of my words
> <u>In this adulterous and sinful generation,</u>
>> Of him the Son of man will be ashamed,
>>> When he comes in the glory of his Father
>>>> With the holy angels."

⁹:¹And he said to them:
> "Truly I say to you
>> That there are some standing here who will not taste death
>> Until they see the kingdom of God <u>having come in power</u>."
>>>>>>>>>>>>>>>>>> —*Mark 8:27—9:1*

Based on the Two-Gospel Hypothesis, Mark 8:27—9:1 represents a lively but balanced combination or blending of Luke 9:18–21 and Matt. 16:13–20 (omitting 17–19). The underlined phrases represent Markan expansions. The first four of these Markan additions are characteristic of Mark's usage. It is evidence against the Two-Source Hypothesis that neither Matthew nor Luke has taken over any part of even one of these Markan phrases. Based on that hypothesis's assumption that both later Gospels copied Mark rather closely, it is unusual that neither has inadvertently taken over any part of these phrases. On the other hand, this evidence supports the view that Mark was composed after Matthew and Luke. Based on this hypothesis, Mark had authorial freedom to expand his text by adding phrases.

Mark is strikingly closer to Luke's shorter version of this text, in that he agrees with Luke in omitting from Matthew the substantive passage:

¹⁷And answering Jesus said to him (Peter):
> "Blessed are you, Simon Bar-Jonah,

Because flesh and blood
   Have not revealed this to you.
      Rather my Father who is in the heavens
        (has revealed this to you).
[18]And I say to you that you are 'Petros,'
   and on this 'petra' I will build my church,
     And the gates of hell will not prevail against it.
[19]I will give to you the keys of the kingdom of the heavens,
   And whatever you bind upon the earth shall be bound in the heavens,
   And whatever you loose upon the earth shall be loosed in the
   heavens."   —*Matt. 16:17–19*

Mark 8:32 follows the text of Luke 9:22 rather closely, adding in Mark's characteristic language: "And he was speaking the word in public."[4] Then Mark, as he often does, turns his attention to the text of his other main source—Matthew, in this instance—to incorporate the substance of Matt. 16:22–23, which Luke had omitted.

By omitting (with Luke) the pro-Petrine tradition of Matt. 16:17–19 while retaining the anti-Petrine tradition of Matt. 16:22–23 (omitted by Luke), Mark, based on the Two-Gospel Hypothesis, gives every appearance of having a strong anti-Petrine tendency. On the other hand, whatever reason Luke had for omitting Matt. 16:17–19, that is, that it was inconsistent with Matt. 18:22–23, would have been sufficient reason for Mark as well to omit these verses. In any case, his decision to include Matt. 16:22–23 involved him in no internal inconsistency.

It is noteworthy that Mark, like Luke, is internally self-consistent. It is even more noteworthy that Mark is also consistent with both Matthew and Luke. Mark seldom if ever contradicts either Matthew or Luke on any matter of substance. This relationship of both internal and external consistency is easy to explain based on the Two-Gospel Hypothesis because, by composing his Gospel with Matthew and Luke in view, Mark has the authorial freedom not only to maintain internal consistency but also to avoid external inconsistency with his sources. In this way, Mark commends his Gospel to readers who value Matthew or Luke, or both, but who also value a version that is shorter than either of its predecessors, while going into greater detail in many descriptions of specific episodes in Jesus' ministry.

Going back to Mark 8:33, these words certainly represent a warning to Peter. They are words of censure: "Get out of my sight, Satan." They are harsh words indeed. The charge against Peter of being a "man pleaser" reminds us of Paul's need to defend himself against a similar charge (Gal. 1:10). But it should be noted that while Mark preserves the words, " Get out of my sight, Satan," he omits the following charge against Peter in Matt. 16:23, "you are a stumbling block in my path." In this sense, Mark's text can be construed as softening the more conflictive text of Matthew. Matthew has it read: "Get out of my sight, Satan, you are a stumbling block in my path"; while Mark writes only: "Get out of my sight, Satan." If Mark, assuming the validity of the Two-Gospel Hypothesis, truly had an anti-Petrine tendency, why would he have omitted Matthew's more stringent underlining of the offense in Peter's behavior?[5]

After incorporating the substance of Matt. 16:22–23 into his Gospel, Mark includes one of his characteristic transitions: "And after calling together the crowd . . . "[6] Mark continues to follow the text of Matthew as it lies open before him (Matt. 16:24–28 || Mark 8:34b–37). Then Mark, possibly from memory, includes Luke 9:26, which Luke added to his version of Matt. 16:24–26. We should not think that Mark's knowledge of Matthew and Luke was merely perfunctory. On the contrary, it is more likely that Mark not only knew the texts of the two earlier Gospels well, but that he had a lively understanding of their content and could readily retell the stories in Matthew and Luke utilizing his own diction while often retaining the language of his sources. This would not preclude Mark from looking closely at the texts and working closely with them, rather than relying simply on his memory of these very familiar texts.

Mark closes his account (Mark 9:1) with a blending of Matt. 16:28 and Luke 9:27, adding: "having come in power." In 8:38, Mark added the colorful words: "In this adulterous and sinful generation." Another noteworthy feature of Mark's text is the addition near the end of verse 35 of his characteristic expression "and the gospel."[7] Only Mark among the evangelists uses the word "gospel" in the absolute way in which Paul uses it: "the gospel."

Finally, in verse 31 we find the expression "and he began to teach them." This is characteristic Markan usage.[8]

In conclusion, based on the Two-Gospel Hypothesis, we can offer a credible account of the development of the Gospel tradition, from Matthew to Luke to Mark. The later evangelists, Luke and Mark, can be seen exercising their authorial freedom in ways that are in accordance with their known literary practice.

Peter and the Keys of the Kingdom and the Two-Source Hypothesis

Assuming the validity of the Two-Source Hypothesis, Matthew and Luke have independently copied Mark and Q. In this instance there is no need to appeal to the hypothetical Q source. Everything appears to be explainable simply by assuming that Matthew and Luke independently used the text of Mark 8:27—9:1. Based on this hypothesis, it would appear that because the giving of the keys of the kingdom to Peter is not found in Mark, this part of the Jesus tradition is not attested by the church's earliest Gospel. This tradition is preserved in Matt. 16:17–19, but it is not present in the Gospel of Luke. The absence of these words of Jesus from the Gospel of Luke supports the view that they probably were not in Luke's copy of Mark. Based on the Two-Source Hypothesis, all indications can be seen to converge in support of the conclusion that these words probably have been added by the evangelist Matthew to the story as it is preserved in the earlier Gospel, Mark.

There are serious problems with this conclusion, however. And some adherents of the Two-Source Hypothesis have already acknowledged the problems. Professor Rudolf Bultmann, on the basis of the form-critical point that the confession calls for a response, has argued that the words of Jesus preserved in Matt. 16:17–19 are probably the original conclusion to the story preserved in Mark 8:27–29 and Matt. 16:13–16 and Luke 9:18–20. Bultmann concludes that "Mark has dispensed with" this "original conclusion retained in Matt. 16:17–19."[9]

Because of Professor Bultmann's importance in the history of biblical interpretation and in shaping Protestant and Catholic theology in the second half of the twentieth century, it is best to cite more fully his writing on this point.

Under the heading "Peter's Confession," Bultmann writes:

> This passage is to be characterized as legend. . . . The fact that Jesus takes the initiative with his question itself suggests that this narrative is secondary, as does the content of the question altogether. Why does Jesus ask something on which he is bound to be every bit informed as were his disciples? The question is intended simply to provoke the answer, in other words, it is a literary device.[10]

In Bultmann's view, the "confession of Peter" is a "legend of faith." The disciples represent the church, and the text expresses "the specific judgement which the church had about Jesus," in distinction from the judgment of outsiders. In this story: "faith in the messiahship of Jesus is traced back to a story of the first messianic confession which Peter made about Jesus."

Bultmann notes that "the narrative (in Mark) is fragmentary, since it must have originally contained an account of the attitude Jesus himself took to the confession he had stimulated." Bultmann regards the instruction "to keep silent," the prophecy of the passion, and the "rejection of Peter" as later Markan formulation. None of this is considered as belonging to the original continuation of the confession.

Of that original continuation of the confession, Bultmann writes: "I think that the original conclusion has been retained in Matt. 16:17–19." Bultmann continues: "Mark has dispensed with it (the original conclusion) and has on top of that introduced a polemic against the Jewish-Christian point of view represented by Peter (a polemic Mark has taken over) from the sphere of hellenistic Christianity of the Pauline circle." Here Bultmann is referring to Mark 8:32, where Peter is castigated by Jesus in the Pauline fashion for not walking in a straightforward manner with reference to the "truth of the Gospel," because he is guilty of pleasing men, not God (Gal. 1—2).

Bultmann argues that, in contrast to his later Hellenistic [Pauline] polemic against Peter, the words of Jesus preserved in the narrative's original continuation go back to "an old Aramaic tradition." Note that Bultmann does not say that these words are authentic words of Jesus. That is a separate question which he addresses in detail in another publication.[11] Bultmann notes that the original continuation of the confession story— dispensed with by Mark but preserved by Matthew in 16:17–19—"can hardly have been formulated in any other place than in the Palestinian church, where Peter was looked up to as the founder and leader of the church and the blessing of Peter was put into the mouth of the risen Lord."[12]

In other words, for Bultmann the words of Jesus promising to give the keys of the kingdom to Peter were created in the Palestinian church, not uttered by Jesus during his earthly ministry. On the other hand, these words preserved in Matthew's text of Peter's confession are more original than the text of Mark's version of the confession story. They go back earlier than the date of the composition of the Gospel of Mark. They go back to the Aramaic-speaking membership of the early apostolic mission to the circumcision led by Peter (Gal. 2). The documentation for an early Palestinian origin for this tradition is given by Bultmann in his discussions of the topic: "Peter as the authority in the new community."[13]

What we should note at this point is that a linguistic analysis of the Gospel tradition preserved in these parallel texts of Matthew, Mark, and Luke does not support the Two-Source Hypothesis. On the contrary, it supports the Two-Gospel Hypothesis. Matthew's text turns out to be more original than either the text of Mark or Luke as far as the history of Matt. 16:17–19 bears on that question. Furthermore, the text of Matthew in this case gives no evidence that it has been expanded by the evangelist, while the parallel texts of Luke and Mark both show clear signs of the addition of words and phrases characteristic of the authors of these Gospels.

It will help the reader to visualize the situation if we reconstruct the text of Bultmann's hypothetical "Ur-Markus." We begin by assuming with Bultmann that both Matthew and Mark had access to the text of Ur-Markus. When these two evangelists agree, we have a secure text of Ur-Markus. We also assume with Bultmann that Matthew has preserved Jesus' response to Peter's confession. Following Bultmann's methodological presuppositions, we reconstruct the text of Ur-Markus as follows:

Ur-Markus

Jesus went out into Caesarea Philippi. He questioned his disciples saying: "Who do men say that I am (or that the Son of man is)?" And they said: "John the Baptist, others Elijah, and others one of the prophets." And he answered them: "And who do you say that I am?" And Peter answering said: "You are the Christ." And Jesus answering said:

"Blessed are you, Simon Bar-Jonah,
> Because flesh and blood
>> have not revealed this to you.
>>> Rather my Father who is in the heavens
>>> (has revealed this to you).
And I say to you that you are 'Petros,'
> and on this 'petra' I will build my church,
>> And the gates of hell will not prevail against it.
And I will give to you the keys of the kingdom of the heavens,
> And whatever you bind upon the earth shall be bound in the heavens,
> And whatever you loose upon earth shall be loosed in the heavens."

Bultmann regarded this as the essential part of Peter's confession and Jesus' response. But the reader may say that this reconstructed text is virtually the same as the text in the Gospel of Matthew! Yes, that is exactly the point. As a consequence, we can see that one is able to get the same results based on the Two-Source Hypothesis as on the Two-Gospel Hypothesis, provided one is willing to double the number of major hypothetical documents by adding an Ur-Markus to Q. But doubling the number of major hypothetical sources further weakens the scientific credibility of that hypothesis. Assuming the validity of the Two-Gospel Hypothesis, neither Q nor Ur-Markus is needed. On scientific grounds, this is a great difference.[14]

Epilogue

During this past century, considerable attention has been focused on whether Jesus promised to give Peter the keys of the kingdom. This resulted in large part because of the role this passage has played in the development of Catholic doctrine making claims for the pope's jurisdictional primacy. In the furor over these claims, many Christians have overlooked the related but separable promise of Jesus that his church will prevail against all hellish efforts to destroy it (Matt. 16:18b). This divine assurance is the theological basis of the doctrine that the church will endure until the end of time. Take away this scriptural support, and the basis for this important doctrine is weakened, opening the door to doubts about the essential role of the church in the divine economy of salvation. Until the end of time, so long as there are nations to be discipled and saved, the church will be present in the world as the chief instrument of the Holy Spirit in reconciling the world to God. Individuals may defect, parties within the church may defect, but the church as the body of Christ will not defect. This is a faith claim based on the doctrine of the indefectibility of the church, and this doctrine in turn rests on the divine assurance in Jesus' promise that the gates of hell shall not prevail against the church.

It is well understood that the blood of the martyrs, the seed of the church, is the blood of both men and women. Assuming the Christian's belief in the (1) indefectibility of the church and (2) the blood of the martyrs as the seed of the church, let us ask what the connection between the two beliefs might be. In posing this question, we are led back to the church's understanding of the work of the Holy Spirit.

In every age some Christians have responded to the Holy Spirit, no matter what the cost. The Christian believes that there will always be members of the body of Christ who will respond to the call of the Holy Spirit no matter what the cost, and that the members of the body of Christ who respond to this call will include men and women.

The martyrdom of women and men as a consequence to this response to the Holy Spirit is the closest we can come to offering an explanation for why Christians are ready to believe the promise of Jesus that the gates of hell shall not prevail against his church. In other words, Christians believe in this promise, not simply because it comes to them in the scriptures, but also because of the church's experience. Beginning with the example of the Chief Martyr of the church, Jesus Christ, the power of the Holy Spirit is well attested by saints and martyrs being raised up in the church, saints and martyrs who are prepared to follow this example.

To penetrate more deeply into the mystery of the church's staying power, we begin by turning to a passage composed by Clement of Rome, who possessed a lively and living memory of the preaching and martyrdom of Peter and Paul. After testifying to these apostles' glorious witness during the church's persecution under Nero, Clement informs the church in Corinth that around these two apostles gathered a great throng of the faithful who gave the church in Rome the finest example of endurance in the midst of persecution. Clement makes clear that among those persecuted were women who suffered terrible and reprehensible acts of violence. He specifically notes that some of these women were faithful unto death and received the highest and most noble recognition that the church can give.

On the basis of this faithful witness of women and men in the church of Rome, Clement pleads with the church in Corinth to lay aside vain and useless concerns and to go straight to the glorious and venerable "norm" handed down in the church of Jesus Christ. We may ask: What was this norm? Clement writes, "Let us fix our gaze on the blood of Christ, realizing how precious it is to God since it was shed for our salvation and brought the grace of repentance to all the world."[15]

From these words, the bishop of Rome is endorsing the canon espoused by the apostle Paul at the close of his letter to the churches of Galatia, namely, "the cross of our Lord Jesus Christ on which the world has been crucified to me and I have been to the world."[16] In exhorting the Corinthians to fix their "gaze on the blood of Christ," Clement is asking that the church focus on the sacrifice made by Christ in offering up his body and blood for us.

Three generations later, the church in southern France was experiencing persecution similar to that in Rome under Nero. As in Rome, women as well as men were persecuted violently, and women as well as men were obedient unto death.

Standing in the same Eucharistic tradition as Clement, an unknown writer of the second century focused her or his readers' attention on the spectacle of the faithful young woman Blandina hanging on a stake where she was being offered as prey to wild beasts. The text reads:

> She seemed to be hanging in the shape of a cross, and by her continuous prayer she greatly encouraged those around her who were contending. For, in their torment, they beheld with their outward eyes in the form of their sister him who was crucified for them. The effect was to persuade those who believed in him that all who suffered for the glory of Christ have eternal fellowship with the living God. And as none of the wild beasts then touched her she was taken down from the stake and cast into prison.[17]

Here we see a woman representing Christ in a way that encourages others to remain faithful in their hour of trial. And what of Phoebe, whom Paul had recommended as a sister and co-worker to Christians in Rome (Rom. 16:1–2)? Did the Christians in Rome who rallied around Paul and Peter and shared with these apostles the sufferings of Christ include church leaders like Phoebe? Was the witness of these women, who stood by the apostles, inspired by a realization that in the new creation of Jesus Christ all are one, including men and women (Gal.3:28)? Does this answer our question?[18]

This analysis suggests that a basis for the Christian's faith that the gates of hell shall not prevail against the church of Jesus Christ is the fact that Christian faith can sustain both men and women in the face of persecution unto death. Such a community of faith can withstand the demonic power to break down community solidarity (especially that power that works by threatening violence against women who hold in their wombs and hearts the primary source of an endangered community's power to reassert itself). The more the church is persecuted, the stronger becomes the faith of those who are prepared to respond to the Holy Spirit, no matter what the cost.

What difference does it make whether one looks at Christian faith in terms of the Two-Source Hypothesis or the Two-Gospel Hypothesis? In this case, the difference can be measured in terms of how the Two-Source Hypothesis affects the scriptural basis for a belief that the gates of hell shall not prevail against the church. In a phrase, the Two-Source Hypothesis weakens scriptural support for this belief. It does this by underscoring that Jesus' assurance that the gates of hell shall not prevail against his church is not found in the Gospel of Mark. This assurance is also not found in Q. It is not attested in either of the two earliest and most reliable sources, assuming the validity of the Two-Source Hypothesis.

The same can be said about the tradition in which Jesus promises to give the keys of the kingdom to Peter. The Two-Source Hypothesis also weakens scriptural support for the belief that authority in the church is in some unique way related to the person of Peter. All those who doubt that Jesus made this promise to Peter will find support for their reservations, assuming the validity of the Two-Source Hypothesis, because these words are absent from both Mark and Q. Conversely, Christians who hold that Jesus promised to give Peter the keys find scriptural support for this conclusion under the Two-Gospel Hypothesis.

Based on the Two-Gospel Hypothesis, Christians have in the Gospel of Matthew direct access to faithful copies of the text that has been handed down by the church as the text of the earliest Gospel. Based on the Two-Source Hypothesis, Christians at best have problematic access to a hypothetical Ur-Markus, which must be reconstructed from later sources by human ingenuity and with considerable use of the imagination. In fact, some adherents of Markan priority dismiss Bultmann's reconstruction as pure speculation on the grounds that no historical evidence of Ur-Markus exists. British scholars are particularly skeptical of Ur-Markus. B. H. Streeter of Oxford University thought of Ur-Markus as a ghost that was best exorcised from the study of the scholar.[19] The Gospel of Matthew is not devoid of problems, but it is less problematic than a text that does not exist, except in the head of scholars who by scholarly conjecture reconstruct that text. That a scholar is able to write such a text down and publish it does not mean that it exists with any more authority than it already has in his or her head. It exists only as a product of creative imagination. This applies to Q as well as Ur-Markus.

We noted at the beginning of this chapter that recent research and reflection have improved our understanding of the role of the Roman Catholic Church within the body of Christ by moving the discussion away from a too narrow dependence on the Peter passage in Matthew. It focuses attention rather upon the early normative (canonical) tradition where the church of Rome's importance rests on the dual witness of its founders, the chief apostles, Peter and Paul. Both of these apostles were obedient unto death, as had been their sovereign Lord and Savior Jesus Christ.

In the light of what we have learned from Clement's letter to the Corinthians, it is possible to understand much better why Irenaeus wanted all churches to be in communion with the church of Rome. This is the church that Irenaeus knew had benefited most directly from the normative witness of the chief apostles as measured, on the one hand, by the example of Christ (cf. 1 Peter 2:21) and, on the other, by the faithful response unto blood of men and women in that church to this apostolic witness. The witness of these early Christians in Rome was also apostolic insofar as it conformed to the norm followed by the apostles. Why should not Irenaeus, the bishop of the church in Gaul where Blandina made her witness, have wanted his church and all other churches to be in communion with the church of Rome? This was the church whose membership was formed by those who had thronged around the apostles Peter and Paul and who, by faith, drew life from the seed of their martyred brothers and sisters. To be in communion with this church was to be in communion with the church founded by the two chief apostles, Peter and Paul. Undergirding this apostolic witness unto blood was their power to confess the faith that Jesus, Son of the living God, Son of David according to the flesh, was the Suffering Servant of the Lord, through whose sacrificial and redeeming love all nations are saved.

It is only fair to include the topic of the keys of the kingdom along with others that are affected by the source hypothesis we use. In the preceding chapters all readers will readily perceive the consequences that follow for Christian faith and practice if one relies on one hypothesis or the other. Readers may differ in the degree to which they do or do not welcome the difference it makes. But all careful readers, whatever their ecclesial identity, will readily recognize that the source theory a Christian follows will make a difference. That is, it will make a difference unless one takes heroic measures to transform the Two- Source Hypothesis into a theory that functions very much the same as the Two-Gospel Hypothesis.

By way of summary, we can say that Peter's relationship to the church has a more central role in Christian faith if one assumes the validity of the Two-Gospel Hypothesis. The Two-Source Hypothesis has a converse effect. The issue of gender is less clearly affected. The way this issue has been stimulated by reflection on the indefectibility of the church is noteworthy. However, it is a topic with only an indirect logical link to the synoptic problem. It illustrates, nevertheless, the rich possibilities for exegesis that are being opened up by use of the Two-Gospel Hypothesis.

How does the question about the authority of Peter in the church affect contemporary theological discourse? Matthew 16:17–19 at present rests like a volcanic rock embedded with numbing effect in the midst of ecumenical dialogue. Because of the close relationship between ecumenical dialogue and scriptural exegesis, real dialogue leading to dependable results is hindered. On the one hand, this text is presently understood to be too hot to handle because it is potentially divisive. On the other hand, significant progress in ecumenical discussions awaits a Spirit-guided, fair, impartial, faithful, and comprehensive study of this passage.[20]

PART 4

How, Why, Where, and When Did the Idea of Markan Primacy Originate?

CHAPTER 10

The Idea and Reality of Markan Priority

The Criterion of Length

The Gerasenes

I

²⁸And when he came to the other side, to the country of the Gadarenes, two demoniacs met him, coming out of the tombs, so fierce that no one could pass that way.

²⁹And behold, they cried out, "What have you to do with us, O Son of God? Have you come here to torment us before the time?"

³⁰Now a herd of many swine was feeding at some distance from them.

³¹And the demons begged him, "If you cast us out, send us away into the herd of swine."

³²And he said to them, "Go." So they came out and went into the swine; and behold, the whole herd rushed down the steep bank into the sea, and perished in the waters.

³³The herdsmen fled, and going into the city they told everything, and what had happened to the demoniacs.

³⁴And behold, all the city came out to meet Jesus; and when they saw him, they begged him to leave their neighborhood.   —*Matt. 8:28–34 (RSV)*

II

²⁶Then they arrived at the country of the Gerasenes, which is opposite Galilee.

²⁷And as he stepped out on land, there met him a man from the city who had demons; for a long time he had worn no clothes, and he lived not in a house but among the tombs.

²⁸When he saw Jesus, he cried out and fell down before him, and said with a loud voice, "What have you to do with me, Jesus, Son of the Most High God? I beseech you, do not torment me."

²⁹For he had commanded the unclean spirit to come out of the man. (For many a time it had seized him; he was kept under guard, and bound with chains and fetters, but he broke the bonds and was driven by the demon into the desert.)

³⁰Jesus then asked him, "What is your name?" And he said, "Legion"; for many demons had entered him.

³¹And they begged him not to command them to depart into the abyss.

³²Now a large herd of swine was feeding there on the hillside; and they begged him to let them enter these. So he gave them leave.

³³Then the demons came out of the man and entered the swine, and the herd rushed down the steep bank into the lake and were drowned.

³⁴When the herdsmen saw what had happened, they fled, and told it in the city and in the country.

³⁵Then people went out to see what had happened, and they came to Jesus, and found the man from whom the demons had gone, sitting at the feet of Jesus, clothed and in his right mind; and they were afraid.

³⁶And those who had seen it told them how he who had been possessed with demons was healed.

³⁷Then all the people of the surrounding country of the Gerasenes asked him to depart from them; for they were seized with great fear; so he got into the boat and returned.

³⁸The man from whom the demons had gone begged that he might be with them; but he sent him away, saying,

³⁹"Return to your home, and declare how much God has done for you." And he went away, proclaiming throughout the whole city how much Jesus had done for him.   —*Luke 8:26–34 (RSV)*

III

¹They came to the other side of the sea, to the country of the Gerasenes.

²And when he had come out of the boat, there met him out of the tombs a man with an unclean spirit,

³who lived among the tombs; and no one could bind him any more, even with a chain;

⁴for he had often been bound with fetters and chains, but the chains he wrenched apart, and the fetters he broke in pieces; and no one had the strength to subdue him.

⁵Night and day among the tombs and on the mountains he was always crying out, and bruising himself with stones.

⁶And when he saw Jesus from afar, he ran and worshiped him;

⁷and crying out with a loud voice, he said, "What have you to do with me, Jesus, Son of the Most High God? I adjure you by God, do not torment me."

⁸For he had said to him, "Come out of the man, you unclean spirit!"

⁹And Jesus asked him, "What is your name?" He replied, "My name is Legion; for we are many."

¹⁰And he begged him eagerly not to send them out of the country.

¹¹Now a great herd of swine was feeding there on the hillside;

¹²and they begged him, "Send us to the swine, let us enter them."

¹³So he gave them leave. And the unclean spirits came out, and entered the swine; and the herd, numbering about two thousand, rushed down the steep bank into the sea, and were drowned in the sea.

¹⁴The herdsmen fled, and told it in the city and in the country. And people came to see what it was that had happened.

¹⁵And they came to Jesus, and saw the demoniac sitting there, clothed and in his right mind, the man who had had the legion; and they were afraid.

¹⁶And those who had seen it told what had happened to the demoniac and to the swine.

¹⁷And they began to beg Jesus to depart from their neighborhood.

¹⁸And as he was getting into the boat, the man who had been possessed with demons begged him that he might be with him.

¹⁹But he refused, and said to him, "Go home to your friends, and tell them how much the Lord has done for you, and how he has had mercy on you."

²⁰And he went away and began to proclaim in the Decapolis how much Jesus had done for him; and all men marveled.   *—Mark 5:1–20 (RSV)*

The basic concept supporting Markan priority in nineteenth-century Germany, its birthplace, was that the shortest Gospel is the earliest. Even today, this idea is very influential, and for many it remains compelling. It is easy to visualize how a shorter narrative could be expanded so that the later versions of that narrative would be longer. Simply put, it is intellectually satisfying for many scholars to think of Mark as being the earliest Gospel, with Matthew and Luke having produced longer, more developed, and more complex narratives. Reduced to its simplest form, the enduring idea of Markan priority has been this: Mark is first because Mark is shortest. So much for the *idea* of Markan priority. What can be said about the *reality* of this idea?

We can test this criterion of length by measuring how adequately it explains the three versions of the same story. The first version is the shortest—seven verses and 162 words—and simplest of the three. According to the idea that "shorter is earlier," we would expect it to be Mark's version. The second version, fourteen verses and 293 words, follows the story outline of the first but expands the narrative by adding much new information. The third version has clearly followed the basic story outline of the first but has not neglected to include a large part of the additional information in the second. In the course of combining the two earlier versions, the author of the third has produced a version that is somewhat longer—twenty verses and 325 words— than either of the other two.

It seems clear that the author of the third version had the advantage of working with the two earlier versions because his text sometimes agrees more closely with the first and at other times more closely with the second. The very first sentence in the third version illustrates how elements from the two earlier versions are blended in the third.

Thus, the author of the third version follows the first in his use of the expression "to the other side" and then makes the text more specific by adding "of the sea." Then he agrees with the text of the second version in identifying the region as that of the Gerasenes, rather than that of the Gadarenes, as in the first version. We need not think that the third author has intentionally in any pedantic or mechanical way woven together the texts of his predecessors' narratives. Rather, we can assume he has read them both and then composed his own text, telling the story in his own way. It is perfectly natural that, in working with the earlier versions, he would produce a text that generally conformed to his sources, sometimes following one more closely, and at other times following the other more closely, with much of his text reflecting his own wording. Such a procedure is perfectly natural. It fully explains the third text.

The shortest and simplest version of this narrative is found in Matthew. Luke's version is second longest, and Mark's version is longest of the three. Moreover, this pattern is generally found throughout the Gospels. Matthew generally provides us the shortest narrative. Luke's parallel text is generally longer than Matthew's, and Mark's version is generally the longest of the three.

Based on a test using the criterion, "shorter is earlier," the idea of Markan priority is ambiguous at best. Some would say that it is downright self-contradictory. While Mark's Gospel may be shorter than Matthew or Luke in overall length, story for story Mark generally uses more words in his narration than either Matthew or Luke. And yet this idea "shorter is earlier" provides the most compelling justification that has ever been provided for Markan priority. We conclude that the idea of Markan priority is illusory and fails the reality test.

Is there an alternative idea that can pass the test of being adequate to the realities of Gospel interrelationships? Yes, there are several. For example, we can say that "shorter is sometimes later," when an author seeks to abbreviate a longer text. A shorter version of an exisiting text may be needed under many circumstances, and an abbreviated text can result from the attempt to meet this need. One of the most common circumstances under which abbreviation takes place is where a community or organization needs a more self-consistent version of an important document. Inconsistent elements are often deleted.

A shorter Gospel also could be a matter of economy. It was expensive to reproduce documents in antiquity because they had to be copied by hand. The need for a shorter Gospel to tell the essential story of Jesus' ministry—and because of overall length can be more readily reproduced—is sufficient reason for abbreviation.

Another matter is appropriateness. Why were certain materials retained while other materials were omitted? One answer is that a shorter Gospel can be composed by omitting material from earlier Gospels that has caused problems for some part of the church. Certainly some of the very Jewish material in Matthew became problematic for the later, more Gentile-oriented churches. Mark in these respects can be said to meet the needs of a Gentile-oriented church by providing a Gospel that is internally self-consistent and relatively free of problem-causing tradition in preexisting Gospels like Matthew or Luke. Jesus' acidic condemnation of scribes and Pharisees in Matthew 23 would have been troublesome for Christian communities in Rome wishing to avoid provoking influential members of Jewish synagogues in that city.

On first sight, Mark can be viewed as an abbreviation of either Luke or Matthew. Augustine first recognized this possibility and at first decided that Mark had abbreviated Matthew. For more than seven hundred years, from the Scholastics to the present, it has been held that the church taught that Mark was the abbreviator of the Gospel of Matthew. The authority cited for this view has been Augustine, *Harmony of the Gospels*, book 1. However, this idea has a problem. If Mark was an abbreviator, why does he so often expand the text from Matthew?[1] Because of this apparent self-contradiction, some scholars, like the reformer John Calvin and many Enlightenment scholars after him, rejected Augustine's idea of the evangelist Mark as an epitomizer or abbreviator.

In 1981, while reading Augustine's *Harmony of the Gospels*, a young research scholar came upon a passage in book 4 that Calvin and all modern scholars had completely overlooked. Of course, Augustine himself had no interest in the synoptic problem. But the idea that Mark was the abbreviation of Matthew profoundly shaped the discussion of the Gospels' chronological sequence developed during the Enlightenment. While this is indeed the idea that Augustine put forward in book 1 of his *Harmony of the Gospels*, David B. Peabody discovered that Augustine, after completing his study of the Gospels, changed his mind and in book 4 put forward another idea, which he said was more probable than the one in book 1.[2] In book 4, Augustine proposed the idea of Mark as a unifier. There is a great difference between an abbreviator and a unifier. The evangelist Mark, writes Augustine, has taken the kingly emphasis of Matthew and conjoined it with the priestly emphasis of Luke to produce a human figure of Christ related to both. Few discoveries in biblical science can match Peabody's rediscovery of Augustine's belief on the most probable way to understand Mark in relationship to Matthew and Luke. Mark, regarded by Augustine as the central Gospel of the church, is a unifying Gospel.

The unifier can seek to achieve its purpose in various ways. In some cases, the more unified text will be longer than its sources. An example would be Tatian's *Diatessaron* (meaning "through four"), a second-century harmony of the four Gospels, Matthew, Luke, Mark, and John. The *Diatessaron* is longer than any of Tatian's sources. But in other cases, the more unified text can be shorter. It all depends upon the author's purpose.

If the author seeks to produce a text that will replace those presently in use, he may sometimes follow the method of Tatian. But if his purpose is to advance the cause of his community or organization by establishing common ground, he may build his new text on any essential "coming together" he finds in his basic sources. Such an author is employing the idea of convergence. All communities and organizations find this idea helpful from time to time, especially during a period of crisis. It follows that "shorter can be later" when the author's purpose is to unify through adhering to common ground, and (while avoiding conflicting teachings) promoting common and complementary motifs in his separate sources. In a time of crisis, such a Gospel can elevate evangelical rhetoric to a more passionate level of intensity and effectiveness. Once the crisis is past, this shorter Gospel could take its place alongside the earlier and longer Gospels and in time be accorded an honored place in the church's canon. Meanwhile, all of the practical advantages of a briefer Gospel, reproducible in a shorter time and at lower cost, would continue to accrue to Mark. On the mission field, Mark traditionally has been and often is today the first Gospel to be translated.

We can now see that the idea "shorter is sometimes later," when applied to the length of the Gospel as a whole, is an idea that fits the facts of Mark as the third Gospel. It is also an idea that coheres with the reality of the life of the church as it is known through a study of its beginnings. The idea of Markan priority fails this test, and it conflicts with what we know about the sequence of the Gospels from church history. As was mentioned in chapter 2, Eusebius, the great historian of the early church, preserves for us information going back to the primitive elders of the church in the first quarter of the second century. Eusebius informs us that the Gospels with genealogies (certainly including Matthew and Luke) were composed before those without genealogies (Mark, John, the *Gospel of Peter*, and *Thomas*, and possibly Marcion's Gospel). This clearly implies that Mark was composed after Matthew and Luke. It is very important to emphasize that nothing in church history supports the idea of Markan priority. To find out how this idea gained a foothold in the modern church's intellectual life, we have to turn back to the history of Germany in the nineteenth century and study the role of the state-controlled German universities in the political and social life of the German nation.

The German people's basic problem at the beginning of the nineteenth century was their political disunity. The first German Reich was established by Charlemagne. Ever since the breakup of Charlemagne's empire, the German people had been divided into smaller princely states. Of all these states, Prussia was the strongest militarily and the most ambitious to expand its influence. Essential to its prosperity was the reconciliation of explosive elements within its population; movements toward unity were encouraged. With state encouragement, the Lutheran and the Reformed churches formed themselves into a single evangelical church. This was a beginning for a modern state-sponsored civil religion in Germany. The Prussian state negotiated an agreement with the Vatican by which the state exercised civil authority over its Catholic minority. With this agreement in hand, the state encouraged the formation of a Protestant-dominated national Christian consensus, including both Protestants and Catholics, that would provide the essential religious base for a unified Germany.[3]

Recognizing Mark as the central Gospel of the church fit the ideological needs of a divided Germany bent on unification. The absence of birth narratives in Mark enabled Germans to avoid conflict over the role of Mary in the new civil religion. This was especially important after 1854, when the Roman Catholic Church issued its decree on the Immaculate Conception of the Virgin Mary.

Also missing from Mark were traditionally anti-Jewish texts such as the "woes against the Pharisees" (Matt. 23), and this absence served to diminish polemic over the Jewish question. The new civil religion would also pave the way for good German Jews to work together with good German Christians. Any Gospel serviceable to Germany's aspirations for a strong national unity would eventually find favor in intellectual circles open to the claims and promises of the new civil religion. Under these circumstances, Mark, traditionally associated closely with the apostle Peter, eventually became the darling of many German intellectuals. In the first instance, these were intellectuals who fed at the trough of state largesse, specifically the German theological professorate. By way of contrast, David Friedrich Strauss, who in 1839 was ousted from the German professorate, regarded the Markan hypothesis as "the swindle of the century!"[4]

The history of Markan priority is inseparable from modern Germany's social history. This idea became popular during the period of German political consolidation 1830–1870[5] and was confirmed as a German dogma during a church-state struggle that wracked the nation during the first decade of the Second Reich, 1870–1880. Theology professors in German universities were subsequently wed to this idea. Forty years after Markan priority had been seriously challenged in scholarly books published by university presses in the United States and Great Britain, the German professorate maintained a united front against a scientific reinvestigation of the question. This academic boycott was maintained in the face of widespread international cooperation on the synoptic problem among experts from Great Britain, the United States, Canada, Denmark, Sweden, Norway, Belgium, France, Switzerland, Italy, Greece, Israel, India, Korea, Australia, Nigeria, and South Africa.

The first German-sponsored, full-scale academic conference on the question in more than a century came only after the fall of the Berlin Wall. This conference was held at the University of Göttingen in August 1991.[6] The second conference was held a year later at Bochum University.[7] Long in preparation, these two academic conferences are a part of the same social history that led up to the fall of the Berlin Wall. Both the fall of this political division and the collapse of German resistance to scientific reinvestigation of outdated academic dogma are, in significant ways, to be fully understood only in relationship to modern German social and religious history culminating in the Third Reich and the Holocaust, followed by the reconciling influence of Vatican II. To understand the decisive history of the idea of Markan primacy, we must, however, go back in time to 1870, the time of Vatican Council I, an event that at first converged and then momentarily collided with the establishment of the second German Reich (see chapter 11).

The Argument from Order

> The order of incidents in Mark is clearly the more original; for wherever Matthew departs from Mark's order Luke supports Mark, and whenever Luke departs from Mark, Matthew agrees with Mark.   —*B. H. Streeter*

The above text is taken from *The Four Gospels: A Study of Christian Origins*. While the idea that the shortest Gospel is the earliest is still an important consideration for Markan priority in the twentieth century, the idea that the "order of incidents in Mark is the more original" is most often cited in those twentieth-century textbooks that give the main reasons for Markan priority.

Let us examine Streeter's statement carefully. If Matthew has copied Mark, we must say that sometimes he follows the order of incidents in Mark and sometimes he departs from Mark's order. Similarly, if Luke has copied Mark, we must conclude that sometimes he follows the order in Mark and sometimes he departs from Mark's order. But under these circumstances, because Matthew and Luke are independently copying Mark and neither knows what the other has done or is going to do, would it be expected that where Matthew departed from Mark's order, Luke would support Mark, and where Luke departed from Mark, Matthew would agree with Mark? Would this not be a rather remarkable coincidence? How would this be possible? How would Matthew independently of Luke manage to follow the order of incidents in Mark in every case where Luke departed from Mark's order? Because Matthew could not have known when Luke had or would depart from Mark, there is no way to explain why he always follows Mark's order when Luke departs from Mark. The same would hold true for Luke. So, the fact is that the situation accurately described by Streeter, far from being a reason to accept the priority of Mark, is a reason to question the idea that Matthew and Luke have independently copied Mark. If Matthew and Luke copied Mark, one or the other would appear to have known what the other had done with Mark's order and then, with that knowledge in mind, the third synoptic writer could have managed to support Mark wherever the one who had written second had departed from Mark's order. Then, if the one who wrote third was careful never to depart from Mark except in cases where the other had followed Mark, it would be possible to reproduce the situation that Streeter describes.

On the other hand, how much simpler it is to explain the situation if we assume the validity of the Two-Gospel Hypothesis. First Matthew composed his Gospel, arranging the incidents in an order that suited his purposes. Then Luke, following Matthew, often took over incidents as he found them in Matthew, but sometimes he rearranged incidents to suit his considerably different purposes. Then Mark, with copies of the two earlier Gospels available for him, decided to basically follow the order of incidents in Luke, always being free to follow the order of incidents in Matthew when his purposes called for this literary procedure. Under these circumstances, Mark had knowledge of the order of incidents in both Matthew and Luke. Because Luke frequently followed the order in Matthew, both Matthew and Luke frequently had the same order. Where Matthew and Luke had the same order of incidents, Mark had a good reason to follow that order. Where Matthew and Luke had a different order, Mark could have departed from both Matthew and Luke or followed one or the other. Where Matthew and Luke had a different order, Mark had no other option. Based on the Two-Gospel Hypothesis, Mark rather evenhandedly now followed the order of one and then the order of the other. This is a perfectly understandable literary procedure for an author in Mark's position.

In sum, the argument from order of incidents, contrary to popular opinion, works against Markan priority. On the other hand, the agreement and disagreement in order of incidents described by Streeter is readily explained under the Two-Gospel Hypothesis.

Some defenders of Markan priority contend that they can explain why Matthew and Luke have departed from Mark better than they can explain why Mark would have departed from Matthew and Luke. However, in every case, these scholars have divided the Gospels and studied them in pairs. They study Matthew in relation to Mark, and Luke in relation to Mark. They never study the three Gospels together. As a consequence, they always miss the evidence that Mark knew the order of incidents in both Matthew and Luke. By always asking, "How can I explain why Mark would have departed from Matthew?" without looking at the Gospel of Luke, they will always miss the answer. Mark has departed from Matthew in this case because he has decided to follow the order of Luke. One then has to go back and ask why Luke departed from the order of Matthew at this point. But the advocates of Markan priority seldom if ever bother to do so.

In conclusion, this argument for Markan priority will not satisfy those who recognize that the synoptic problem is, by definition, how to explain the literary relationship among all three of the synoptic Gospels looked at together. It will only satisfy those who insist that they have the right to divide the Gospels into pairs and study them two at a time. But, as we have seen, to do so ignores the very evidence these scholars say they are looking for, namely, the reason that Mark departed now from Matthew, and then from

Luke. Assuming the validity of the Two-Gospel Hypothesis, Mark's reason for doing this is always at hand. It was always to follow his other source.[8]

The Minor Agreements

Jesus Is Mocked

[67]Then they spat on his face and slapped him and hit him,
[68]saying:
> "Prophesy to us, O Christ,
>> Who is it who is striking you?"   —*Matt. 26:67–68*

[63]And the men who held him, mocked him, beating him,
[64]And blindfolding him, they questioned him,
> saying:
>> "Prophesy,
>>> Who is it who is striking you?"
[65]And they spoke many other words against him, reviling him.—*Luke 22:63–65*

[65]And some began to spit on him and to cover up his face and to slap him and to say to him:
> "Prophesy";
And the attendants received him with blows.   —*Mark 14:65*

All verbatim agreements in Greek between Matthew, Luke, and Mark are underlined in the above texts. The term "minor agreement" is used to refer to agreements between Matthew and Luke against Mark in passages where Mark contains a parallel passage. The agreements as a whole between Matthew and Luke against Mark are rather striking. Matthew and Luke agree with one another against Mark in using the participial form of "to say": *saying*, and then they agree with one another against Mark in including the question: "Who is it who is striking you?" The problem for those who advocate the Two-Source Hypothesis is that, according to that hypothesis, neither Matthew nor Luke had access to the other. Both have independently copied Mark. How then, based on this hypothesis, can one explain the above agreements between Matthew and Luke? The word "prophesy" could have been copied from Mark because it is present in the parallel text of Mark. And the agreement in using the participial form of the verb "to say" instead of the infinitive as in Mark, could be explained as due to a stylistic preference on the part of Matthew and Luke. But the presence in the texts of both Matthew and Luke of the question: "Who is it who is striking you?" cannot be explained as having been copied from Mark, because those words are not in Mark's text.

Defenders of Markan priority have been unable to explain this evidence to the satisfaction of most scholars. In most cases, the minor agreements are explained by defenders of Markan priority as due to stylistic preference. But many cannot be so easily explained. Sometimes extensive agreement between Matthew and Luke against Mark is explained by conjecturing what is called an overlap between Mark and Q.

In these instances, it is suggested, Matthew and Luke have copied Q and not Mark. But no one has ever suggested the overlap theory to explain the presence of the question "Who is it who is striking you?" in Matt. 26:68 and Luke 22:64. This would require Q to have a passion narrative, and few defenders of the Two-Source Hypothesis would want to assume that.

Based on the Two-Gospel Hypothesis, Matthew has presented Jesus being distracted by his tormentors and taunted with the words: "Prophesy to us, O Christ, who is it who is striking you?" For the distracting effect of being spat upon, Luke substitutes the act of blindfolding, to bring out the cruelty of Jesus' mistreatment. How could Jesus possibly see who was striking him after his tormentors had blindfolded him?

Mark's account includes the spitting in Matthew as well as the covering of his eyes in Luke, and includes the other harassing treatment—slapping and hitting. By omitting the question, "Who is it who is striking you?" and closing his account with the words: "and the attendants received him with blows," the reader is allowed to imagine Jesus' tormentors relentlessly escalating violence against him, from the physically harmless though insulting: "being spat upon," through mildly violent "slapping," to Jesus being violently beaten following the terse and mocking command to "prophesy."

The agreements among all three accounts can be explained on this sequence of composition. The agreements between Matthew and Luke are explained by Luke's use of Matthew, and the agreements between Mark's account and those of Matthew and Luke are explained by Mark's use of these two earlier Gospels. Objections to this sequence can be raised, but so far the objections are based on subjective considerations, such as: Why would Mark have done this or that? Or why would Luke have modified Matthew in this way or that way? There is no hard literary evidence against the Two-Gospel Hypothesis that equals the importance of the agreement between Luke and Matthew against Mark found in the minor agreement, "Who is it who is striking you?"

There are both positive minor agreements and negative minor agreements. The minor agreement in the mocking incident just discussed is an example of what scholars term a "positive minor agreement," a case where Matthew and Luke agree against Mark by the positive act of including a question that is not found in Mark. The other kind of agreement is created when Matthew and Luke agree in not having something that *is* found in Mark. This is called an "agreement in omission." Some scholars term this a "negative agreement" of Matthew and Luke against Mark. Although these negative agreements in omission have in the past been given less attention than the positive agreements of Matthew and Luke against Mark, in recent years they have been playing a more important role in the international discussion of the minor agreements.

For example at the 1991 Symposium on the Minor Agreements in Göttingen, Germany, under the sponsorship of the theological faculty of the University of Göttingen, the agreements in omission between Matthew and Luke against Mark played an important role. To illustrate the significance of this kind of minor agreement, we will discuss the call of Matthew.

The Call of Matthew

[9]And Jesus passing along from there saw a man called Matthew seated at the customhouse, and he says to him:
      "Follow me."
    And getting up he followed him.   —*Matt. 9:9*

[27]And after these things he went out and he observed a tax collector, by name Levi, seated at the customhouse, and he said to him:
      "Follow me."
[28]And leaving everything, after getting up he began to follow him.
                                          —*Luke 5:27–28*

[13]And he went out again beside the sea; and all the crowd was coming to him, and he taught them.
[14]And passing along he saw Levi, the son of Alphaeus, seated at the custom-house, and he says to him:
      "Follow me."
    And after getting up, he followed him.   —*Mark 2:13–14*

Matthew's account of the calling of the disciple Matthew is the shortest of the three. Luke expands this account by adding the temporal clause: "And after these things he went out." Luke gives the name Levi for Matthew and further expands the text by specifying that the man sitting at the customhouse was a tax collector. Luke again expands that account by adding the phrase "leaving everything" before telling his readers in words close to the text of Matthew that "after getting up" he began to follow him.

Mark, on the other hand, expands the text of Luke considerably at the beginning of the story. In place of Luke's, "And after these things he went out," Mark has, "And he went out again beside the sea; and all the crowd was coming to him, and he taught them." Mark specifies that Levi was the son of Alphaeus, after omitting Luke's redundant information that the man sitting at the customhouse was a tax collector.

Assuming the validity of the Two-Source Hypothesis, Matthew and Luke have agreed to omit the very important information that Jesus went out "again beside the sea; and all the crowd was coming to him, and he taught them." This agreement of omission has four component parts. First, Mark uses the word "again," which characteristically means "retrospectively" in his writings. "Again" here refers to Jesus going out by the sea for the first time at Mark 1:16. There, Jesus called the two sons of Zebedee, James and John. Here at Mark 2:13, Jesus issues his third call to discipleship to Levi (Matthew) as he sits at the customhouse.

The second component part is "by the sea." The third is "and all the crowd." And the fourth is "and he taught them." All four of these component parts have been shown by Peabody to be characteristic of Markan usage.[9]

A close study of the parallel texts of Matthew, Mark, and Luke will show that the patterns of agreements among the three accounts is most easily explained if Mark is seen to be blending the texts of Matthew and Luke. It is striking that every word and phrase in this passage of Mark that cannot be traced to Matthew or Luke, or both, is characteristic of Mark. Conversely not one of the words and phrases in Mark that are parallel in Matthew or Luke is characteristic of Mark. This consistent pattern of positive and negative correlations suggests that Mark has freely recomposed the loosely parallel texts of Matthew and Luke and, in doing so, has used many of his own characteristic words and phrases. That is, what is not characteristic of Mark can be explained as having been taken over from Matthew and Luke. The rest can be explained as coming from Mark. Nothing is left over. To reverse the explanation would be to suggest that Matthew and Luke have managed to omit only what is characteristic of Mark, each independently taking from Mark only what is not characteristic of Mark. That goes against all normal expectations of how authors compose. How would two authors independently using the same source accomplish such a nice example of meaningless literary discrimination, even if for some reason that is what they wanted to do?

If one is looking for compelling evidence that serves to falsify the Markan hypothesis, what kind of literary evidence outweighs this? To refuse to accept this literary evidence is to opt out of the discipline of literary criticism as it is practiced in all fields of literature.

The Göttingen Symposium on the Minor Agreements marked the first time that scholars were asked to study the minor agreements not only within the compositional contexts of smaller separable units, which had been done before on a selective basis, but also within their larger compositional contexts.

At this symposium it was demonstrated that the Greek word *palin* (usually translated "again") "used retrospectively uniting two or more separated smaller literary units" is a literary characteristic of the author or composer of the narrative framework of Mark's Gospel. Peabody, in his book *Mark as Composer*, had shown fourteen examples where *palin* is used retrospectively to unite two or more separated paragraphs.[10] At the Göttingen symposium, the participants were presented evidence that a certain compositional structure existed for a large part of the Markan Gospel, which therefore has the highest probability of coming from the author's hand. The fourteen examples of *palin* used retrospectively to unite two or more separated smaller literary units all serve to structure major sections of the Gospel of Mark, including, at least Mark 1:16—4:2; 4:35—5:43; 6:34—8:26; 9:35—10:12; and 10:32—13:1.

In an oral presentation at the 1989 annual meeting of the Society of Biblical Literature in Anaheim, California, Peabody had already demonstrated that not one of these examples of *palin* ever appears in the parallel texts of Matthew or Luke.

Assuming the validity of the Two-Gospel Hypothesis, this compositional evidence is easily explained if Mark has added this feature to the highly dramatic text he created from his major sources, Matthew and Luke.

On the other hand, assuming the validity of the Two-Source Hypothesis, one would be constrained to say that in independently working with Mark's text, Matthew and Luke have accidentally agreed in omitting every single one of the fourteen instances of what may well be the most striking compositional feature of their source.

In conclusion, it has been demonstrated that the criterion of length and the criterion of order of incidents, both of which have been used to argue *for* the priority of Mark, can easily be reversed and used to argue *against* Mark being the earliest Gospel. It has also been demonstrated that the "minor agreements," which have always worked *against* the Two-Source Hypothesis, recently have come through the work of David Peabody to be recognized as offering significant support *for* the Two-Gospel Hypothesis. The Two-Gospel Hypothesis, therefore, enjoys more support from this set of literary tests than does the Two-Source Hypothesis.

Further Considerations

The Parable of the Lost Sheep in Matthew and Luke

[12]What do you think?
> If a man has a hundred sheep,
> > and one of them goes astray,
> does he not leave the ninety-nine,
> > and go to the mountains
> > > to seek the one that is astraying?
[13]And if he should find it,
> > assuredly, I say to you,
> he rejoices more over that sheep
> > than over the ninety-nine
> > > that did not go astray.

—Matt. 18:12–13

⁴What man of you,
> having one hundred sheep,
>> if he loses one of them,
> does not leave the ninety-nine in the wilderness,
>> and go after the one which is lost until he finds it?

⁵And when he has found it,
> he lays it on his shoulders, rejoicing,

⁶and when he comes home,
> he calls together his friends and neighbors,
> saying to them:
>> "Rejoice with me,
>>> for I have found my sheep which was lost."

⁷I say to you:
> that likewise there will be more joy in heaven
>> over one sinner that repents
>>> than over ninety-nine righteous persons,
>>>> Who need no repentance.   *—Luke 15:4–7*

It is generally held that these are two different versions of Jesus' parable of the lost sheep. Matthew's version appears to have been modified to apply to the situation in the life of the church where some members are wandering away. The teaching is that God rejoices more over finding the member who is going astray than over ninety-nine who are remaining faithful.

The Lukan form, on the other hand, appears to fit well the life situation of Jesus in Luke 15:1–2, where Jesus is being criticized by the righteous for accepting and having table fellowship with sinners. Jesus tells this parable to rebuke the self-righteousness of persons who resent God's mercy, which Jesus shows to the repentant sinners who draw near to hear him and who, after being accepted by him, share table fellowship with him. The teaching is that it is appropriate for Jesus to eat with these repentant sinners in celebration of their repentance because in heaven there is "more joy over one sinner who repents than over ninety-nine righteous persons who have no need for repentance."

Luke's Use or Disuse of Matthew

The famous North African bishop Augustine first made the point that a careful study of the Gospels teaches us that no one of the evangelists wrote in ignorance of what his precedessors had written.

So if Luke was written after Matthew, it is not unreasonable to explain most of the verbatim agreement between the texts of these two Gospels on the hypothesis that the evangelist Luke copied the text of Matthew.

At this point, however, we encounter a serious problem. Sometimes Luke appears to have preserved an earlier version of a story or saying of Jesus. Jesus' teaching about the lost sheep is an example. Luke's version of this story is said by many scholars to fit the life situation of Jesus better than its parallel in Matthew.

This can be explained, however, by pointing out that in every case where Luke may have preserved an earlier version of a story or saying, the amount of verbatim agreement is so slight that one can think of Matthew and Luke preserving different forms of the same story or saying. One is not required to think of one evangelist copying the other in such cases. Luke could have copied Matthew extensively and still have utilized other source material here and there. In his preface, Luke tells his readers that he has access to eyewitness accounts, and Matthew would have been only one of those accounts. In some cases, this other source material may have preserved an earlier form of the story or saying than that recorded in Matthew. All hypotheses presuppose a period of oral tradition bridging the time of Jesus' ministry and the time when the Gospels were written. Different forms of the stories of Jesus could have developed during this oral period. The two different forms of the parable of the lost sheep probably represent an example. Thus, this particular problem can be solved.

But another problem continues to cause difficulties for some scholars in understanding how Luke made use of Matthew. In the first two-thirds of the Gospel of Luke, and especially in chapters 3—9, Luke has stories and sayings of Jesus that are also found in Matthew, but they are arranged in a very different and somewhat perplexing way. This situation, taken with the fact that sometimes one and sometimes the other preserved an earlier form of a story or saying, led some nineteenth-century scholars to postulate that Luke and Matthew were independent of one another. This was a fundamental departure from the view of Augustine, but the internal evidence seemed to these scholars to require this hypothesis. The best solution appeared to be Matthew and Luke independently copying some earlier Ur-Gospel. The scholars who promoted this solution did not think of Mark as having copied the earlier Gospel. The chief advocates of this solution were the one-time Berlin professors Friedrich Bleek and Wilhelm De Wette, both of whom believed Mark used Matthew and Luke. Bleek and De Wette were leading Griesbachians. Their Griesbachian hypothesis is to be distinguished from the Two-Gospel Hypothesis. While they held that Mark was the third Gospel, they did not begin with the two Gospels of Matthew and Luke. They began with an Ur-Gospel that was longer than Mark and included everything that Matthew and Luke have in common.

Matthew, Luke, and Mark and
the History of the Two-Source Hypothesis

In the estimation of Bleek and De Wette, the foremost proponents in their day of the idea of Mark being third, the best way to understand the evangelist

Mark was to recognize him as an author who had produced a new text out of the narratives of Matthew and Luke. Because Mark has very little information about Jesus that could not be explained as having been taken from either Matthew or Luke, and because the only chronology known to Mark was that shared by Matthew and Luke, it seemed clear that Mark was written after Matthew and Luke and (in accordance with the commonsense view of Augustine), was not written in ignorance of his predecessors' work.

Other scholars had proposed, on the contrary, that Mark was the earliest Gospel,[11] and still others had already proposed earlier hypothetical Gospels.[12] By the early 1860s, everything appeared to be in flux. In this situation of scholarly confusion came a young scholar, Heinrich Holtzmann, who was inspired by the vision of a united Germany and a desire to bring rival parties together, a man who today is seen by some historians as a leading theologian of civil religion in Germany.

This young German patriot was chosen by Bleek's widow to take charge of her distinguished husband's literary remains. Holtzmann's first service was to complete and publish the final edition (1862) of the deceased scholar's *magnum opus.* This made the younger scholar famous at the age of thirty. He quickly came out with his own book (1863) and in this book he found the key to success in his observation that, in the face of all the disunity in German Gospel scholarship, it was possible to appeal to one cardinal point of agreement. To make clear what this point of agreement was, Holtzmann settled on a particular but ambiguous use of the word *Grundschrift*. The only point on which all experts agree, he said, was the belief that behind all the Gospels, there was a common *Grundschrift*. If we translate *Grundschrift* as "fundamental writing," we will have missed this young scholar's intention. For he proposed, following the views of a scholar named Weisse, that this singular *Grundschrift* was in fact made up of two basic sources. By this semantic finesse Holtzmann, like his hero Bismarck, facilitated the working together of conflicting parties. The one source, termed *alpha* after the first letter of the Greek alphabet, stood for the earliest Gospel. The other basic source, termed *Lambda* for the first letter of the Greek word *Logia*, stood for a collection of sayings of Jesus.[13]

For the young scholar Holtzmann, the *Grundschrift* behind all the church's Gospels, which alone guaranteed access to the truth about Jesus and the origin of Christianity, was divided into two parts: an Ur-Gospel named *Alpha,* and a collection of the sayings of Jesus, which he named *Lambda* and which later came to be known as Q. Thus came into effective being the fluid Two-Source Hypothesis, sometimes known as the Two-Document Hypothesis. Both of these sources (or documents) in the beginning were hypothetical. All the church's Gospels were based in one way or another on this dual *Grundschrift*. Eventually, Holtzmann's hypothetical Ur-Gospel or Ur-Markus gave way to Mark itself, so that the original, more fluid version of Holtzmann's nineteenth-century Two-Source Theory developed into its less fluid twentieth-century version: the priority of Mark and the existence of Q. Necessity is the mother of invention. Holtzmann's Two-Source Hypothesis was born out of invention—an invention that met the needs of the time. It was never presented, let alone defended, as a coherent theory until the twentieth century, when it had already been academically sanctioned as offering common ground for all German scholars.

This is the essential genealogical history of the Two-Source Hypothesis. Meanwhile, however, some serious scholars now contend that scientific support for this theory has evaporated. Most of these scholars hold to the view that Luke made use of Matthew. Nonetheless, equally serious scholars deny this and continue to defend the Two-Source Hypothesis. In addition to those who advocate the Two-Gospel Hypothesis, a significant body of scholars follow the critical tradition of French scholars like Joseph-Marie Lagrange and Xavier Léon-Dufour. These scholars have also operated with an Ur-Gospel, but they reject the Two-Source Hypothesis in its Germanic form. Their criticism rests on the recognition that it requires the "Judaization" of Mark to produce Matthew. In other words, they recognize the difficulty of positing a return trip of the Gospel from Rome to Palestine for the sake of obtaining a Semitic cultural cast. These exegetes are allies of the Two-Gospel Hypothesis insofar as they recognize the primary character of Matthew's text, but they are not willing to see Mark as an evangelist who drew upon and blended the narratives of Matthew and Luke.[14] This book will not review the history of this ongoing scholarly debate. The most complete bibliography documenting the essential scholarly discussion can be found in Professor David L. Dungan's article in the *Anchor Bible Dictionary* on the Two-Gospel Hypothesis. This article outlines the essential case for the Two-Gospel Hypothesis—which is juxtaposed to the Two-Source Hypothesis in this book.[15] Since Professor Dungan wrote his article, a newly rediscovered book has appeared that throws even more light on what happened in the nineteenth century and further documents the essentially unscientific character of Holtzmann's famous synthesis, relying as it did on a now universally discredited idea of a common *Grundschrift.*[16]

This newly rediscovered book was originally published in 1866 by a young Dutch scholar, Hajo-Uden Meijboom, a younger contemporary of Holtzmann. His story of the Markan hypothesis culminated with Holtzmann's 1863 effort to bring order out of chaos in German Gospel studies. Meijboom analyzed Holtzmann's work and demonstrated its critical weakness. Today we know with certainty that Holtzmann did not establish the Two-Source Hypothesis on a firm scientific basis. The esteemed Marburg successor of Bultmann, Professor Werner G. Kümmel, once wrote in his *History of New Testament Research* that

Heinrich Julius Holtzmann . . . summed up all previous research in magnificent fashion. He not only demonstrated most convincingly by an appeal to the primitive character of its narrative style and diction, that Mark's Gospel was a source of the two other synoptics, but also showed just as convincingly that we must assume a second source back of Matthew and Luke, one that consisted mainly of discourses.[17]

We know now, however, that Kümmel was writing without knowledge of the critical tradition in which Holtzmann stood. This has been demonstrated by David B. Peabody in his well-documented study of Holtzmann's uncritical reliance on the linguistic work of Markan priorist C. G. Wilke. Peabody's research makes clear that no reliable scholarly consensus in New Testament studies can be achieved as long as influential scholars continue to deny the history of the Two-Source Hypothesis.[18]

As for the question of how Luke's apparently perplexing use of Matthew is to be explained based on the Two-Gospel Hypothesis, one begins by recognizing that Luke, in working with Matthew's text, works forward through Matthew, drawing material from Matthew according to his own purposes and uniting that material with stories and sayings from other source material available to him. Once he reaches a point in the later chapters of Matthew where he finds nothing ahead in the text that he wishes to incorporate into his writing, Luke returns to an earlier point in Matthew's Gospel. In doing this, Luke often takes up a saying of Jesus from Matthew's Sermon on the Mount, and from that point he once again works his way forward in Matthew, following the same compositional procedure. Luke makes this forward compositional sweep through the text of Matthew several times until finally he has taken from Matthew all the material he wishes to incorporate into his text.

If one follows Luke carefully, always asking whether his literary procedure is compatible with the compositional freedom of an author, one never finds this evangelist violating normal literary procedure. Only when utilizing the kind of modern synopsis invented by Griesbach—where all the episodes and sayings in each Gospel are arranged in separate and parallel columns according to the principle of similarity of content—is the impression created that differences in the order of episodes and sayings in Matthew and Luke are so complex that it is unimaginable how one could have drawn material directly from the other.

It is a well-kept secret among synopsis makers that no one synopsis can enable the reader to see all the evidence as it should be seen to understand how the Gospels are related to one another. But at no point is the inadequacy of the modern synopsis more serious than at the point of enabling the reader to understand how Luke used Matthew. Assuming the Two-Gospel Hypothesis, one would need a separate synopsis for each of the compositional moves forward in Matthew made by Luke. As it is, all of these forward compositional sweeps in Luke are simultaneously superimposed upon one another in all modern synopses, creating the illusion of utter literary confusion. The student who has not followed Luke's procedure step by step is drawn to the ill-considered conclusion that Luke must be compositionally independent of Matthew. No one ever objected to Luke's use of Matthew on literary grounds until after the invention of the modern synopsis. It is important to note that J. J. Griesbach, inventor of the modern synopsis, was never able to explain Luke's use of Matthew. It is a great mistake to confuse the Griesbach Hypothesis with the Two-Gospel Hypothesis. The only thing they have in common is that both hypotheses assume that Mark made use of Matthew and Luke. As we have seen, the Griesbach Hypothesis at the hands of Holtzmann, helped pave the way for the Two-Source Hypothesis. The Two-Gospel Hypothesis, however, rejects the major premise of the Two-Source Hypothesis, namely, the independence of Matthew and Luke.

Under the guidance of Professor Peabody, scholars in the Society of Biblical Literature have devised a reasonable explanation of Luke's use of Matthew. This group is engaged in doing redaction criticism of Matthew, Mark, and Luke assuming the Two-Gospel Hypothesis.[19]

Conclusion

Arguments in favor of Markan priority can be refuted. According to the criterion of length, the text of Mark—episode by episode—tends to be longer than the text of Luke and generally is longer still than the text of Matthew. Thus applied, the criterion of length indicates that Mark could be later. If Mark used Matthew and Luke, we should expect Mark to be shorter because Roland Mushat Frye (see note 1) has discovered that this is generally the case when a third author is using two narrative sources on the same subject.

As for the agument from order, Streeter's classic formulation in favor of Markan priority actually argues in favor of Mark coming after Matthew and Luke.

In the case of the minor agreements of Matthew and Luke against Mark, the evidence not only argues against the view that Matthew and Luke were independent of one another, but it also argues for Mark being third. The best way to explain why Matthew and Luke agree in not having so many of Mark's characteristic phrases and usages is to assume that Mark was third and created his own unique version of the Gospel making use of Matthew and Luke. In every case—with the criterion of length, the argument from order, and the minor agreements—the reader has had actual texts to read. All that the reader has been asked to do is to reflect on the evidence in these texts. And in every case the evidence argues against Markan priority.

The preceding section, "Further Considerations," shows how it is possible to answer the objections that have been raised against the view that Luke used Matthew.

In sum, arguments in favor of Markan priority do not stand up to close scrutiny, while objections to Luke's use of Matthew turn out to be based on a failure to understand Luke's compositional method.[20]

CHAPTER 11

A Social History
of Markan Primacy

Introduction

In 1977, the world of theological scholarship was rudely shocked when the venerable German publishing house of Vandenhoeck & Ruprecht brought out a book by Hans Herbert Stoldt questioning the Two-Source Hypothesis.[1] No one could have foreseen that Vandenhoeck & Ruprecht, one of the most distinguished academic presses in Germany, would have been willing to publish a book questioning the single most "assured" result of nineteenth-century German scholarship. Professor J. Y. Campbell of Westminster College, Cambridge, England, once said: "If we cannot be sure of Markan priority and the existence of Q what can we be sure of?" Professor Van Harvey, now of Stanford University, once said that those who questioned Markan priority must be wrong, "because it is inconceivable that all German New Testament scholars could be mistaken on such a fundamental point."

The author of this surprising new book was an expert on eighteenth- and nineteenth-century German literature. Thus, he was intellectually well equipped to investigate circumstances in nineteenth-century Germany that could account for a critical mass of scholarly opinion in support of Markan priority—even though most learned scholars in Germany never accepted this conclusion. The scholars who never accepted Markan priority are a who's who of relevant nineteenth-century scholarship.[2] Most of these scholars regarded Mark as third. Stoldt came to the same conclusion with regard to Mark.

This conclusion obligated Stoldt to explain an unlikely development where a valid hypothesis that was once widely held was replaced by a radically different hypothesis—a hypothesis that Stoldt's research indicated was completely false. Why was the more valid hypothesis abandoned? That was the question that Stoldt set out to answer. He discovered an answer in the public reaction against the sensational *Life of Jesus* by David Friedrich Strauss (1835). Strauss was a student of F. C. Baur, professor of church history at the University of Tübingen, who was widely recognized as the greatest New Testament scholar of his generation and was the head of what was known as the Tübingen school.

The work of Baur and his students, who dated the Gospels very late, was considered radical by moderate liberal scholars like Heinrich Ewald. Ewald first introduced nationalism into the scholarly debate by accusing Baur and his school of bringing shame on German scholarship. Feelings were running high, and the public outcry against Strauss only added fuel to the fire. Strauss became a darling of the left in that era's political struggles, and the Tübingen school, under attack from the right for both theological and political reasons, was demonized.

In England, where Germany's intellectual turmoil was followed closely, the source theory adopted by Baur and Strauss was known in establishment circles as the Tübingen theory and was believed to be tainted by theological and political radicalism. Strauss and Baur presupposed the prevailing view that the Gospel of Mark was composed after Matthew and Luke and had made use of both. Theological and political animosity against these prominent scholars appears to have carried over to, and adversely affected, the future reception of the source hypothesis on which their work was founded.

No doubt, reaction against the Tübingen school indirectly served to discredit this source hypothesis. But had Stoldt overstated his case? A young British scholar named Christopher Tuckett believed that he had.[3] The ensuing scholarly discussion led to the rediscovery of a brilliant but long-forgotten book written in 1866 by a young Dutch scholar named Hajo-Uden Meijboom, who was intimately acquainted with the contemporary scholarly discussions going on in Germany. In his book, Meijboom established in great detail the decisive importance of reaction against D. F. Strauss's *Life of Jesus*.

According to Meijboom, proponents of Markan priority like C. H. Weisse explicitly acknowledged that they intended to offer the German people a critical alternative (including an alternative source theory) to the dangerous views of the Tübingen school. So Meijboom's book, once rediscovered, offered strong support for Stoldt's thesis. But it did more than this. Meijboom's book carried a devastating critical analysis of a famous work by Heinrich Holtzmann.

Holtzmann's work is generally credited with having put the Two-Source Hypothesis on firm scientific ground.[4] Stoldt had also shown the critical weakness of Holtzmann's work. But once Meijboom's work was rediscovered, and it was recognized that the academic sham of Holtzmann's case for the Two-Source Hypothesis had been exposed as early as 1866, only three years after its publication in 1863, the question naturally was asked: "How then can we account for the fact that Prussian state authorities appointed Holtzmann to the prestigious position of professor at the newly reconstituted University of Strasbourg?" This appointment, in 1874, provided a boost to the Two-

Source Hypothesis at a crucial period in Germany's history and eight years after its scholarly refutation. What was going on?

Meijboom's book, now available in English translation,[5] has recently stimulated further research into the history of nineteenth-century Gospel criticism. Two scholarly conferences bringing together specialists in the history of biblical criticism (under the leadership of Professor H. Graf Reventlow of Bochum University) with specialists in the history of the German universities (under the leadership of Professor Charles McClelland of the University of New Mexico) have been held in recent years. The first meeting was held in Latrobe, Pennsylvania, in 1990, and the second in Bochum, Germany, in 1992. On both occasions, considerable time was devoted to discussing developments in the German universities after 1870, focusing upon archival research into the Holtzmann appointment of 1874.

The reaction against Strauss in the first half of the twentieth century helps to explain how a once-dominant view fell into popular disfavor and how the more popular Two-Source Hypothesis took its place. It does not, however, explain how Markan priority, a literary hypothesis, was transformed into the Protestant dogma of Markan primacy. We need to know how the priority of Mark was converted in the second half of the nineteenth century from a relatively more conservative "scientific" hypothesis into what Professor Bo Reicke has termed a *theologumenon* of liberal Protestant theology.

Markan Primacy and the *Kulturkampf*

Part A

To designate Markan primacy a *theologumenon* is to recognize that this hypothesis took on the function of religious dogma. When did this happen? This dogmatic function was sealed in the intense but largely forgotten church-state conflict known as the *Kulturkampf*,[6] which dominated relations between Germany and the Vatican during the 1870s. This conflict arose after the close of the First Vatican Council and pitted Chancellor Otto von Bismarck against Pope Pius IX. It was a question between church and state. Constantine had announced to the church's bishops that he had received a revelation that he would exercise the office of bishop on all matters outside the church, just as they were to exercise jurisdiction on all matters internal to the life of the church. Therefore, it has always been tempting for the head of any government in Christendom to presuppose the right to exercise sovereignty over Christian subjects. Kaiser Wilhelm was no exception, and Bismarck was his prime minister. Pius IX, on the other hand, was the inheritor of a tradition according to which, as the head of the Catholic Church, he was responsible for every Catholic, including those who were German citizens.

At issue was whether Catholics were to obey the pope or the Iron Chancellor. The conflict broke out when a Catholic teacher in the *gymnasium* (preparatory school) at Braunsberg in East Prussia, having refused to assent to the Vatican decrees of 1870 on the supremacy and infallibility of the pope, was excommunicated and deprived of his right of giving instruction in the Catholic faith.[7] It helps to know that, although this teacher was giving instruction to Catholics, he in fact had been appointed by government officials, and his salary was paid by the state. Ordinarily, this arrangement worked well, because such appointments were made in consultation with church authorities. The state in turn took for granted that no local bishop would dismiss such a government appointee without due cause.

And here we come to the crux of the matter. What caused a breakdown in a system that for so long had worked well in maintaining a viable relationship between Prussia and its Catholic minority?

At issue was the way the Vatican Council decrees were to be implemented, not only in Germany where Bismarck could control the situation through his influence within its dominant state, Prussia, but in France and Austria, whose governments were vulnerable to pressure from ultramontane (pro-Vatican) forces.

It was from the ultramontane elements in French and Austrian society— with their reaction against Enlightenment tendencies embodied in some forces behind Bismarck—that the Jesuits had found support for their plans to persuade the pope to call the Vatican Council. The aim had been to strengthen the papacy by issuing decrees on universal papal jurisdiction and papal infallibility. A strengthened papacy was perceived as offering the best hope for maintaining a defense against a ruinous tide of social unrest.

Meanwhile, in response to this teacher's excommunication, the Prussian minister sent a response to the local bishop demanding that Catholic students should continue to receive religious instruction from the same teacher. The bishop protested. The state responded by issuing a statement that "in the eyes of the state, the excommunicated teacher remained a member of the Catholic Church."[8] The Prussian bishops sent an immediate protest against "the interference of the state in the church's internal sphere of faith and right." In response, the German sovereign communicated to Pius IX that "the Prussian government had acted in strict accordance with the existing law" as hitherto approved by the pope. A high-ranking official of the government issued a declaration that "the state was under no obligation to treat the adherents of the unchanged Catholic Church as seceders from it." In August, the *Provinzial-Korrespondenz*, the publication through which the government clarified its views for the benefit of the public, explained that no bishop could be permitted to compel teachers under state control "to give their assent to a dogma imperiling the relations between the state and the Church of Rome."[9] How could the dogma of papal infallibility imperil relations between Germany and the Church of Rome? The answer is clear. Protestant principles were dominant in Germany, and this dogma seemed to Protestants to be anti-Protestant to the core!

The decrees had been promulgated in St. Peter's on July 18, 1870. One month later, the *Allgemeine Augsburger Zeitung* delivered this judgment:

> The monstrosity has taken place. The paramount party in the Church [the Roman Catholic Church] has committed the crime of declaring to be a heresy the oldest principle of the Catholic faith that revealed truth is made known only by the continuous consent of all churches, and, on the other hand, has declared as a dogma by the mouth of the unhappy Pius IX the crazy opinion of mere human origin that the Pope by himself is infallible. It has ventured to threaten with excommunication from the Church all those who may decline to agree to this overbearing outrage. It was not a formally valid resolution of the Council which delivered this verdict. It was merely a remnant of the Vatican gathering. . . . This remnant of a sickly corporate body has attempted to turn the Church upside down by the overthrow of its constitution, and Pius IX has lent himself to confirm this criminal undertaking.[10]

From 1830 onward, the unification of Germany had required a *modus vivendi* between Protestants and Catholics. In response to this ideological need, German liberalism had carefully worked its will within both communions.

Lillian Wallace, in *The Papacy and European Diplomacy, 1869–1878*,[11] writes that in the period before the Vatican decrees were issued:

> The leading German churchmen had been building up a powerful Catholic party which [1] aimed at harmony with the world of science, [2] resented Jesuit influence over the Pope, and [3] strongly opposed further centralization of power in papal hands.[12]

Wallace goes on to note that "the ambitions of this group were clearly grasped and set forth" by the papal nuncio in Munich, who wrote to Cardinal Caterini as follows:

> Almost all of these people pride themselves on forming what they call the great party of German savants. Their aspirations consist in general of encouraging and pursuing to their furthest limits of scientific progress, and that with liberty, complete independence, maintaining dogma intact but sacrificing certain doctrines which are associated with it and have not been defined by the Church; their aspirations also consist of laying aside old-fashioned methods of scholasticism, these antiquities of the Middle Ages, as they call them, which are incompatible with modern progress; most important, their aspirations consist of rendering the scientific research of Catholicism as similar as possible to the scientific research of Protestantism, in order to demonstrate the superiority of Catholic theology over Protestant theology; finally, their aspirations include

giving to biblical, philological, and historical studies a very large place, leaving only a very small place for true and positive theology. This party is dominated by pride. It resents the rein of authority which according to its view hinders progress. It takes little account of the decisions of the Roman congregations; it esteems highly the university system of "learned" Germany and prefers it to the seminaries of foreign lands; it regards with an eye of pity, if not scorn, the degree of scientific culture possessed by other countries, and considers theological science in the seminaries of Italy, France, and other nations as in a state of infancy.[13]

It should be noted that this party aspired to render the research of Catholicism as similar as possible to the research of Protestantism. This clearly included biblical and historical studies. The fact that Germany's state-controlled universities, which dominated biblical research, were financially dependent upon the government appeared to these Catholics to pose no threat.

If we analyze this letter, we find that it confirms the view that these Catholics were implicated in facilitating the assimilation of the Catholic intelligentsia within a dominantly Protestant regime. Of course, there needed to be a compatible Protestant majority equally willing to abide by the *modus vivendi* that would emerge out of this cultural accommodation.

Let this one point be underscored: It is the German university system and more precisely German science (*deutsche Wissenschaft*) that is to provide the national magisterium in the struggle for salvation of the German state. How shortsighted this reliance on the German universities was only began to become clear during the Third Reich.

Part B

A society's ideological needs inevitably affect how that society's literature is interpreted. However, in the world of biblical scholarship, this is not always recognized. There is today a reluctance to recognize how the ideological needs of nineteenth-century German society have influenced the way in which the Bible was and continues to be interpreted in our theological schools and our universities.

Among the ideological needs of Germany was a *modus vivendi*, not only between a Protestant majority and a Catholic minority but also between a Christian majority and a Jewish minority. These culturally diverse citizens had to accommodate their differences if the empire was to fulfill its role in world politics.

Nineteenth-century biblical criticism served German society well by enabling it to meet these ideological needs. It is shocking to see how far German Jews were willing to go to become a "better" German. Not only were the dietary laws abandoned, but some synagogues were even willing to move their main worship services to Sunday. Enlightenment biblical criticism, which became state-supported biblical scholarship, smoothed the way.

Sacrifices made by the Christian majority were less radical. However, all scripture passages that had fed anti-Semitism needed to be discounted. This meant that the words in Matthew "let his blood be upon our heads" needed to be relativized, as did the condemnations of the Pharisees in Matthew 23. This was achieved by denying the foundational role of Matthew in the church's constitution, and by turning this role over to earlier hypothetical sources from which passages used for anti-Jewish polemic were sanitized as much as possible.

Part C

Let us return now to the struggles between Bismarck and Pius IX. Each of these titans lived within and represented his own world of discourse. That of Pius IX was Catholic; Bismarck's was Protestant. At issue is the figure of the apostle Peter, and how the pope is to be understood in relationship to Peter.

We must bear in mind that the protagonists from these two worlds of discourse are playing out their roles on a stage where both sides have committed themselves to religious toleration. Blood must not be shed over this issue. There must not be torture, nor capital punishment—there can only be arrests, trials, banishments, or imprisonments. It is against this background that measures taken by Bismarck to break down Catholic resistance are so shocking. By 1876 every Prussian bishop either was in prison or had left the country.[14] It is estimated that at the height of the controversy, as many as 989 Prussian parishes were without priests.

How were these measures initiated? In May 1871, Bismarck told the Prussian legislators that

> the Prussian cabinet is determined to take measures which shall henceforth render it impossible for Prussians who are priests of the Roman Catholic Church to assert with impunity that they will be guided by canon rather than by Prussian law [Bishop Kremenz of Ermeland had so expressed himself]. . . . We shall maintain the legislative power of the state against all comers.[15]

The next month, Bismarck told a government official that he "proposed to move vigorously against the clerics." Wallace conjectures that this decision was possibly the result of a report from Rome that "the papacy was assuming an anti-German attitude."[16] No doubt the Vatican authorities were concerned over actions by the Prussian authorities.

Three days later an article appeared in the *Neue Preussische Zeitung* declaring that the Jesuits were responsible for the formation of the Center Party (the Catholic Party). Although the Papal See, it went on, had at first greeted establishment of the German empire with approbation, Rome's action had belied its word. Germany would never consent "to strengthen a party whose sole aim was to resurrect the powers of the papacy." This article, in Wallace's view, was the clarion call to arms in the *Kulturkampf*.[17] This was June 22, 1871.

Two days later, an article in the periodical *Germania* concluded that an "ultramontane, that is a Catholic, cannot love his German fatherland; he is a stranger in his own house."[18] The conflict escalated and, according to one count made early in 1875, 136 editors had been arrested, 20 confiscations of newspapers had been executed, 210 Center (Catholic) Party members had been arrested, 74 house searches had been executed, 55 dissolutions of meetings and organizations had occurred, and 103 expulsions and internments had been ordered.[19]

On May 14, 1872, a bill was introduced in the Reichstag calling for the expulsion of the Jesuits from Germany. Speeches were heated, and the supporters of the bill proved to be unstoppable. Following a day of debate, songs were performed in the theater about the Jesuits, the pope, and infallibility.[20]

One month later, after word about the debates in the German Reichstag had reached the pope, he addressed the German reading club in Rome. While he could agree that God wants citizens to obey magistrates, God also wants them to fight error, the pope said.

> We find ourselves under [a] persecution [that has been] prepared for a long time, but [is] now making itself felt. It is the minister of a powerful government who after great success on the battlefield [victories over Austria and France] has placed himself at the head of this persecution. I have let him know (it is not a secret, the whole world may know) that triumph without moderation cannot last, that a triumph which combats truth and the Church is the greatest madness. Who knows if soon a little stone may be detached from the height to break the foot of the colossus? . . . If God wills that other persecutions follow, the Church is not afraid. On the contrary! In the persecution it will be purified, strengthened, and surrounded with new beauty.[21]

Bismarck was displeased. Everyone realized that "the stone and the colossus" referred to the German empire and particularly to Bismarck. The Jesuits were banned, and the *Kulturkampf* was actively under way by the summer of 1872.[22]

The following January, the first repressive laws were introduced into the Prussian legislature.[23] They can be summarized as:

> Priestly offices could only be confirmed on candidates of German birth, who, after passing the school-leaving examination, had studied theology for three years in a German university, and had received a sound scientific training tested

by the state. Certain exceptions notwithstanding, this rule was manifestly aimed at theological seminaries on whose behalf an outcry at once arose. Still more contentious . . . was the subjection of the appointment of candidates duly trained to the veto of the state. . . . Appointments made without the approval of the state were null and void; and the making of such appointments or the leaving open of clerical offices beyond the period of a year, was to be punishable by fines. Heavy fines were also to be imposed on priests illegally appointed (even if they should only) exercise spiritual functions—a provision which had the effect of depriving a parish served by such a priest of the ordinary comforts of religion.[24]

These laws were passed, 245 to 110, by the lower legislative body. After long debate and a speech by Bismarck alleging that it was "the conviction of the king and the government that the foundation of the state is in danger," this legislation also passed in the upper house, 87 to 53, on May 1. The Catholic bishops prepared for resistance, informing the government that they were "unable to cooperate in carrying out these enactments."[25]

Six months later, Pius IX lamented certain things, including the May Laws that were causing Prussian Catholics so much suffering. He nonetheless advised courage and reminded everyone that the church would be triumphant in the end. "Heaven and earth may pass away, but my words will not pass away." The pope said the words Jesus referred to were: "Thou art Peter, and upon this rock I will build my church." Those who oppose the church, history teaches us, have been defeated in the end, while the church itself "gleams brighter than the sun,"[26] Pope Pius said. Here, he publicly called attention to what Jaroslav Pelikan has designated as "the charter of Roman Catholic Christianity," the passage in Matthew where Christ bestows on Peter the keys of the kingdom (Matt. 16:18–19). This passage undergirds papal claims of universal jurisdiction and infallibility.[27] It was only a matter of time before the other protagonist, Bismarck, would level an exegetical counterattack against this papal appeal to holy writ. Meanwhile, the bishops were required to take an oath to keep the state's laws conscientiously and without reservations. Catholic legislators in both the Prussian and imperial parliaments opposed these measures and spat out their defiance at the Iron Chancellor. On occasion they reduced their tormentors to silence. One day their spokesperson stood up in the Prussian parliament and said:

> You have power to torment us, to wound our hearts. You do not have the power to take our faith away from us. When you shall have closed all our churches we shall assemble in the forests, we shall imitate the Catholics of France during the [Reign of] Terror.[28]

Bismarck's campaign against the Catholic Church was most intense in 1874, the year of Holtzmann's appointment, with passage of the law on the "internment or expulsion of recalcitrant priests." With all Catholic bishops in

Prussia either in prison or in exile, with hundreds of priests incarcerated, and several hundred parishes priestless, the pope on February 5, 1875, cried out against the May Laws. Because the church no longer had control of the education of its priests and thus, for example, could not be sure that its charter would be left intact, the pope could hold that this anti-Catholic legislation overturned the constitution of the church. Catholic bishops who were shut up in prison, he held up as martyrs.

> For it is not to the powers of this earth that the Lord has submitted the bishops of His Church, but to Peter to whom he has entrusted his sheep and his lambs. This is why no temporal power . . . has the right to despoil of their episcopal dignity those who have been named by the Holy Spirit to administer the Church. . . . It is necessary to obey God rather than man.[29]

It follows that Bismarck is not contending with a mere human being but with Peter, prince of the apostles, who by faith is perceived by Catholics to be authoritatively present in the person and office of the pope. This resistance of the Catholic bishops, urged on by the ultramontane forces of other Catholic countries, tormented Bismarck beyond endurance.[30]

This defiance of the pope evoked this response in a government newspaper:

> The fact of this open outspoken message leaves no doubt that the relations of the Papal See to secular government have been fundamentally altered through the newest development [i.e., the appeal to scripture to justify resistance to the ultimate authority of the May Laws].

The pope's message, the writer maintained, was a revolutionary challenge to the state's authority. By virtue of its unmistakable purpose, the government's course was clear: the Catholic Church must be made to learn who is sovereign in Prussia.[31]

Bismarck had no question about the decisive role in all this of both the Vatican Council decrees on papal infallibility and papal supremacy. Only two months after the pope had last called attention to his Petrine authority, on April 15, 1875, Bismarck leveled a bitter counterattack against Pius IX. The Catholic Church, he said, is now nothing else but the pope. Before the Vatican Council, German bishops exercised the right to at least think for themselves. However, complained Bismarck, they no longer exercised this independence from the pope. And now, going for the jugular, Bismarck juxtaposes Peter to the pope, saying that Pius IX was not really Peter's successor, since the apostle Peter had not been infallible; Peter had sinned, wept bitterly, and repented; Bismarck closed his attack with these words: "From the pope, I think, we need not expect that."[32] This adroit use of biblical exegesis strongly suggests that Bismarck and his advisers understood the importance of scripture's polemical role in the ongoing political struggle. They would have understood the way in which the special interests of the state would be served by a university-endorsed counterargument. Of course, the argument could not be effective unless and until it was supported in most influential universities of the realm. Essential to this development would be a professorate that was sensitive (but not openly subservient) to the interests of the state, and a government that knew how to work with local university officials.[33]

Markan primacy offered support for discounting the claims for a papal authority, which rested on the Peter passage in Matthew that was absent in Mark. To have well-placed professors who supported Markan primacy would serve the state interests. Conversely, any professor whose published work had Matthew as the earliest Gospel would be out of step with the interests of the state and could expect to wither on the vine. This is exactly what happened to Adolf Hilgenfeld, whose negative review of Holtzmann's book did little to slow growing support for Markan primacy. Protestant pastors caught up in the spirit of the times simply ceased to recommend to young theologians that they hear Hilgenfeld. It was not necessary to take his views into account.[34]

And now we approach the point of our essay.

Markan primacy, as Professor Bo Reicke has noted, became a German *theologumenon*. It was taught to children in the schools without question. How did this happen? In 1870, the Markan hypothesis was no more than a scholarly hypothesis with a growing following. But certainly by 1914, and possibly as early as 1880, this hypothesis implicitly was converted into a liberal dogma. Why? In the struggle between church and state, the ideas of Markan primacy and the existence of Q took on ideational roles. That is, they began to function ideologically within the university-dominated Protestant magisterium. It is probable that this function of the "Two-Source" Hypothesis was largely unconscious. In any case, these university-endorsed ideas served to undercut the basis for the decrees of the First Vatican Council.

The immediate reaction of the Catholic hierarchy was resistance. Bismarck, however, found a way around this resistance by going over the heads of German Catholics and negotiating with the new pope an end to the *Kulturkampf*. Leo XIII, elected in 1878, wanted to normalize relations between Germany and the Vatican. This eventually freed German Catholic liberals—who, in the face of persecution, had joined forces with conservative Catholics—to resume assimilation through university-sponsored German scholarship. This paved the way for German Catholic scholars like Baron von Hügel to recommend Markan primacy and the existence of Q even in the face of Vatican opposition.

During the *Kulturkampf*, the German universities were more unified in support of Bismarck than was the Prussian legislature, some of whose members opposed the May Laws. No such opposition developed in the universities. We must bear in mind that all professors at German universities, Catholics as well as Protestants, were appointed by the state. After 1875, for a brief period, German scholars who would publicly question Markan primacy would be endangering "the foundation of the state." They would be denying a decisive defensive weapon against the use the Vatican was making of the Peter passage, a Matthean passage notably absent in Mark!

This intense conflict lasted only two or three years. When Pius IX died, Leo XIII made peace. Persecution of Catholics in Germany abated, but the die had been cast. The Gospel of Matthew was henceforth associated with ultramontanism. In this situation, a critical mass of scholarly opinion formed in favor of Markan primacy—in the absence of serious historical and literary evidence and indeed in the face of compelling counterevidence. Therefore, the conclusion that other interests were exercising an influence is unavoidable. Some of these other interests were discussed in the histories of Meijboom and Stoldt. To these may now be added state interests. While the conflict between Bismarck and the Vatican eventually subsided, anti-ultramontane feelings in Germany persisted and remained strong throughout the Second Reich.

It may be arugued that no university professor would have allowed himself to be influenced by nonscientific considerations. But is such an argument tenable? And in any case, would these scholars also be free from all national sentiment? For example, would Catholic professors during the Second Reich be immune from pressure emanating from a prejudice that a Catholic "cannot love his fatherland"? Within this context, we will find the answer to the question: "How did Mark displace Matthew as the foundational Gospel for Christian faith?" Once the nineteenth-century, politically correct Markan hypothesis had become an alternative to the radical Tübingen hypothesis, this transformation happened unconsciously in response to the need of the German state for a theological defense against a perceived Catholic threat. This perceived threat was triggered by Pius IX and his close advisers who were seen as having bulldozed through the Vatican Council, over the opposition of liberals from northern Europe and the United States, the decrees on papal surpremacy and papal infallibility. These decrees were expected to rally a coalition of ultramontane forces against Protestant Prussia—decrees that proceeded from the Peter passage found only in Matthew. Liberal German Catholic scholars at the First Vatican Council, after the *Kulturkampf* was over, eventually regrouped, and at Vatican Council II, with the assistance from moderates, their goal of a Catholic biblical criticism as close as possible to Protestant biblical criticism won the day. Meanwhile, however, they had learned an important lesson. By Vatican Council II, they had come to recognize who was sovereign in Germany. It was Mark, not Matthew.

It is important to recognize that this reading of history does not require that the state exercised explicit pressure on university professors. Gordon A.

Craig refers to *Selbst-Gleichschaltung* (self-censorship), by which he means "the voluntary, preemptive acceptance of the conformity ordered or expected by the regime." "It signifies submission out of a whole range of motives. . . . The regime had a calibrated sense of how to apply censorship and terror, which encouraged voluntary submission."[35] Craig is writing about the Third Reich and, among other things, refers to the collapse of responsible resistance to Hitler in all German universities. But self-imposed conformity operates at all levels in every society. And all that is required to explain the virtual collapse of critical resistance to a problematic Markan primacy in the Second Reich by most, indeed almost all, university professors (Theodor Zahn and Adolf Schlatter are the two most notable exceptions) is a commonsense recognition by the professorate that state interests called for "voluntary, preemptive acceptance of a conformity." No one was asked to sign on the dotted line; no oath was required. Everyone was free to make up his own mind and to speak and act in accordance with his own conscience. But this did not preclude a scholar from considering his perceived duty as a servant of the state and exercising a voluntary self-censorship that would bring him into line with his colleagues and all higher authorities.

Serious research on the synoptic problem virtually halted. Individual scholars carried out their independent research interests in new directions, along lines that enabled them to maintain their personal integrity as scholars. Through the power to appoint, state interests would eventually prevail. It is true that once one becomes a professor, one is free to follow his conscience. But to become a professor, a measure of *Selbst-Gleichschaltung* (self-censorship) is essential in all universities.

The sovereignty of Mark in the Second Reich was quickly passed to all societies outside Germany that had a symbiotic relationship with the Second Reich through the agency of German scholarship.

It may be asked whether scholars at Oxford and Cambridge would take over Markan primacy from their German colleagues. In fact, they did.[36]

Epilogue

The historian can seldom pinpoint the exact beginning of any social phenomenon. But, in June 1871 conditions prevailed that can account for when and why the tradition of Matthew as our earliest Gospel became anathema for Protestant theology. Bismarck decided then to move vigorously against priests of the Roman Catholic Church. If Wallace is correct in suggesting that this decision was the result of a report from Rome that the papacy was assuming an anti-German attitude, we can explain what happened.

The previous month, in May 1871, Bismarck had forced the pope's hand when he told the Prussian legislators that the cabinet was determined to make it "impossible" for Catholic priests in Prussia to "assert with impunity" that they would be guided by canon rather than by Prussian law. It is important to grasp the nature of the crisis that this juxtaposition of "canon" and "Prussian" law entailed. Canon law rests on the Bible. The New Testament is the norm of the Christian Bible. And the Gospels provide the norm of canon law because they represent the legislative voice of the Son of God. Within this fourfold Gospel canon, the first Gospel has been foundational for the church. There, Christ, as the new Moses, reveals his law for his church. "All authority in heaven and earth has been given to me. Go make disciples of all nations . . . teaching them to keep my commandments. And I will be with you until the close of the age" (Matt. 28:18–20).

The Gospel of Matthew is the backbone of canon law. To break that back was to break the resistance to Prussian authority. Bismarck could hardly have thought consciously in these terms because Matthew is scripture and Lutherans honor scripture. But canon law could be attacked because that was identified as "Catholic."

Let there be no mistake: ecclesiastical authority as it is expressed in Matthew inspired the pope and stood in Bismarck's path. In addition to the Peter passage, there is the apostolic discourse:

> You will be dragged before governors and kings for my sake, to bear testimony before them and to the nations. When they deliver you up, do not be anxious how you are to speak or what you are to say; for what you are to say will be given to you in that hour; for it is not you who speak, but the Spirit of your Father speaking through you. . . . He who endures to the end will be saved. . . . So have no fear of them; for nothing is covered that will not be revealed, or hidden that will not be known. And do not fear those who kill the body but cannot kill the soul; rather fear him who can destroy both soul and body in hell. . . . He who does not take his cross and follow me is not worthy of me. (Matt. 10:18–38)

This apostolic discourse brought the Roman Empire to its knees and continues to steel the martyrs of the church. The Second Reich with its Protestant Kaiser resurrected the specter of Caesars of old. And Bismarck's *Realpolitik* was bringing the crisis to a head.

Sociologically, Markan primacy leads to a deconstruction of canonical authority. As most Lutherans think, however, it is less Matthew than Paul who establishes the norms of the New Testament. In Lutheran circles where the authority of the Gospels, especially the canonical authority of Matthew, was under a cloud, Rom. 13:1–5 was absolutized to serve state *interests*. This meant that Bismarck could count on the support of a Protestant-dominated Prussian legislature in his move to imprison Catholic priests and bishops who resisted the authority of the German state. But such measures could only bring temporary relief.

To guarantee that the German Catholic Church had suitable leadership, Bismarck turned to the state-controlled university system. By requiring all clerics to be educated in the state universities, Bismarck intellectually neutered the Catholic Church in Germany and drafted the German university professorate into his forces. The result of Bismarck's move was to eradicate ultramontanism from German Catholicism.

No official directions from Berlin were required; they would have been counterproductive. Many German professors in the first half of the nineteenth century had fought against princely government authorities in behalf of a strong, united Germany. Now that Bismarck had brought about German unity, these professors were more than willing to support an empire that respected and honored the German professor. These privileged servants of the state were perfectly capable of grateful self-censorship in behalf of a strong Germany. One consequence of this was an increasing tendency to consent by silence to the Protestant shibboleth of Markan primacy. In this sense, the historian can say that Markan primacy won by default. This helps to explain how a critical mass of scholarly opinion, despite convincing evidence to the contrary, formed in favor of Markan primacy, so that during the first half of the twentieth century it became possible for almost all scholars to believe (what today almost all scholars have come to disbelieve) that the Two-Source Hypothesis was an "assured result" of nineteenth-century German scholarship.

If students of the social history of nineteenth-century Gospel criticism have learned anything, it is this: broadly speaking, the transitional Second Reich stands between the cosmopolitan scholarship coming from German universities at the beginning of the nineteenth century and the malevolent influence of the state on the German universities under Hitler. Much of biblical scholarship (but not all of course) coming from the German universities in the period—as well as much of twentieth-century exegesis based on that legacy—is often misleading and sometimes downright wrongheaded.[37]

Part 3 illustrated the difference it makes when scholars use the Two-Source Hypothesis rigorously. In every case, the results based on the Two-Source Hypothesis are seriously misleading and unnecessarily problem-causing for sound Christian theology and vibrant church leadership. This hypothesis also is seriously counterproductive for a church that must steel itself for redemptive sacrifice in a world scarred by ethnic cleansing and divided by unacceptable disparities in economic and political resources. Part 4 has highlighted the problematic character of the ideas of Markan primacy and the existence of Q. A return of the Two-Gospel Hypothesis, first Matthew, second Luke, and third Mark, will guarantee nothing. But it will be a creative move in the right direction for all the reasons that have been reviewed in this book.

PART 5

What Is behind the Current Interest in Q?

CHAPTER 12

A Dismantling
of the Church's Canon

The Claremont-Harvard Connection

This book has focused on an idea and on that idea's social function. But, to be influential, ideas must be embodied. This book would not be complete without some attempt to represent how scholars and their academic institutions have embodied—literally given flesh and blood—to the idea of Markan priority and its corollary, the existence of Q. We focus now on the Q hypothesis and the way Q has been used by two especially distinguished and influential New Testament scholars, Professor James M. Robinson of the Claremont Graduate School and Professor Helmut Koester of Harvard University.

This chapter seeks to document how Professors Robinson and Koester have worked together in using the idea of Q to achieve their stated purpose of dismantling the categories of New Testament scholarship to reshape our understanding of Christian origins. We will focus on the way each has utilized and endorsed the ideas of the other to illustrate how competent scholars can promote and multiply the problematic consequences of outdated ideas.

How Did We Get Where We Are Today?

No one book has been more influential in setting the stage for the present upswing in Q research than James Robinson and Helmut Koester's *Trajectories Through Early Christianity*, published simultaneously in English and German.[1]

Among the essays in that volume, none is more often cited in the Q literature than Robinson's chapter on Wisdom Sayings.[2] This essay was republished with other selected essays from the Bultmann volume in an English edition.[3]

Never before has one essay received such a boost in the same year from four different publishing houses, on both sides of the Atlantic. As we have noted, the year was 1971. It is important to note the time of publication—because this was just one year after the Pittsburgh Festival on the Gospels for which James Robinson and David Dungan produced opposing papers on the origins of the Gospel tradition. There is no indication in LOGOI SOPHON, hereafter referred to as "Wisdom Sayings," that Robinson is willing to consider the scholarly contention that this whole Q edifice may be based on faulty premises.[4]

Let us take up the Robinson-Koester volume *Trajectories* and examine it carefully. If we turn to the introduction, which is entitled "The Dismantling and Reassembling of the Categories of New Testament Scholarship," and focus on the first page, Robinson and Koester say that they both "studied under Rudolf Bultmann. Both are involved in the current indigenization [i.e., domestication] of the Bultmann tradition on American soil."

Something very far-reaching in its implications captures our attention in Koester's concluding essay, entitled "The Intention and Scope of Trajectories," where we read: "The distinctions between canonical and noncanonical, orthodox and heretical are obsolete. . . . One can only speak of a 'History of Early Christian Literature.' "[5]

We now have more than an inkling of what "dismantling" implies. This promises to be a dismantling of the church's canon. Robinson writes:

> Walter Bauer's epochal work *Orthodoxy and Heresy in Earliest Christianity* drew attention to a bifurcating trajectory: out of a fluid, amorphous primitive Christianity there gradually emerged a polarized antithesis between secondary developments, known to us as orthodoxy and heresy, as the initial plurality gave way to the dominance of the Roman view.[6]

Robinson argues to two conclusions important for his program of "Reassembling the Categories of New Testament Scholarship." First, that it is possible to trace back into the canonical Gospels themselves the beginning of Wisdom Sayings as a designation for the literary category of collections of sayings, and second, that the development of this designation in the canonical Gospels has significant parallels with *Thomas*—a writing that offers an alternative vision of the significance of Jesus' life to the vision in the canonical Gospels.[7]

We will turn now to the first conclusion. To be sure, collections of written materials, including sayings materials, were available to the evangelists. At issue is: how good a case can be made for the position that the Gospel writers themselves knew of some primitive genre, Wisdom Sayings, and were influenced by those sayings in composing their Gospels.

Crucial to Robinson's case is Matthew's use of the term *logoi* related to collections of sayings. At issue is whether such collections were ever designated as Wisdom Sayings in the period prior to the composition of this Gospel. In five instances[8] the final redactor of Matthew has concluded a collection of sayings with the transitional editorial formula: "And it came to pass when Jesus finished . . ." Between the fixed formula: "And it came to pass when Jesus finished" and the continuation of his text, the evangelist always uses some expression that refers to the sayings in the collection being closed. Thus in Matt. 13:53, at the conclusion of a collection of parables, he writes: "And it came to pass when Jesus finished these parables he withdrew from there." And at 11:1 at the close of his apostolic discourse, he writes, "And it came to pass when Jesus finished commissioning his twelve disciples, he withdrew from there in order to teach and preach in their cities." In 7:28 and 19:1 the evangelist simply writes: "And it came to pass when Jesus finished these sayings . . . " And in 26:1 he only adds the adjective "all" to the phrase "these sayings."

The question to be asked is whether Matthew, in using *logoi* (sayings), is reflecting the existence of a Wisdom Sayings literary form, so that the use of parable in 13:53 and "commissioning his twelve disciples" in 11:1 are to be regarded as variants from "the basic form of the formula" that utilizes *logoi* (sayings); or whether this formula in all four of its variant forms simply represents a flexible summary formulation used by Matthew as he created his Gospel, as seems more probable.

Robinson continues to develop his argument without having established that a Wisdom Sayings literary form known to the evangelists actually existed. He then writes: "Thus we seem to be able to trace the beginnings of a designation for the *Gattung* (literary form) of collection of sayings back into the earliest of such collections in the primitive church."[9]

But upon what evidence is this conclusion based? What is actually written in this connection is as follows:

> If one may discern in Mark 4 traces of a pre-Markan collection, it is possible that what we know in expanded form as the Sermon on the Mount (or Plain) is the outgrowth of another such early cluster of sayings and parables. It uses as its conclusion a double parable exalting Jesus' *logoi* in much the same way as does Mark 13:31. For the double parable Luke 6:47 || Matthew 7:24 (cf. v. 26) begins: "Every one who comes to me and hears my *logoi* and does them." Hence the term *logoi* may have functioned as a designation for this early collection. In that case it would be the trend toward alluding, near its end, to such a collection as *logoi*, which would have provided Q with the catchword for connecting this collection to the rest of the Q sayings. . . . For here Q presents the story of the healing of the centurion's servant, oriented to the centurion's trust in the authority of Jesus' word (Luke 7:7 || Matthew 8:8). It would be this same trend at work in Matthew that leads to the fixed formula with which he concludes his five sayings collections, the first occurrence of which follows directly upon the double parable (Matt. 7:28).[10]

Then follows: "Thus we seem to be able to trace. . . . "

What we have in fact—which Robinson suggests is a "trend"—is the use of *logoi* to refer to sayings (and *logos* to refer to a specific saying) under somewhat diverse circumstances, including the use of *logoi* in a saying at the end of a collection in Matthew, and near the end in a collection in Mark.[11]

It would appear to the reader that Robinson has set forth a hypothesis for which he provides the reader with insufficient evidence.

Making use of the earlier work of Koester, Robinson argues:

> In 1 Clement[12] 46:7–8 the quotation formula is followed by a woe and two threats. Comparison with a double tradition in the synoptics leads Koester to the conclusion: "There remains only the assumption that 1 Clement 46:8 is related to a stage behind the synoptics, and one doubtless thinks of Q. Indeed all the sayings in 1 Clement 46:8 that are related to the synoptics could have stood in Q. Thus one may assume that such collections were familiar to Clement, and also that excerpts from such collections were introduced with the quotation formula cited above making use of the plural form of *logoi*."[13]

Robinson builds his argument upon a thought that occurred to Koester and that Koester believes would occur to others. In other words, the Claremont-Harvard connection represented by the collaboration between Robinson and Koester lacks a secure basis in a sound scholarly method. One plays off the other, both parlaying their collective gamble for all that it is worth. So long as no one questions their credit, each is free to make ever more risky "academic" wagers.[14]

Koester's use of "assumption" is quite correct. However, it is clear that Koester assumes the existence of Q. His assumption concerning *1 Clement* is thus based upon an assumption.

It follows then that the conclusion: "Thus one may assume . . . " is assumed in the premise, and thus the argument is fallacious.

One should note how the author continues to depend on Koester's admitted speculation. Robinson writes:

> In 1 Clement 13:2 the quotation formula is followed by a chain of seven sayings. They are partly attested in the Gospels (mostly in the Sermon on the Mount), partly elsewhere; yet they can be derived from no surviving source. Hence Koester concludes: "Perhaps the author is making use of some written collection of sayings of the Lord no longer known to us, but perhaps earlier than our Gospels. . . . Perhaps it is the reproduction of an oral, though firmly formulated, local catechism."[15]

The careful "Perhaps . . . perhaps . . . perhaps . . ." construction makes clear how speculative Koester's thinking is at this point. All we are given here are some highly educated guesses. But these guesses all fit a theory with far-reaching consequences. These consequences are clearly stated by Koester in his essay GNOMAI DIAPHOROI,[16] which is published immediately following Robinson's "Wisdom Sayings" in *Trajectories Through Early Christianity*. Koester writes:

Further light [on *Thomas*] can be expected from more detailed studies of the *Sitz im Leben* ["life situation"] and theological function of the sayings, the *logoi*, in the early church. An important step in this direction has been taken by James M. Robinson ["Wisdom Sayings"]. A direct consequence of his study can be formulated in this way: The Gospel of Thomas continues, even if in a modified way, the most original *Gattung* of the Jesus tradition—the *logoi sophon*—which, in the canonical Gospels, became acceptable to the Orthodox Church only by radical critical alteration, not only of the form, but also of the theological intention of this primitive *Gattung*. Such critical evaluation of the *Gattung*, *logoi*, was achieved by Matthew and Luke through imposing the Markan narrative-kerygma (message) frame upon the sayings tradition represented by Q.[17]

In social historical terms, we have an endorsement by a Harvard University professor of an idea stemming from and useful to Professor Robinson. The argument does not proceed from reliance on sound historical method. Rather, the author is engaged in making synthetic judgments which presuppose tendentious speculation. The reference to Wisdom Sayings (*logoi sophon*) as *the most original* literary form of the Jesus tradition is a case in point. What remains here at issue is presupposed as a stated fact. In a footnote, readers are referred to Robinson's earlier work "The Problem of History in Mark, Reconsidered,"[18] where Robinson says: "I have tried to trace this *Gattung*, whose gnosticizing proclivity is blocked by Matthew and Luke by embedding Q in the Markan Gospel form."

Whether scholars should work together is not at issue. At issue is whether the early church ever had a literary form called "sayings" which, as Koester argues, was "the most original *Gattung* of the Jesus tradition." The Robinson-Koester argument for such a literary form presupposes the existence of what is only hypothetical, namely Q. Their argument is thus circular at best.

What Difference Does It Make?

The far-reaching consequences of this particular Robinson-Koester enterprise may be measured by the fact that all the canonical Gospels feature passion narratives where Jesus Christ is represented as suffering under Pontius Pilate; these Gospels, unlike their gnostic counterparts, all tell the story of the flesh-and-blood martyrdom of the Son of God. This story, important in the tradition of the church known to the apostle Paul (including such details as what happened on the night when Jesus was delivered up), would not represent the most original form within which the words of Jesus were to be understood, as with his sayings as they are preserved in the Gospels. The "most original" form would be that of the hypothetical Wisdom Sayings (*logoi sophon*). And where do we have that form best represented? As a complete document, we have only one example: *Thomas*.

The canonical Gospels of the church all depart from the original form. Thus this line of reasoning not only raises crucial issues for a historical reconstruction of earliest Christianity, but also has substantial theological ramifications as well.

To what is *Thomas* related—our canonical Gospels or Q? Were the *logoi* of Jesus *ever* socially transmitted in isolation from the redemptive message of salvation? Was there an apostolic community in the earliest days of Christianity that had no use for the cross and resurrection of the kerygma?

In the final analysis, what is the bottom line of *Trajectories Through Early Christianity*? This book carries a word of hope. And what is that hope? Christianity—shackled by a deadly orthodoxy, moribund in hoary tradition, compromised on all sides by its unholy alliance with principalities and powers—can, through eyes of faith opened to insight from extracanonical materials, enable us to perceive a thin ray of light at the end of the dark tunnel of contemporary theology. That thin ray of light is coming from the east—from eastern Syria and Egyptian Christianity, to be specific. For this Christianity escaped the western tendency to block the gnosticizing proclivity of the primitive church.

Egyptian Christianity preserved the Nag Hammadi[19] treasures with its chief jewel: *Thomas*. This is the bright center of the ray of light we are expected to discern at the end of our dark tunnel. With the aid of patient scholarship (reconstructing the hypothetical text of Q), and guided by light from the extracanonical materials, scholars can reconstruct the other Christianity that did not block the gnosticizing proclivity, but allowed the Wisdom Sayings to develop in an eastern manner into the form eventually reached in the third or fourth century in the Coptic *Thomas*.

This is a grand vision, and not since Constantin Tischendorf's famous visits to St. Catherine's monastery in the Sinai desert has the western world been treated to such a romance. But is the romance of it all blinding us to some of the realities of the matter? The existence of Q, the font of all these speculations, is questionable and today is more seriously contested than at any other time in our century. This is clearly recognized by some of the leading members of the Q Section in the Society of Biblical Literature. Its chairperson, Professor J. S. Kloppenborg, acknowledges some of the problems facing advocates of Q and perceptively discusses a wide range of scholarly literature that expounds the Two-Gospel Hypothesis.[20]

Ironically, at the very time Robinson was beginning a rehabilitation of the Q hypothesis, David Dungan, at the Pittsburgh Festival of the Gospels in 1970, was signaling its ultimate demise. In reviewing the considerations weighing against critical confidence in Q's existence, Dungan noted the bottom line on the matter. C. S. Petrie had examined the seventeen reconstructions of Q printed in James Moffatt's *Introduction to the New Testament* and had made the astounding discovery that "not a single verse of Matthew was common to all seventeen reconstructions and only eighteen verses from Luke."[21] Dungan continues:

> Petrie understandably enough considered this "absence of even a mild display of unanimity" to be something of a disgrace in the household of advanced biblical science, something the neighbors in "the hard sciences" probably ought not to find out about. Indeed, he has moved to make the following caustic observation: "the malleability of this nebulous hypothesis makes Q a letter to conjure with. Its protean nature allows the magician to endow his production with whatsoever characteristics he may choose, and he is encouraged to adopt for Q the principle that Humpty Dumpty paraded when Alice sought for a definition of glory: "It means just what I choose it to mean—neither more nor less."[22]

Critical doubt about the Two-Document Hypothesis is not going away.[23] There is growing recognition of the secondary character of Mark whose priority is recognized as the first pillar of this thesis.[24] There is also a growing recognition that scholars can dispense with Q. Nonetheless, it appears that Q has the staying power to remain in orbit long after it has been separated from the booster rocket of Markan priority.

In our view, the present spectacle of theologians writing books about the theology of the Q community is like children making castles in a sandbox. But unlike children's sand castles, these theologians' Q plaything is not always designed to entertain. The effort has far-reaching consequences when Q is parlayed with Gnostic sources like *Thomas* into fanciful reconstructions, that imply the existence of a primitive apostolic community for which the death and resurrection of Jesus Christ was (contrary to the New Testament) of little or no importance.

James M. Robinson's Drew Lecture on Q

In a lecture on "The Sayings of Jesus: Q," delivered at Drew University in October 1983,[25] James Robinson has made more explicit the christological implications of the present theological interest in Q. In this lecture, the canonical claims made for Q are clear and uncompromising. We may consider the following statement: "Even if it has survived only incompletely, Q is surely the most important Christian text we have." This implies not only that Q is more important than Romans or 2 Corinthians, but also that it is more important than any of the canonical Gospels: Matthew, Mark, Luke, or John.

Robinson proceeds without interruption to state that Q's purported status as the most important Christian text "should not be contested, in spite of the recognition of the ongoing debate about the synoptic problem, and with all due respect to the canonical books of the New Testament."[26] Following this line of reasoning, Professor Robinson's view should be immune from criticism. By one stroke of his pen, he has given his claims for Q a status that would make them academically infallible. For Professor Robinson, it is all but irrelevant that colleagues are raising critical questions about the existence of Q.

Contra Robinson, would it not be more reasonable to conclude that if the ongoing debate about the synoptic problem raises questions about whether Q ever existed, which it certainly is doing, should not he and all scholars who build on Q acknowledge the hypothetical character of their reconstructions? Should they not admit that their various projects depend upon a premise that may be false—a premise that more and more competent scholars are prepared to say probably is false?[27]

What christological consequences follow from Q? Two quotes from Robinson will serve to point up what is at stake in this whole matter. "The saving significance of Jesus, according to Q, does not consist in Jesus having died for our sins, . . . but in that he did not let himself be turned off by the fear of death in presenting the definitive guide for understanding the Torah."[28] This is unclear. Is the death of Jesus for the Q community redemptive or not? Is Professor Robinson straining to retain a place for his reconstruction of the Q source in the life of the church?

Robinson acknowledges that the main consequence of Q for Christology is to depict an apostolic community that did not make the kerygma of cross and resurrection central, but then he makes an interesting qualification: "If the whole theology of Q is best known for the absence of the kerygma of cross and resurrection, this should not be taken to mean that the Q community did not know that Jesus had died for them."[29] To be sure, but if this hypothetical community did know that "Jesus had died for them," would that not make the Christology of Q, where the Christology of the cross and resurrection is absent, all the more unusual? Where in the history of the church, or the Jesus movement, does this Christology belong?

Epilogue

Is there any reason to hope for some critical progress in settling the disputed question of a literary need for the Q hypothesis? We have already noted the ongoing research by scholars in the Society of Biblical Literature who have now made significant progress in explaining Luke's use of the Gospel of Matthew, thus reducing the need for the hypothetical Q source. Some of these same scholars participated in the Symposium on the Minor Agreements organized by Professor Georg Strecker at Göttingen University in Germany in 1991.[30]

In the nineteenth century, investigation of these agreements led some German critics who held to the Two-Source Hypothesis to recognize that Luke had used Matthew.[31] But Anglo-American scholars were temporarily thrown off track by B. H. Streeter's rejection of this idea. Streeter reasoned that if Luke knew Matthew, there would be no need for Q. Streeter's prodigious effort to explain away these minor agreements succeeded for a time in sustaining critical confidence in the independence of Matthew and Luke and their independent use of Mark.

Streeter's achievement lasted for thirty years until the Q parties at Oxford, when Austin Farrer, after exposing the weaknesses of Streeter's critical treatment of the minor agreements of Matthew and Luke against Mark, concluded that Luke had used Matthew and that therefore there was no need for Q.[32] In 1971, the Swiss scholar Robert Morgenthaler published a statistical study in which he argued that the minor agreements of Matthew and Luke are best explained by acknowledging that Luke used Matthew. However, unlike the British, Morgenthaler (like the later Holtzmann) did not reason that this justified giving up Q.[33]

In 1974, Frans Neirynck of Louvain published a compilation of the minor agreements of Matthew and Luke against Mark.[34] For twelve years at the annual meetings of the Society for New Testament Studies seminar on the synoptic problem, Michael Goulder relentlessly pressed the point that these agreements meant that Luke knew Matthew and that one could, with Austin Farrer, dispense with Q.[35]

Another member of that seminar, Professor Albert Fuchs, championed the view that these minor agreements between Matthew and Luke against Mark were best explained by a theory of Deutero-Markus, that is, a theory that someone produced a later version of our canonical Mark in which certain changes were introduced, a *second* Mark, and that Matthew and Luke copied this second Mark, not the earlier and original Mark that we have in our canon. This theory is implausible because it requires us to believe that although this second Mark was so important and so well-known that two different evangelists in two different places used it in preference to the original Mark, yet wonder of wonders, all copies of this second Mark have vanished and all surviving manuscripts of Mark preserve the text of the original Mark, which neither Matthew nor Luke bothered to copy! Possible? Yes. Plausible? No! Nonetheless, implausible as it is, this hypothesis appears to be gaining ground in Germany. It was well represented at the 1991 symposium on the minor agreements organized by Professor Georg Strecker. Scholars like H. Conzelmann had long admitted that these minor agreements remain unexplained on the Two-Source Hypothesis. With the acceptance of Deutero-Markus we may be seeing the beginning of at least a crack in the heretofore rather solid wall of German defense of the Markan hypothesis.

A shift from the prevailing view that canonical Mark was independently copied by Matthew and Luke to the view that it was a later version of that Mark that Matthew and Luke independently copied may in turn open the door to consideration of less implausible alternatives to the Two-Source Hypothesis. For the theory of Deutero-Marcus is in some ways like a halfway house, from which it can be expected that some of its adherents will want to move on.

Also worthy of note, the more far-reaching solution of Austin Farrer has been gaining ground in England. These minor agreements of Matthew and Luke against Mark are explained, not only by Michael Goulder of Birmingham University but also by John Drury and John Fenton of Oxford University, by recognizing that Luke used not some hypothetical Q text, but the actual text of Matthew *as well as Mark*. We see then that while these Anglican scholars are willing to jettison Q, they continue to assume, following their German cousins, the primacy of Mark.

Meanwhile, on this side of the Atlantic, as noted above, there appears to be an increasing willingness to recognize the secondary character of Mark's text. In addition to Helmut Koester, one thinks readily of Pierson Parker of Claremont, California; Thomas Longstaff of Colby College, Maine; David Dungan of the University of Tennessee; Lamar Cope of Carroll College, Wisconsin; George Buchanan, formerly of Wesley Theological Seminary, Washington, D.C.; David Peabody of Nebraska Wesleyan University; Alan McNicol of the University of Texas; and William Walker of Trinity University, San Antonio.

Finally, we take up the conclusions of E. P. Sanders, better known as a specialist in Pauline studies but from his early days of scholarship, a competent student of the synoptic problem.[36] With Margaret Davies, Sanders has recently coauthored an advanced textbook for students of the synoptic Gospels.[37] In this book, it is stated that students interested in synoptic-source criticism should carefully evaluate four major hypotheses. These are (1) the Two-Source Hypothesis, (2) the Two-Gospel Hypothesis, (3) the Austin Farrer hypothesis, where Markan priority is retained, but it is allowed that Luke used Matthew so that it is proper to dispense with Q, and (4) the Boismard hypothesis, which postulates a multiple-source theory, with many different earlier versions of the canonical Gospels. Of these four hypotheses, according to Sanders and Davies, three are critically tenable. Only one is critically untenable, they say: the Two-Source Hypothesis. And why do they come to this conclusion about the Two-Source Hypothesis? To do justice to their work, the reader would need to consult the lengthy and detailed discussion of the Gospel texts treated by Sanders and Davies. But it can be fairly reported that the minor agreements play a leading role in the discrediting of the Two-Source Hypothesis at the hands of Sanders and Davies.[38]

As the older generation of Robinson and Koester bows out, a well-disciplined corps of younger synoptic scholars is ready to take its place. This includes critics like J. S. Kloppenborg, who assumes the existence of Q and is a coworker of Robinson and Koester. But it also includes scholars who question Q, like E. P. Sanders, Margaret Davies, David L. Dungan, and David B. Peabody. The wheels of scholarship grind slowly, but they do grind fine. Meanwhile, now that readers have an answer to the question, "What difference does it make?" there should result an increased interest in the research by this younger generation of synoptic experts.

It can be expected that research assuming the existence of Q will continue. But the prospect of agreement among Q scholars appears dim in view of the disagreement with Koester-Robinson-Kloppenborg coming from advocates of Q in Germany.[39]

PART 6

Summary and Conclusions

CHAPTER 13

The Gospel of the Lord Jesus

The Heart of the Gospel

> [1]Moreover, brethren, I declare to you the Gospel which I preached to you . . .
> which also you received . . .
> [2]By which also you are saved . . .
> [3]For I delivered to you first of all that which I also received:
>> That Christ died for our sins
>>> According to the scriptures. . . .   —*1 Cor. 15:1–3*

We begin the concluding chapter with this text because it provides the historical and theological peg on which all that follows logically hangs. What follows in this chapter need not be taken up in the order here presented. The reader is free to read ahead in this chapter as his or her interests dictate. The argument that follows is logical. But the inherent logic does not require that the texts or topics should be read in the order in which they are here presented. Of primary importance is that the reader realizes that the gospel preached by Paul and by which the Corinthians were saved began with the message:

> Christ died for the forgiveness of sins
>> According to the scriptures.

This passage is of the greatest importance because it defines the essence of the gospel in terms of salvation through the forgiveness of sins *according to the scriptures.*

All scholars agree that the scriptures referred to include and indeed center on Isaiah 53. Unlike Paul, who uses the noun "gospel" regularly, Isaiah uses only the verb: "to proclaim good news." This is the same as "to proclaim the gospel" or "to bring glad tidings." These are all acceptable ways to translate the verb used by Isaiah to which the noun gospel as used by Paul is closely related.

The noun gospel was used in antiquity in the secular sense, to refer to "good news" of various kinds, including good news of political victory or of coming prosperity. The fact that Paul in 1 Corinthians connects the gospel he preached with the good news that

Christ died for our sins
    According to the scriptures . . .

means that this gospel is defined essentially by that particular scripture according to which "Christ died for our sins." That particular scripture, all agree, is Isa. 53:5–12.

He was wounded for our transgressions
    tortured for our iniquities;
upon him was the chastisement that made us whole,
    and by his blood drawn by the whip we are healed. . . .
He poured out his soul to death
    and he was counted among the transgressors;
yet he bore the sins of many,
    and made intercession for the transgressors.

How did the message that Christ died for our sins constitute good news? It was good news because it pointed to the essential fulfillment of the conditions set by God for the salvation of his people (including Israel and the Gentiles). Christians knew that the whole creation had been groaning together[1] until the fulfillment of this condition. Particularly since the time of Alexander the Great, the human family had been led to look for the unity of warring nations and the salvation of all peoples. The hope of salvation was still alive under Roman rule. But the reign of Rome, enforced by the sword, had failed to bring about a just peace among the nations. The God of Israel through the prophet Isaiah's oracles had revealed a different mode of salvation for his people, one that envisioned salvation by the redemptive suffering of the righteous. That salvation, so long awaited and hungered for by the righteous, which was promised for Jews and Gentiles alike, was now being actualized. That was the good news that the apostles were sent to proclaim. God's promise that the nations would beat their swords into plowshares was being fulfilled as Jews and Gentiles individually and collectively laid down their weapons of war and lifted up the cross of reconciliation and redemption as brothers and sisters in Christ.

This was the new creation of which Paul writes.[2] The accord or harmony between Isa. 53:5–12 and the suffering and redeeming death of Jesus Christ focuses our attention on the heart of the gospel preached by Paul. But where did he get this gospel? Paul himself tells us he preached the faith that he once as a persecutor of the church had tried to destroy. The gospel that Paul preached is none other than the gospel preached by those who were apostles before him.[3]

Let us see what content there was to this gospel besides the initial point that

Christ died for our sins
    According to the scriptures.

The text in 1 Corinthians goes on to add:

> And that he was buried
>> And that he rose again on the third day
>>> According to the scriptures.

We have here a threefold structure:

> Christ died for the forgiveness of sins,
>> Christ was buried,
>>> Christ rose again.

This is the nucleus of the Gospel story. Isaiah does not specify that the Servant of the Lord would rise "on the third day." He does mention, however, that the Servant of the Lord had his grave made with the wicked (Isa. 53:9) and that he would "prosper, be raised up, and be exalted to the heights" (Isa. 52:13). "The Lord will prolong the life of his servant and the Lord's pleasure shall prosper in the hand of the servant" (Isa. 53:10b).

The correspondence between the sketchy and episodic story of Isaiah's Servant of the Lord, on the one hand, and the gospel that Paul preached, on the other, serves to ground this gospel in the Lord's universal plan of salvation[4] on three counts: (1) a redemptive death of the Servant (being offered up for the forgiveness of sins), (2) a burial of the Servant's lifeless flesh-and-blood body in a grave, and (3) an exaltation of the Servant who made "his soul an offering for sin."

To see that this Gospel story is structurally present in the scriptures on which Jesus reflected, it is well to take the time to reflect on the following words of the prophet Isaiah:

> [52:7]How beautiful upon the mountains
>> are the feet of him who brings glad tidings,
> who publishes peace,
>> who brings good news,
> who publishes salvation,
>> who says to Zion: "Your God is sovereign."
> [8]Hark, you watchmen, lift up your voices
>> and shout together in triumph;
> for with their own eyes they see
>> the return of the Lord to Zion.
> [9]Break forth together in singing,
>> you waste places of Jerusalem;
> for the Lord has comforted his people,
>> he has ransomed Jerusalem.
> [10]The Lord has bared his holy arm
>> before the ages of all the nations;
> and all the world from the ends of the earth
>> shall see the salvation of our God. . . .

¹³Behold, my servant shall prosper,
    he shall be raised up,
    exalted to the heights.
¹⁴As many were astonished at him—
    his appearance being marred
    beyond human likeness,
    and his form beyond that
    of the sons of man—
¹⁵so shall he startle many nations;
    kings shall curl their lips in disgust at sight of him.
  For they see what they never expected to see,
    and things never heard of before fill their thoughts.
⁵³:¹Who could have believed what we have heard,
    and to whom has the arm of the Lord been revealed?
²For he grew up before the Lord like a young plant,
    with its roots thirsting in dry ground.
  He had no beauty or majesty to attract our eyes,
    no graceful appearance to draw us to him.
³He was despised and rejected by men;
    a man of sorrows, and acquainted with grief;
  as a thing from which people turn away their eyes,
    he was despised, and we discounted him.
⁴Surely he has borne our suffering
    and endured our torments;
  while we accounted him smitten by God,
    struck down and afflicted by disease.
⁵He was wounded for our transgressions,
    tortured for our iniquities;
  upon him was the chastisement that made us whole,
    and by his blood drawn by the whip we are healed.
⁶All we, like sheep, have gone astray;
    each of us has gone his own way;
  and the Lord has laid on him
    the guilt of us all.
⁷He was oppressed, he submitted to being struck down,
    and he did not open his mouth;
  like a lamb that is led to the slaughter,
    and like a ewe that is dumb before its shearers,
  so he did not open his mouth.
⁸After arrest and judgment he was taken away;
    and as for his fate, who gave it a thought,
  how he was cut off from family and friends,
    stricken to death for the transgression of my people?
⁹He was buried with the transgressors,
    given a grave among the refuse of mankind;
  although he had done no violence,
    and there was no word of treachery in his mouth.

> ¹⁰Yet the Lord took thought for his tortured servant,
>> and healed him who had offered himself a sacrifice for sin;
>> so shall he prolong his life, and see his children's children,
>> and in his hand the Lord's cause shall prosper.
> ¹¹After all his travail he shall be bathed in light;
>> after his disgrace he shall be fully vindicated;
>> so shall my servant vindicate many,
>> himself bearing the penalty of their guilt.
> ¹²Therefore, I will allot him a portion with the great,
>> and he shall share the spoils of victory with the triumphant
> because he poured out his soul to death
>> and was counted among the transgressors;
> yet he bore the sin of many,
>> and made intercession for the transgressors.
>>> —*Isa. 52:7—53:12* ·

For a moment, set aside the question of the origin of the "Gospel story" as we know it in the birth, life, suffering, death, burial, and exaltation of Jesus as told in the church's Gospels, and focus on the concept of "gospel" itself. We note the following: the gospel in the book of Isaiah functions as a Gospel of the Lord. The glad tidings are that the Lord will comfort his people, and will ransom Jerusalem, baring his holy arm before the eyes of all nations. It is the good news that all the world from the ends of the earth will see the salvation that comes to the Lord's people with his return to Zion and the establishment of his sovereign reign.

However, this Gospel of the Lord is concretely related to the mission of the Suffering Servant. The Lord's ransoming and saving activity for Israel and all the nations is carried through by the Suffering Servant. So the Gospel of the Lord in Isaiah is the good news that God's promise to save his people (including all the nations of the earth) is being fulfilled through the redeeming activity of the Servant.

It is of the greatest importance to recognize that Paul did not go to Isaiah and draw directly from the text some original meaning it could have had in its own right. Paul read the text of Isaiah in the light of the reality of the subsequent death and resurrection of Jesus. But because that death and resurrection took place within the life of Israel, where Isaiah was read in the synagogue, it was inevitable, beginning with Jesus himself, that this death and resurrection, both as anticipated and later as experienced, would influence the way in which Isa. 53:5–12 would be understood in a community that believed Jesus had died on behalf of the sins of members of that community—*according to the scriptures.* This particular scripture had to be important for such a community, and its meaning would certainly have been enriched by the concrete way in which that community had experienced the redeeming death and vindicating resurrection of its savior.

Thus we may note the creative way in which Paul reads Isa. 52:7 and 53:1 in his letter to the Romans:

> And how shall they preach unless they are sent?
> As it is written:
>> How beautiful are the feet of those who preach good news
>>> who bring glad tidings and good things?
>> But they have not all obeyed the Gospel;
>>> for Isaiah says:
>> Lord, who has believed our report?
>>> So then faith comes by hearing,
>>>> and hearing by the preaching of Christ.
>>>>> —*Rom. 10:15–17*

When Paul writes: "But they have not all obeyed the Gospel," he uses the noun form of the verb "to preach good news." It is clear from this text that the only gospel that Paul is concerned with is the gospel originally referred to in Isaiah. This is the same gospel according to the truth of which all those who are sent by Jesus Christ are to walk in a straightforward manner.[5] But what it meant to the apostles to walk in a straightforward manner according to the truth of this gospel was profoundly influenced by the way in which they had learned to walk in response to the teaching and example of Jesus, who on the night he was offered up identified his forthcoming death with that of the Servant in Isaiah by taking the cup and after giving thanks, saying:

> Drink from it, all of you:
>> For this is my blood of the new covenant[6]
> Which is shed for many
>> For the remission of sins.
>>> —*Matt. 26:27–28 (See chap. 5 above)*

Professor Otfried Hofius of Tübingen University, in a paper read to a congress of Bible scholars meeting in Madrid in August 1992, pointed out how Isa. 53:7–12 is creatively interpreted by Paul in the light of the love of Christ:

> For the love of Christ constrains us,
>> because we judged thus:
>>> that if One died for all, then all died;
> and he died for all, that those who live
>> should live no longer for themselves
> but for him who died for them,
>> and rose again. . . .
> Therefore if anyone is in Christ,
>> he is a new creation.
> Old things have passed away;
>> behold all things have become new.

Now all things are of God,
>who has reconciled us to himself
>>through Jesus Christ
>>and has given us
>>>the ministry of reconciliation.
That is, that God was in Christ
>reconciling the world to himself,
>>not imputing their trespasses to them,
and has committed to us
>the word of reconciliation.
Now then, we are ambassadors for Christ
>as though God were pleading through us:
We implore you on Christ's behalf,
>be reconciled to God.
For he made him who knew no sin
>to be sin for us[7]
that we might become
>the righteousness of God in him.
>>>>>>>>>>*—2 Cor. 5:14–21*

Clearly, concluded Professor Hofius, Paul says more in his letter to the Corinthians, indeed something other than what he found in the text of Isaiah. It is the reality of the love of Christ that constrains us to interpret, to develop, to reflect on the word of God, in ways that lead us beyond what we can otherwise get from the text absent that love.

Jesus' Self-Understanding and Isaiah 53

Before proceeding, we need to pause and reflect briefly on a point of some importance. It is not a waste of time to reflect on the question of Jesus' self-understanding and Isaiah 53. But where should we begin? Should we begin with the words of Jesus where we can clearly trace the influence of Isaiah 53 on how he formulated his teaching? No, for there are only two such sayings. One is the saying about giving his "life as a *ransom for many*,"[8] and the other is what he uttered when he held the cup in his hands the night he was handed over: "This is my blood of the covenant which is *poured out for many for the forgiveness of their sins*."[9] These two sayings provide too slender a basis on which to begin our reflection, however decisive this linguistic evidence may prove to be, once it is seen in the light of the larger context of all the relevant data.

We begin our reflection with what we can learn from how Paul understood the importance of Isaiah 53 for the self-understanding of those who by faith believe that Christ died for all.[10] We note from the passage in 2 Corinthians that Paul does not reflect on Isaiah 53 in a vacuum. Rather, the apostle enters into the text from a particular perspective, namely, that of the love of Christ, which, as he writes, "constrains" Christian reflection in a particular direction and opens the text to new conclusions.

Paul is presumably a very different person from Jesus. Yet, for all the differences between the two, Paul had become a student in the "Jesus school." He no longer examined the Law and the Prophets through the lens of Numbers 25 with its teaching that salvation was to come through zealous acts of violence against trangressors. Such acts of violence Paul performed against Christians as a persecutor of the church. He now looked at the whole of scripture from the perspective of Isaiah 53, with its teaching that salvation was to come through the redemptive death of the Servant of the Lord. This way of reading the scriptures was not invented by Paul; those who were apostles before him passed it on to him. This is what is meant by Paul having become a student and a teacher within the "Jesus school." This way of reading the scriptures was presumably passed by Jesus to his disciples, who became the apostles who passed it on to Paul. Jesus too, like Paul, presumably read Isaiah 53 within the constraints of a preexisting reality of divine love. In Jesus' case, the love of the God of Israel for his people would have been mediated to him from his infancy by Mary and Joseph. Israel had been redeemed by the love of God. Mary and Joseph understood that. This understanding shaped their spiritual formation and the formation of Jesus in their home. At some point, Jesus began to read and reflect on Isaiah 53 in the light of this divine love. This appears to have shaped his servanthood and the spiritual formation he intended for his disciples. At least that is the case, if we may judge from his words and his actions as they are preserved and handed on by Paul and the evangelists Matthew, Mark, Luke, and John. The contrast with the wisdom of our contemporary world of theological discourse, as expressed in some of the popular academic reflection on *Thomas* and Q, is too painful to dwell on.

The Foolishness of the Gospel

The Gospel of the Lord preached by the apostles is foolishness to those who are perishing, but, to those who are being saved, it is the power of God. Paul writes:

> I will destroy the wisdom of the wise, and the cleverness of the clever I will thwart [Isa. 29:14]. Where is the wise man? Where is the scribe? Where is the debater of this age? Has not God made foolish the wisdom of the learned? For since, in the wisdom of God, the world did not know God through wisdom, it pleased God through the folly of what we preach to save those who believe. For Jews demand signs and Greeks seek wisdom, but we preach Christ crucified, a stumbling block to Jews and folly to the Gentiles, but to those who are called,

both Jews and Greeks, Christ is the power of God and the wisdom of God. For the foolishness of God is wiser than men and the weakness of God is stronger than men.

For consider your call, brethren; not many of you were wise according to worldly standards; not many were powerful; not many were of noble birth; but God chose what is foolish in the world to shame the wise, God chose what is weak in the world to shame the strong, God chose what is low and despised in the world, even things that are not, to bring to nothing things that are, so that no human being might boast in the presence of God. He is the source of your life in Christ Jesus, whom God made our wisdom, our righteousness and sanctification and redemption. . . .

None of the rulers of this age has understood this; for if they had, they would not have crucified the Lord of Glory. But as it is written:

"What no eye has seen, nor ear heard,
nor the heart of man conceived,
all prepared by God for those who love him [Isa. 64:14],"
this, God has revealed to us through the Spirit.   —*1 Cor. 1:19—2:10*

In these words from Paul's first letter to the church in Corinth, Paul cites the text of Isaiah twice (Isa. 29:14 and 64:14). But when Paul mentions to the Corinthians that "God chose what is low and despised in the world . . . to bring to nothing things that are," and writes that God made Christ Jesus "our redemption," he does not cite the Isaiah text, but rather alludes to it. He knows, however, that his readers will resonate to his playing off the text of Isa. 52:7—53:12, cited in full above. This leads us to an important point. One cannot judge the influence of Isaiah 53 by the number of times it is cited. In fact, one can hardly judge the influence of Isaiah 53 even by the times it is alluded to. Let us consider, as a case in point, the creeds of the early church.

Isaiah 53 and the Apostles' Creed

Isaiah 53 was a subtext for early Christians. A subtext, as has been noted, is a text so important and so well known that it is banal to cite it. The profound influence of Isaiah 53 on Christian faith is brought out by Professor Claus Westermann, who has noted a structural similarity between Isa. 52:13—53:12 and the structure of the clause concerning the second person of the Trinity in the creeds of the early church. He observes that this structural similarity is more significant than any explicit citation of this text.

The reference to the suffering death of Jesus Christ in the Apostles' Creed is readily connected with the suffering death of the Servant of God in Isaiah 53. But Westermann found a more extensive structural similarity. First, the servant develops before the Lord as one born of woman. He shares our human existence. We would note that this is unlike Marcion's Christ, whom

Marcion said descended from heaven to earth as a full-grown man at the beginning of his public ministry. Second, the Servant suffers ignominiously. Third, the Servant is put to death. We would note that, unlike Jesus in the *Gospel of Peter* who felt no pain as he hung on the cross, the Servant of Isaiah was acquainted with grief, was "wounded" and "bruised." Fourth, the Servant, like a man of flesh and blood, was buried. (We would add a fifth, the Servant was to be glorified and exalted. He was "to be raised up, exalted to the heights." After his travail, the Servant was to be "bathed in light" and "fully vindicated.") These parallels in the life of the Servant with the (1) birth, (2) suffering, (3) death, and (4) burial of Jesus in the Apostles' Creed were sufficiently striking to Westermann that he called attention to them.[11]

It is especially noteworthy that the burial of Jesus, which could so easily have been omitted, is retained in the creeds of the church. So the fourfold structural similarity noted by Westermann persists, and the evidence suggests that this text from Isaiah has indeed functioned as a norm in the development of the gospel tradition into its creedal forms. Of course, Westermann did not mean to imply that those who formulated the church's creeds were trying to reproduce the structure of the Servant's life in Isaiah 53. We should understand him to assume that his readers would see the continuity we are making explicit in this book. This is a continuity that begins with Isaiah 53 and runs through the ministry of Jesus, the pre-Pauline tradition of 1 Cor. 15:1–3, the Gospels, the canon of faith of the early church, all leading to the formation of the New Testament canon and the earliest creeds. Moreover, I presume that Westermann intended to convey that this whole doctrinal development did not proceed in any simplistic way, but rather that each stage tended to presuppose all earlier stages. Thus the importance of Isaiah 53 was never out of the picture but maintained its canonical influence along with that of the New Testament all the way to the period of creedal formation, and even until today.

The Canon of the Church and the Church's Gospels

We take up now the matter of *canon*, namely, what is *normative* in Christian faith? When Clement of Alexandria, who thrived in the later part of the second and beginning of the third century, refers to the "Ecclesiastical Canon" and defines it as the harmony and correspondence between the Law and the Prophets and the covenant of Jesus Christ, he probably had in mind Paul's recitation of the gospel tradition he passed on to his churches.[12] But Clement, no doubt, also had in mind the church's Gospels. In any case, he could not have cited a more persuasive example of this ecclesiastical rule than the harmony and correspondence between the structure and theology of

Isaiah 53 and the structure and theology of the church's Gospels, especially, assuming the Two-Gospel Hypothesis, the earlier Gospels, Matthew and Luke.

At some time and place in the second century, the fourfold Gospel canon was created to distinguish the Gospels that the church accepted as canonical from those that were eventually denied this status. According to Clement's ecclesiastical canon, none of the apocryphal gospels is canonical. They all reflect the abandonment of this canon. This, of course, includes *Thomas* and the *Gospel of Peter*. And it would have included the "Sayings Gospel Q" if it ever existed.

The forming of the fourfold Gospel canon probably took place around the middle of the second century. At about this same time, the apologist Justin Martyr was referring to these church scriptures as "memoirs of the apostles." He tells us that they were being read as scriptures in the worship services of the church. The text with the inscription, "The Gospel according to Mark" in the fourfold Gospel canon was referred to by Justin as the "Memoirs of Peter." No evidence exists that the early church ever referred to the canonical Gospels as the Gospel of Matthew, the Gospel of Mark, and so on. The gospel was independent from, and earlier than, any of these church documents. Its earliest linguistic form, as we can see from what has been reviewed thus far, clearly originates with God's revelatory activity in the oracles of the prophet Isaiah. But it received an indelible expression and ultimate fulfillment in the life, suffering, death, burial, and resurrection of Jesus of Nazareth as the Christ, Son of the living God, Suffering Servant of the Lord, who came to give his life as a ransom for many (Isa. 53:12). This is why the church refers to the efforts to tell this redemptive story as Gospels, and to their authors as "gospelers" or "evangelists," based on *euangelion*, the Greek word for "gospel."

In chapter 4, we noted that the author of the *Didache* prefaced his version of the Lord's Prayer with an instruction to his readers to pray as the Lord commanded "in his Gospel." While the author of the *Didache* probably knew the text of our canonical Gospel according to Matthew, he does not instruct his readers to pray "as the Lord in the Gospel of Matthew commands." Rather, he thinks in terms of the "Gospel of the Lord," and thus he writes: "Pray as the Lord commanded in his Gospel." And where could his readers find this prayer? They could find it in the document that from the time of the fourfold Gospel canon came to be known as "The Gospel according to Matthew." If the author knew this text as it is found in the church's fourfold Gospel canon, he knew it not as "The Gospel of Matthew," but as "The Gospel of the Lord according to Matthew."

This is probably the way those who formed the fourfold Gospel canon thought about the matter. They thought of the Gospel as good news of the Lord, as that good news is known from reading the Law and the Prophets, and more particularly as it is known from reading the book of Isaiah. From what other source could this expression have arisen? It is likely therefore that the concise ascription affixed to the four Gospels, i.e., "The Gospel according to . . . ," is an abbreviation of the fuller ascription as understood: "The Gospel of the Lord according to . . . "

This way of looking at the matter solves all problems. We begin with Isaiah. Then Jesus teaches his disciples—including teaching them how to read the Law and the Prophets and especially how to read and understand the book of Isaiah. According to this way of looking at the matter, the good news of the Lord, in the first instance, refers to the glad tidings of peace and salvation referred to in Isa. 52:7. The Gospel of the Lord as represented by Jesus' teaching and ministry becomes in effect the Gospel of Jesus. Perhaps we should think in terms of "The Gospel of the Lord Jesus."[13] Jesus personifies and—through faith in the redemptive effect of his death and resurrection, to which he called his disciples on the night he was offered up—institutionalizes this gospel in the church. To walk in a straightforward manner with reference to the truth of this gospel becomes the canon by which apostolic faith is known and approved in the church.[14]

No matter how great an apostle Peter was, he could not depart or defect from the truth of this gospel without making himself vulnerable to the apostolic charge of dividing the church in the interests of a party, the party of James, which was prepared to put at risk God's plan to save the nations by requiring circumcision of the Gentiles, that is, by requiring that they adopt Jewish cultural practices. According to Paul, Christ died for the sins of all, Jews and Gentiles alike: a bold reading of Isa. 53:12: "He poured out his soul to death . . . he bore the sins of many."[15] Gentiles and Jews alike are brought into a right relationship with God through their faith in the God who had the power to make alive the dead, and not through works of the law, but through the faith of Jesus Christ.[16]

The Gospel of Jesus

At this point, we offer the reader a brief recapitulation of the overall argument of this book. The overarching concern has been "the Gospel of Jesus."

In this book I have mounted an argument on two matters: one is the greater adequacy of the Two-Gospel Hypothesis to deal with specific texts in the synoptic Gospels. This was basically carried out in the discussion of a representative set of Gospel texts in part 3. But closely related are the points raised in parts 2 and 4. The second matter is that of relevance. What difference does it make? Here again the work done in part 3 is crucial. I have argued that the Two-Gospel Hypothesis not only makes more sense of the "facts on the ground," but also more adequately accounts for the church's tradition concerning the Gospel narratives and, not insignificantly, allows Christians greater confidence as believing readers that the character and message of Jesus Christ has been faithfully transmitted to them.

This book presupposes a generation of international research into Christian origins by hundreds of scholars. The results of this research have been regularly reported in journals, university press publications, and the ecumenical press.

We may summarize the most important results of this research as follows: Jesus was a literate Jew. His chief reading material was the Law and the Prophets. As a Jew who called disciples to follow him, Jesus preached, taught, and led. From the effect of his teaching and ministry, it is possible to tell how Jesus read the Law and the Prophets. Jesus took a holistic approach to the scriptures. Yet there was a certain focus to the way in which revelation formed Jesus' mind and guided his life. Jesus learned to read the scriptures through the eyes of the prophets, and especially the prophet Isaiah. The Servant of the Lord, especially as set forth in the oracle of Isaiah preserved in 52:13—53:12 became normative for the way in which the whole of scripture was interpreted by Jesus for his disciples. Within the scriptures, Jesus found God's will for Israel, for himself as a son of Israel, and for his disciples, with Isaiah as the hermeneutical key for unlocking the mystery of God's purpose for Israel and the nations.

The chief evidence for this comes from Paul's letters. There, when the apostle writes "Jesus Christ," one can read "the Suffering Servant of the Lord" as depicted in Isa. 52:13—53:12. The rabbis taught that when the Messiah comes, he will come as the Servant of the Lord in Isaiah 53. Here is where the Jewish-Christian dialogue could find significant common ground. Why, for example, did rabbis of old teach that the Messiah, when he comes, will come as the Servant in the book of Isaiah?

The confession that Jesus is the Messiah draws the one making this confession into the community of faith that bears his name. This is the origin of the Christian church. This origin was preceded by divine revelation to Jesus (by which we mean God's self-disclosure to Jesus, through Jesus' reflection on God's Word mediated through reading the scriptures and hearing them read in a faith-strengthening community), and on the basis of this revelation, Jesus' call of his disciples. Then came Jesus' public ministry supported by his disciples, including men and women, culminating with his death and resurrection.

The first point at which our book touched on this outline of Jesus' ministry was found in chapter 5, "The Lord's Supper." There we learned that the words of institution as preserved in the text of Matthew give the strongest evidence of the formative influence of Isaiah 53 on the mind and ministry of Jesus.

Chapter 9, "The Keys of the Kingdom," led us into a discussion of martyrdom in relation to Jesus' promise that the gates of hell would not prevail against the church. Because the blood of the martyrs is the seed of the church, it is clear why that church could not agree with Marcion that Christians should dispense with the Law and the Prophets. This would have cut the church off from its chief root which reaches back through Jesus as the Christ to this central and normative prophecy of Isaiah. Tertullian in his refutation of Marcion's assertion that the compassionate Father of Jesus Christ is a different God from the justice-oriented God of Israel, found his main counterevidence in the book of Isaiah. Thus, whether it is from the side of Gnostics who abjure redemption through the ransoming sacrifice of Christ or from the side of Jews who have traditionally denied that Jesus is the Suffering Servant of the Lord through whom God is saving the nations, the issue is Isaiah and the canonical authority of his oracles for the fulfillment of the promise of the New Covenant found in Jer. 31:31–34, and the fulfillment of a whole series of divine promises found in the Law and the Prophets, beginning with God's promise to Abraham.

The Gospel and Isaiah's Concern for the Nations

We now return to our argument and focus on a central point, namely, the origin of the catholic or universal character of Christian faith. The very word "gospel" in the title of this book can be traced back to the book of Isaiah. "Gospel" means "good news."

> Get you up to a high mountain,
> O Zion, herald of good news [gospel].
> Lift up your voice with strength,
> O Jerusalem, herald of good news [gospel],
> Lift it up, fear not;
> Say to the cities of Judah,
>   "Behold your God!"
> Behold, the Lord God comes with might,
> And his arm rules for him;
> Behold, his reward is with him,
> And his recompense before him.
> He will feed his flock like a shepherd,
> He will gather the lambs in his arms,
> He will carry them in his bosom,
> And gently lead those that are with young.
>   —*Isa. 40:9–11*

Here the good news (gospel) is that the people of God are not to fear, because the Lord God comes with might to feed his flock and to carry the lambs in his bosom. From Isa. 52:7–10 (already cited) it is clear that the good news (gospel) is the announcing of God's salvation and the proclamation to Zion of the kingdom of God. It includes a message to all the nations as well, because "all the ends of the earth" will see the salvation of God. This concern for "the nations" runs from the beginning to the end of Isaiah.

> It shall come to pass in the latter days
> that the mountains of the house of the Lord
> shall be established as the highest of the mountains,
> and shall be raised above the hills;
> and all the nations shall flow to it,
> and many peoples shall come and say:
> > "Come, let us go up to the mountain of the Lord,
> > to the house of the God of Jacob;
> > that he may teach us his ways,
> > and that we may walk in his paths."
>
> For out of Zion shall go forth the commandment,
> and the word of the Lord from Jerusalem.
> He shall judge between the nations,
> and shall decide for many peoples;
> and they shall beat their swords into plowshares,
> and their spears into pruning hooks;
> nations shall not lift up sword against nations,
> neither shall they learn war anymore.[17]
>
> —*Isa. 2:2–4 (RSV)*

> I am coming to gather all nations and tongues;
> and they shall come and see my glory,
> and I will set a sign among them.
> And from them I will send survivors to the nations . . .
> to the coastlands afar off,
> that have not heard my fame or seen my glory;
> and they shall declare my glory among the nations.
> And they shall bring all your brethren from all
> the nations as an offering to the Lord . . .
> to my holy mountain Jerusalem, says the Lord,
> just as Israelites bring their cereal offerings
> in a clean vessel to the house of the Lord.
> And some of them also I will take for priests
> and for Levites, says the Lord.
>
> —*Isa. 66:18b-21 (RSV)*

From these passages it is clear that God's salvation, God's kingdom, is going to include a concern not only for Israel *but for all the nations* (cf., e.g., Isa. 42:1–4). How the salvation of the nations is going to take place is vague, but clearly Isaiah envisions a new world order, including reforms in the central cult life of Israel.

To begin to understand the Gospel of Jesus, we need to enter into the thought world of Isaiah.

> The Lord says to his servant:
> "It is too light a thing that you should be my servant
> to raise up the tribes of Jacob
> and to restore the preserved of Israel;
> I will give you as a light to the nations,
> that my salvation may reach
> to the ends of the earth."
> —*Isa. 49:6*

Here we have the Lord's repeated promise *to save the nations* made explicitly dependent upon the ministry of his servant.

> The Lord of hosts has sworn:
> "As I have planned,
> so shall it be,
> and as I have purposed,
> so shall it stand. . . ."
> This is the purpose that is purposed
> concerning the whole earth;
> and this is the hand that is stretched out
> over all the nations.
> —*Isa. 14:24–26 (RSV)*

For Isaiah, the Lord's plan of salvation is to extend to people of all ethnic groups. How is this to be achieved? As we have seen, the gospel that Paul preached, which he had received from those who were apostles before him, entailed the good news that Christ *died for our sins* in accord with Isaiah 53. But equally important is the compelling truth that *he died for all*.[18] It is implied in the text of the Lord's Supper that Jesus saw the means by which God was to achieve his purpose of saving Israel and the nations, revealed in this same central oracle of Isaiah. The Servant of the Lord was to "pour out his soul unto death." The Servant of the Lord was to "make himself an offering for sin." He was to be a "ransom for many." Whether for Jesus the "many" of Isaiah included all the nations, and not simply Israel, is important. For Jesus, the will of God was decisive, and according to Isaiah, God willed to save "all nations and tongues."[19] Jesus could not have been ignorant of this fact. In our reflection on the question of Isaiah 53 and the self-identification of Jesus, we must bear this in mind.[20]

Isaiah and the Gospel Story

We return now to the question of how all that we can learn from Isaiah bears on the origin and meaning of the Gospel story. According to the canonical Gospels, Jesus had some difficulty in making it clear to his disciples that it was necessary for him to suffer and die. But his death and resurrection opened their eyes, and since then the church has never doubted the importance of the redemptive death of Jesus. So that the reader can experience the full impact of the textual basis for the judgment that the book of Isaiah has been important not only in forming the mind and ministry of Jesus but also in giving shape to the subsequent attempt to communicate the Gospel of Jesus, we will now cite a series of passages from the canonical Gospels. These passages clearly indicate the way in which the Gospel of Jesus was shaped by the influence of the text of Isaiah.

I

Behold, a virgin shall conceive and bear a son,
And his name shall be called Emmanuel
(which means "God with us").

—Matt 1:25; Isa. 7:14

II

Now in the fifteenth year of the reign of Tiberius Caesar, Pontius Pilate being governor of Judea, Herod being tetrarch of Galilee, his brother Philip tetrarch of Ituraea and the region of Trachonitis, and Lysanias tetrarch of Abilene, while Annas and Caiaphas were high priests, the word of God came to John the son of Zacharias in the wilderness. And he went into all the regions around the Jordan preaching a baptism of repentance for the remission of sins, as it is written in the words of the book of Isaiah the prophet, saying:
The voice of one crying in the wilderness:
"Prepare the way of the Lord;
     make his path straight.
Every valley shall be filled
     and every mountain and hill brought low;
the crooked places shall be made straight
     and the rough ways smooth;
and all flesh shall see the salvation of God."
—Luke 3:1–6; Matt. 3:1–3; Mark 1:3; Isa. 40:3–5

III

And Jesus came to Nazareth, where he had been brought up; and he went to the synagogue, as his custom was, on the sabbath day. And he stood up to read; and there was given to him the book of the prophet Isaiah. He opened the book and found the place where it was written:
"The Spirit of the Lord is upon me,
because he has anointed me to
preach good news to the poor,
he has sent me to proclaim release to the captives
and recovering of sight to the blind,

to set at liberty those who are oppressed,
to proclaim the acceptable year of the Lord."

—Luke 4:16–19 (RSV); Isa. 61:1–2

IV

And after leaving Nazareth Jesus went and dwelt in Capernaum by the sea, in the territory of Zebulun and Naphtali, that what was spoken by the prophet Isaiah might be fulfilled:

The land of Zebulun and the land of Naphtali
toward the sea across the Jordan,
Galilee of the Gentiles—
the people who sat in darkness
have seen a great light,
and as for those who sat in the region and shadow of death,
on them light has shone.

—Matt. 4:12–16; Isa. 9:1–2

V

Now when John heard in prison about the deeds of the Christ, he sent word by his disciples and said to Jesus:

"Are you the one who is to come,
or shall we look for another?"

And Jesus answered them:

"Go and tell John what you hear and see:
the blind receive their sight and the lame walk,
lepers are cleansed and the deaf hear,
and the dead are raised up,
and the poor have good news preached to them."

—Matt. 11:2–5; Luke 4:18–19; Isa. 29:18–19; 35:5–6; 61:1

VI

Jesus, aware [that the Pharisees sought to destroy him], withdrew from there. And many followed him and he healed them all, and ordered them not to make him known. This was to fulfill what was spoken by the prophet Isaiah:

"Behold, my servant whom I have chosen,
my beloved with whom my soul is well pleased.
I will put my Spirit upon him,
and he shall proclaim justice to the nations.
He will not wrangle or cry aloud,
nor will anyone hear his voice in the streets;
he will not break a bruised reed
or quench a smoldering wick,
till he brings justice to victory;
and in his name will the nations hope."

—Matt. 12:15–21; Isa. 42:1–4

VII

With them [those who neither see, nor hear, nor understand] indeed is fulfilled the prophecy of Isaiah which says:

You shall indeed hear but never understand,
and you shall indeed see but never perceive.
For these people's heart has grown dull,
and their ears are heavy of hearing,
and their eyes they have closed,
lest they should perceive with their eyes,
and hear with their ears,
and understand with their heart,
and turn for me to heal them.

—*Matt. 13:14–15; Mark 8:18; Isa. 6:9–10*

VIII

Then the Pharisees and scribes came to Jesus from Jerusalem and said:

"Why do your disciples transgress the traditions of the elders?
For they do not wash their hands when they eat."

He answered them:

"And why do you transgress the commandments of God
for the sake of your tradition?
For God commanded:

'Honor your father and your mother,'
and 'He who speaks evil of father and mother,
let him surely die.'

But you say:

'If anyone tells his father or his mother,
What you would have gained from me is given to God,
he need not honor his father.'

So, for the sake of your tradition,
you have made void the word of God.
You hypocrites! Well did Isaiah prophesy of you,
When he said:

'These people honor me with their lips,
but their heart is far from me;
in vain do they worship me,
teaching as doctrines the precepts of man.' "

—*Matt. 15:1–9; Mark 7:1–23; Isa. 29:13*

IX

Jesus called his disciples to him and said:

"You know that the rulers of the Gentiles lord it over them,
and their great men exercise authority over them.
It shall not be so among you;
but whoever would be great among you

must be your servant,
and whoever would be first among you
must be your slave;
even as the Son of man came not to be served
but to serve,
and to give his life as a ransom for many."
—Matt. 20:25–28; Mark 10:42–45; Isa. 53:10–12

X

Now as they were eating, Jesus took bread, and blessed, and broke it, and gave it to his disciples and said:
"Take, eat;
this is my body."
And he took a cup; and when he had given thanks he gave it to them saying:
"Drink of it, all of you;
for this is my blood of the covenant,
which is poured out for many
for the forgiveness of their sins.
I tell you, I shall not drink of the fruit of the vine
until that day when I drink it new
with you in my Father's kingdom."
—Matt. 26:26–29; Mark 14:22–25; Isa. 53:10–12

XI

Then Jesus said to his disciples:
"There are many words which I spoke to you
while I was still with you,
that everything written about me
in the Law of Moses and the Prophets
and the psalms must be fulfilled."
Then he opened their minds to understand the scriptures,
And he said to them:
"Thus it is written, that the Christ should suffer
and on the third day rise from the dead,
and that repentance and forgiveness of sins
should be preached in his name
to all the nations,
beginning from Jerusalem."
—Luke 24:44–47; Isa. 2:2–3; Isa. 53

XII

And Jesus came and spoke to them, saying:
"All authority has been given to me in heaven and on earth.
Go therefore and make disciples of all the nations,
baptizing them in the name of the Father
and of the Son
and of the Holy Spirit,

teaching them to observe all things that I have commanded you;
and lo, I am with you always,
even to the end of the ages."
—*Matt. 28:18–20; Isa. 2:2–4; 14:24–26;*
42:1–4; 49:6; 52:7–10; 66:18b–21

What Difference Does It Make?

All in all, we shall have to conclude that the influence of Isaiah 52:13—53:12 on
the earliest Christian kerygma can hardly be demonstrated. A fortiori there is no
proof that Jesus himself was profoundly or uniquely influenced by this scripture
passage.   —*Marinus de Jonge, Shaffer Lectures, Yale University, 1989*

Professor de Jonge's summary conclusion fits like hand in glove with the
quotation from Professor Helmut Koester that opened the first chapter of this
book. Obviously, the case that has been made in this book leads to a very
different conclusion. To understand how adherents of the Two-Source
Hypothesis like de Jonge can come to the negative judgment on the
importance of Isaiah 53 for Jesus, expressed in the words cited above, and how
this judgment can lead on to the more radical conclusions of the "*Thomas*-Q
school," we need to ask, how is the series of Isaianic passages cited in the
previous section of this chapter understood by adherents of the Two-Source
Hypothesis? One way is to argue that the Gospel story in Mark is essentially
the same as that in Matthew and Luke, so that the influence of Isaiah is basic in
any retelling of the story of Jesus.

The fact that Matthew and Luke contain more passages from Isaiah than
Mark can be partially explained by the circumstance that Matthew and Luke
are longer than Mark. Those who argue this way then divide over whether the
more extensive use of Isaiah in the later Gospels Matthew and Luke is to be
explained as confirming of the importance of Isaiah for understanding Jesus,
or whether this more intensive use of Isaiah does not indicate a development
within the church that began not with Jesus but with an early church struggle
to make sense out of the ignominious and tragic death of Jesus. According to
this way of thinking, it is possible to argue along with Morna Hooker,
professor of New Testament at Cambridge University, that there is no
evidence that Isaiah 53 was of any importance to Jesus. Morna Hooker is an
example of a scholar who has been led to such a conclusion. She is led to this
conclusion by reading the evidence as she believes it should be read assuming
the Two-Source Hypothesis.[21] This way of looking at Christian beginnings is
strengthened even further if one regards the hypothetical sayings source Q as
earlier than and more authoritative than Mark. This Rudolf Bultmann already
tended to do. Then after the discovery of the Nag Hammadi documents, with
the recovery for the first time of the full text of *Thomas*, albeit in a Coptic

translation from the original Greek text, it has been possible to argue that Q itself is the decisive New Testament document to be followed in reconstructing Christian origins. This then results in offering readers a very different Jesus from the one that is known in the church's story of Jesus as expressed in the canonical Gospels.

On the basis of the Two-Gospel Hypothesis, one reaches very different conclusions about Jesus than are reached by those who base their reconstructions on Q. The differences are not so great when compared to results reached by adherents of the Two-Source Hypothesis who use the Gospel of Mark, rather than Q, as the basic source for understanding Jesus. The main difference in that case has to do with the degree of critical confidence one is entitled to have in the reconstructions that result from the use of these two hypotheses.

Conservative books by Markan priorists are generally ignored by Bultmannian adherents of the Two-Source Hypothesis. Where these more conservative reconstructions are thoroughly critical, as with such works as *The Aims of Jesus*, by Professor Ben Meyer, and *Jesus der Messias Israels*, by Otto Betz, the authors employ a sophisticated hermeneutic, according to which the raw consequences of the Two-Source Hypothesis are hidden or obscured by appeal to the theory that later documents can preserve earlier forms of tradition. This truism often leads to the additional hypothesis of an Ur-Markus, if not a "multiple-source hypothesis," where little regard is paid to the straightforward results of the Two-Source Hypothesis. This results in giving little more than lip service to the priority of Mark and the existence of Q. The *Thomas*-Q school finds it easy to ignore the work of scholars like Meyer, Betz, Hengel, and Stuhlmacher on the grounds that they are not following the Two-Source Hypothesis with sufficient rigor, that is, they ignore the importance of Q. But ignoring the work of these more conservative adherents of the Two-Source Hypothesis is also a necessity. Scholars like Robinson, Koester, Crossan, and Mack would die of critical indigestion if they were to chew and inwardly digest the work of these scholars who share with them adherence to the Two-Source Hypothesis. This represents the state of impasse that exists today within the larger Two-Source school.

By way of contrast, the reconstruction outlined in this book utilizes the hypothesis that the Gospels were probably composed in the sequence Matthew, Luke, and Mark without any need for a hypothetical sayings source Q or for any hypothetical Ur-Markus. Any valid benefits from literary criticism, form criticism, redaction criticism, genre criticism, canon criticism, compositional criticism, narrative criticism, reader-response criticism, womanist criticism, social-historical criticism, or Afrocentric criticism are conformable with the results reached by the use of the Two-Gospel Hypothesis. This is a research paradigm that works well with all of these new disciplines.

Finally, there is the claim that the Two-Source Hypothesis has been useful, and for that reason we should be slow to abandon it. Let us ask, useful for whom? Be it noted that on the basis of the evidence reviewed in this book it can be said that the Two-Source Hypothesis can be useful to the following:

1. Those who wish to claim that Jesus never taught his disciples to pray the Lord's Prayer.
2. Those who wish to view the Lord's Supper as a cult legend.
3. Those who separate Jesus from Paul by arguing that Paul's teaching of justification by faith has no point of contact with the teaching of Jesus.
4. Those who conclude that women did not play an important role in the ministry of Jesus.
5. Those who would discount liberation theology's emphasis on God's preferential love for the poor.
6. Those who focus on internal conflict in explaining Christian origins and discount the importance of Peter and any teaching of Jesus concerning the church.
7. Those who want to discount the importance of the Law and the Prophets for the Christian and eventually dismiss as sub-Christian the scriptures read by Jesus and his disciples.
8. Those who wish to think of Jesus as less Jewish than the Gospels represent him to be. (Q, for example, paves the way for readers to believe that the Lukan version of Q is the best source for understanding Jesus, whereas assuming the validity of the Two-Gospel Hypothesis, Q is to be regarded as a tendentious selection made for his Gentile readers by Luke, from the very Jewish sayings of Jesus in Matthew.)
9. Those who think it is appropriate to dismantle the church's canon.
10. Those who think that Q and *Thomas* plus other apocryphal Christian literature afford us a way of understanding Christian origins equally valid to that provided by a study of the New Testament against the background of the Law and the Prophets.
11. Those who have concluded that the redemptive death of Jesus was not normative on the basis of *Thomas* and the sayings source Q.
12. Those who have concluded on the basis of Q that the earliest Christians (at least as far as the Q community is concerned) did not give any importance to the redemptive character of the death of Jesus.
13. Those who would assert that there is no evidence that Isaiah 53 was of any importance for Jesus.
14. Those who would see Paul as departing from or corrupting the earliest form of Christianity [best represented by *Thomas* and Q].
15. Those liberal Catholic theologians and Bible scholars who feel alienated from a hierarchically dominated church and welcome the liberation from intellectually restrictive dogmas that comes with the adoption of the liberal German Protestant critical tradition, with its emancipating and intellectually satisfying idea of Markan priority.

It should be pointed out that many scholars adhere to the Two-Source Hypothesis who have no sympathy with any of the pragmatic benefits listed here. But, as has been suggested, many if not most of these scholars are involved in what can be regarded as paying lip service to the Two-Source Hypothesis. They certainly do not milk this research paradigm for all it is worth. In practice, they generally avoid basing any important conclusions on it, covering their bets by citing Mark only where Mark's text is backed up by either Matthew or Luke, or both. This paradigm is, in this sense, largely useless to them. If they say that this hypothesis is useful, and many would make no such argument, they would have in mind the fact that this hypothesis seems to work. Not infrequently, they see something new that has never been noticed before. This can be exciting. No matter how small the point might be, it can often be accepted for publication. In this way, it can lend credence to the view that this hypothesis is useful.

It is quite possible to write a book that would present Markan priority in a very positive light. Such a book might begin with the undeniable way this revolutionary idea has proved to be intellectually satisfying to so many scholars and laypeople. Or one could, for example, begin with the tradition associating the Gospel of Mark with the preaching of Peter, a tradition witnessed to by Papias, Irenaeus, and Clement of Alexandria. But that would be a "conservative" book with quite a different purpose. The purpose of this book has been to highlight in a critical manner the difference it makes whether one begins a quest for understanding Christian origins with Mark and Q or with Matthew and Luke.

Meanwhile, we must be content with making educated guesses as to why the idea of Markan priority rose so high in the intellectual life of the west and has retained its hold on the minds of so many intelligent students of Christian beginnings. From this book, carefully read and inwardly digested, it should be clear that this idea of Markan priority is essentially groundless. The same can be said of the critical basis for its progeny, the *Thomas*-Q line of research. It too is esssentially groundless because it presupposes a hypothetical Q document that in turn presupposes the groundless idea of Markan priority.

We have, on the one hand, endless speculation based largely on nonexisting documents, such as Q and different earlier versions of Mark, and on the other hand, actual texts, namely, the church's Gospels, all of which were written before *Thomas*, which probably made use of the Gospel of Luke and which, while it contains a few sayings of Jesus not found in the canonical Gospels, basically preserves later and on the whole less reliable versions of the sayings of Jesus compared to those preserved in the church's Gospels.

Scholarship is at a crossroads. Faced with these alternate ways to answer the question concerning Christian origins, we can either join a wild goose chase following the lead of the *Thomas*-Q line, or we can settle down and participate in a serious engagement with the texts of the church's earliest sources, Paul's letters and, we would maintain, the Gospels of Matthew and Luke. This latter course is the more promising path to follow because it affords the church a more credible account of its origins and a more adequate basis for its faith.

Some readers will want to know where this leaves the question of the historical Jesus. That is the subject of another book. Certain things should be clear from reading this book. We can see how assuming the Two-Gospel Hypothesis produces very different results from those based on the Two-Source Hypothesis. It is reasonable to expect that a book on the historical Jesus, assuming the Two-Gospel Hypothesis, would present a reconstruction conformable to the sketch that emerges from the "Gospel of Jesus" as outlined in this book. Following the historical method, and benefiting from all the new disciplines mentioned above, one would flesh out this sketch with the full range of evidence available to the historian, critically evaluated. The bulk of this evidence, but not all, would be drawn from Paul's letters, the Gospels of Matthew and Luke, and the works of Josephus, supplemented by the rich background material illuminating life in the Mediterranean world, philosophy, history, and so on, the archaeological evidence from the Herodian period, and including all relevant written sources like the Qumran, intertestamental, and Nag Hammadi material. There is no evidence that cannot be grist for the mill of the historian. But unless the historian has a focus, there is no story to tell. This book provides a focus.

The Two-Source Hypothesis as a Methodological Criterion in Synoptic Research[1]

In 1941, Rudolf Bultmann published a lengthy discussion of the authority of Matt. 16:17–19, where Jesus is presented as giving Peter the keys of the kingdom.[2] Here we want to focus on Bultmann's use of the Two-Source Hypothesis as a criterion for deciding the authenticity of Jesus' sayings. This matter is important on two grounds. The first is the church's interest in the interpretation of this particular passage. The second is the need for an exegetical method of dealing with the synoptic tradition as a whole that is as free as possible of any unnecessary ambiguity. That contemporary synoptic research has unresolved ambiguity is the thesis of the following discussion.

The specific occasion of Bultmann's article was Oscar Cullmann's published view arguing for the authenticity of this Matthean passage. Bultmann noted that, if Cullmann were right, his conclusion would reverse a judgment that had been previously regarded as a reliable result of historical criticism. Bultmann proceeded to review the history of the question beginning with C. H. Weisse, *Die evangelische Geschichte* (1838), taking into account the views of H. J. Holtzmann, A. Loisy, J. Wellhausen, J. Weiss, J. Kreyenbühl, B. H. Streeter, M. Goguel, E. Meyer, K. G. Goetz, M. Dibelius, W. G. Kümmel, J. Haller, and B. S. Easton in order to show that there was little ground in the views of these critics for the authenticity of this passage. Bultmann considered it self-evident that conservative Protestant research, as well as Catholic, regarded this passage as authentic, and he then devoted the rest of his discussion to difficulties inherent in regarding this passage as the authentic words of the historical Jesus.

Bultmann concluded that the ecclesiastical language and thought of Matt. 16:17–19 is foreign to the best authenticated sayings of Jesus. His reasoning proceeded as follows: the word *ekklesia* is found in the sayings of Jesus only in Matthew and the importance of this fact is grounded in the correlate that *ekklesia* is not found in the sayings of Jesus preserved in Mark or in Q. Obviously, Bultmann assumed that the sayings of Jesus found in Mark or Q are more likely to be authentic than those found in Matthew or Luke. He wrote: "Now it is naturally not precluded that sayings of Jesus deriving from early tradition are to be found in the Special Materials of Matthew and Luke. But in every single case that is first to be established as probable; and in so doing it must be held on to as a criterion, that such sayings should fit together in language, conceptuality, and interest with the sayings of Jesus which can be regarded as early on the basis of their having been preserved in Mark and the sayings source [Q]. For Matt. 16:17–19 this is clearly not the case."[3]

To understand this statement, one has to assume that Bultmann is presupposing and is methodologically dependent on the Two-Source Hypothesis. This hypothesis was first formulated by Christian Hermann Weisse in 1838,[4] then popularized through the epoch-making work of Holtzmann published in 1863[5] and thereafter adopted by an ever-increasing number of critics until by Bultmann's student days before World War I, it was regarded in many universities as an assured result of nineteenth-century New Testament criticism. According to this hypothesis, Mark and Q are thought of as being the two most primitive and best authenticated sources of early reliable tradition concerning Jesus. Bultmann clearly adheres to this hypothesis. He does not deny that Matthew and Luke might have preserved authentic sayings of Jesus not found in Mark or Q, but he believes that in such a case the burden of proof rests on those who think this to be true. Thus arguing for the authenticity of a saying of Jesus, the critic must test the language, the conceptuality, and the interest of the saying concerned in terms of the corpus of more primitive sayings of Jesus preserved in Mark and Q. If the saying fits with the nucleus of the more primitive sayings in Mark and Q, then this argues for its authenticity; if not, then this argues against its authenticity. Bultmann speaks of this procedure as the criterion by which the authenticity of those sayings not found in Mark and Q is to be discerned.

While Bultmann himself was a pioneer of the form-critical method, which does not in principle depend on the Two-Source Hypothesis, he remained in perfect continuity with the late nineteenth-century source criticism of liberal scholarship and continued to think in terms of an essentially pre-form-critical orientation toward the synoptic tradition, namely, in terms of the Two-Source Hypothesis. This points to an inherent incoherence in Bultmann's work. The results of form criticism call into question the results of the methodological criterion that Bultmann advocates and depends upon. This will become clear as we proceed. It is worth noticing, however, that Bultmann in his treatment of Matt. 16:17–19 does not make any further use of this criterion, nor does he in his subsequent writings ever again appeal to this criterion. Could this omission indicate Bultmann's growing lack of confidence in the criterion or even a realization of the inherent incoherence resulting from adherence to both form criticism and the Two-Source Hypothesis? Still, it is possible, to trace the influence of the Two-Source Hypothesis in the rest of his work even though this criterion is not explicitly followed.

If a critic analyzes the tradition preserved in the Gospels according to form-critical methods, isolates those literary units that seem most likely to represent authentic sayings of Jesus, and then attempts to find a central core—some self-consistent, comprehensible, historical nucleus of Jesus' sayings concerning whose authenticity there is the very least reason for doubt—he will find at the center of that historical core such literary units at Luke 15; Matt. 20:1–6; Luke 18:9–14; Matt. 21:28–32; Matt. 9:10–13; || Mark 2:15–17 || Luke 5:29–32; Matt. 18:21–35; Matt. 5:44–45 || Luke 6:35–36; Matt. 13:44–46; Matt. 7:7–11 || Luke 11:9–13; Luke 11:5–8; Luke 18:1–8; and Luke 14:28–32. These sayings and others would by all form-critical considerations belong to the basic core of Jesus' teaching. Luke 13:6–9; Matt. 25:1–12, and many other sayings could be included here. After this analysis, it is clear that those sayings of Jesus, preserved in the Gospels and possessing the highest claim to be considered authentic by form-critical principles, are best represented not in Mark or Q, but in materials found only in Matthew on the one hand, and only in Luke on the other. This conclusion remains unchanged no matter how much the basic core of most probable authentic tradition is extended. This does not imply that Mark and Q, assuming the latter's existence, do not contain authentic sayings of Jesus. They undoubtedly do. But it becomes evident that Bultmann's criterion for determining the authenticity of a particular saying of Jesus in the special materials of Matthew and Luke draws no support from form criticism. The opposite is true. Form criticism calls into question this criterion. It seems clear that the basic core of authentic sayings of Jesus is better represented in materials found only in Matthew and only in Luke, than in Mark or Q.

To make the sayings of Jesus preserved in Mark and Q a norm by which we establish the authenticity of sayings found only in the special materials of Matthew or Luke, gives preference, on the one hand, to a restricted and atypical parabolic tradition in Mark that is mysteriously esoteric, and on the other hand, to a gnomic tradition in Q that is unintelligible when isolated from the parables of Jesus in the special materials of Matthew and Luke. To rely on such a questionable methodology is to measure the relatively more certain by the relatively more problematic. Jesus' sayings that enable one to understand how Mark's parables of the kingdom can be held together with the ethical material from Q are found, for the most part, in the parabolic tradition preserved in the special materials of Matthew and Luke.

Bultmann was able to make sense out of Jesus' message in his book *Jesus and the Word*, but for this he depended heavily on parabolic material found only in the special materials of Matthew and Luke.[6] This is especially clear in the decisive final section of his reconstruction.

Nothing set forth above is intended to establish that Matt. 16:17–19 is an authentic saying of Jesus, but simply to suggest that the question of its authenticity cannot be settled satisfactorily by the application of criteria that owe their rationale to the kind of methodological dependence on the Two-Source Hypothesis we find Bultmann advocating. This is true of the whole gospel tradition. This leads us to conclude that all New Testament research resting upon a naive acceptance and dependence upon one particular nineteenth-century solution to the source problem needs to be reworked with this point in mind, especially in light of the fact that this solution is being increasingly called into question by developments in New Testament research.

In sum, form criticism calls into question the priority of Mark. For example, the tendency of the imagination to identify anonymous persons is noted by Bultmann, but he does not point out that this happens more often in Mark than in Matthew. Furthermore, Bultmann notes that the evangelists follow a custom characteristic of pagan miracle stories when they reproduce the wonder-working word in a foreign tongue, and he cites as examples *Talitha cumi* (Mark 5:41) and *Ephphatha* (Mark 7:34), without acknowledging that this phenomenon occurs only in Mark. Moreover, in his treatment of the biographical apophthegmata, Bultmann not infrequently reconstructs as the more original form behind Mark a form of the tradition that is closer to Matthew and Luke than to Mark. Some instances are Mark 10:13–16; 11:15–19; 12:41–44; 13:1–4; and 14:3–9.[7]

Bultmann's mentors took for granted that Mark was the earliest Gospel. On what basis did they do that? It was the phenomenon of the order of the narratives in the three synoptics that convincingly indicated to them that Matthew and Luke were later Gospels. This phenomenon of the order of the narratives refers to the peculiar pattern of agreement and disagreement in the sequence of material among the three synoptics. Frequently all three agree. Often Matthew and Mark agree against Luke. Often Mark and Luke agree against Matthew. But Luke and Matthew almost never agree against Mark. This was evidence to Bultmann's mentors that Matthew and Luke independently copied Mark, because the order of material in Mark is almost always supported either by Matthew or Luke and often by both. Holtzmann and Paul Wernle are often cited in this connection.

The argument from order was first formulated by Karl Lachmann in 1835.[8] To this argument flocked many of the strong advocates of Markan priority, including B. H. Streeter, who often sarcastically dismisses other New Testament critics who doubt Markan priority.[9]

That the argument from order is not a valid argument for the priority of the Gospel of Mark over Matthew and Luke was demonstrated by H. G. Jameson in 1922,[10] by J. F. Springer in 1924,[11] and by John Chapman in 1937.[12] But it was not until 1951, when Cambridge University Press published B. C. Butler's *The Originality of Matthew*, that New Testament scholars generally began to note the fallacious character of this argument for Markan priority. It was a significant occasion in the history of synoptic criticism when G. M. Styler, an advocate of Markan priority, admitted in 1962 that Butler's careful analysis of this argument demonstrated once and for all that the argument from order was not a valid argument for the priority of Mark.[13] Ever since Butler, the argument from order has suggested only that Mark occupies a medial position between Matthew and Luke but not that Mark was the first Gospel.

It is true that many scholars have gone on to find what they regard as corroborating evidence for Markan priority in their Gospel studies. But for many, the argument from order remained decisive and they presupposed Markan priority from the very beginning of their Gospel studies. Thus, it is very difficult to know to what extent supporters of the Two-Source Hypothesis are involved in a kind of circular argumentation in which they think they have found evidence to support a hypothesis that they have uncritically used as a methodological presupposition. All investigative work is plagued by this difficulty. We may safely assume then that if Bultmann had not believed that the priority of Mark was an assured result of nineteenth-century criticism, he would have been the first to note that the application of form-critical methods frequently produces results that call Markan priority into question.

Later advances in historical and literary criticism have further called into question Markan priority. Pierson Parker in *The Gospel Before Mark* has set forth important historical considerations that stand in the way of thinking that Matthew is dependent upon Mark.[14] The literary considerations to which B. C. Butler[15] and Austin Farrer[16] have drawn attention also serve to highlight the uncertainty of the Two-Source Hypothesis.

Some advocates of Markan priority argue that Mark's text is more primitive than the texts of Matthew and Luke.[17] Still others argue that the theological interests of Mark are less developed than those in Matthew and Luke. The most popular argument for the Two-Source Hypothesis, however, has been what may be termed the "usefulness" argument, on which the use of this hypothesis is defended on the grounds that it has proved its usefulness. This argument is primarily used by critics deeply involved in redaction criticism, in whose hands the argument is in danger of becoming circular, for the same critics use the Two-Source Hypothesis as a basic methodological presupposition. They would have an argument if these critics were to carry through their redactional analyses of the Gospels based on different source hypotheses, publish the results of their research, and then demonstrate that the Two-Source Hypothesis produces more useful results than the alternate source hypotheses. This has never been done.

While some may question that the Two-Source Hypothesis is especially useful today, it is possible to show that it was particularly useful in the nineteenth century. For example, the nineteenth-century need for a categorical imperative was met by the stringent ethic of the Sermon on the Mount in Q. The nineteenth-century need to ground the notion of progress and development in the teachings of Jesus was met by the parables of growth in Q and the parable of the seed growing secretly in Mark. Indeed, it can be argued that some of the main developments in synoptic criticism in the nineteenth century are but footnotes to the history of dogma in that century.[18] For example, it can be demonstrated that the church's need in the nineteenth century to get back behind its non-eyewitness Gospels and to ground its theology in one or more historically trustworthy apostolic sources led first to the discovery of the theological relevance of the Ur-Gospel, then to a practical preference for the Two-Source Hypothesis. The originators of these different useful hypotheses did not always emphasize their theological advantages, but those who popularized these theories did not, and others do not now, hesitate to do so.

Albert Schweitzer recognized the theological importance of the Markan hypothesis when, in reference to the works of Schenkel and Weizsäcker, he wrote:

> What attracted these writers to the Marcan hypothesis was not so much the authentication which it gave to the detail of Mark, though they were willing enough to accept that, but the way in which this Gospel lent itself to the a priori view of the course of the life of Jesus which they unconsciously brought with them. They appealed to Holtzmann because he showed such wonderful skill in extracting from the Marcan narrative the view which commended itself to the spirit of the age as manifested in the sixties. . . . The way in which Holtzmann exhibited this characteristic view of the sixties as arising naturally out of the detail of Mark, was so perfect, so artistically charming, that this view appeared henceforward to be inseparably bound up with the Marcan tradition. Scarcely ever has a description of the life of Jesus exercised so irresistible an influence as that short outline—it embraces scarcely twenty pages—with which Holtzmann closes his examination of the Synoptic Gospels. This chapter became the creed and catechism of all who handled the subject during the following decades. The treatment of the life of Jesus had to follow the lines here laid down until the Marcan hypothesis was delivered from its bondage to that a priori view of the development of Jesus. Until then anyone might appeal to the Marcan hypothesis, meaning thereby only that general view of the inward and outward course of development in the life of Jesus, and might treat the remainder of the Synoptic material how he chose, combining it with, at his pleasure, material drawn from John. The victory, therefore, belonged, not to the Marcan hypothesis pure and simple, but to the Marcan hypothesis as psychologically interpreted by a liberal theology.[19]

The decisive factor in the triumph of the Markan hypothesis was not any scientific argument or series of arguments; rather, that factor was theological. This is undoubtedly an oversimplification of the issue on the part of

Schweitzer, but it is a brilliant attempt to explain something that cries out for explanation. The question is: How was it possible for the theory of Markan priority to triumph so unambiguously in the absence of any compelling proof and in the face of all the serious objections made throughout the nineteenth century? This points to a problem that requires historical investigation.[20]

Notes

1. Introduction

1. The text known as *Thomas* is a fourth-century Coptic document believed to be based on a second-century apocryphal work in Greek. Whether *Thomas* is a gospel remains in dispute.

2. Helmut Koester, *Ancient Christian Gospels: Their History and Development* (Philadelphia: Trinity Press International, 1990), 86.

3. Gal. 2:5, 14.

4. Perhaps the best-known example of this tendency is the work of John Dominic Crossan, *The Historical Jesus: The Life of a Mediterranean Jewish Peasant* (San Francisco: HarperCollins, 1991).

5. Cf. David L. Dungan, "The Two-Gospel Hypothesis," *Anchor Bible Dictionary*.

6. James M. Robinson, "The Sayings Gospel 'Q,' " in *The Four Gospels: 1992 Festschrift Frans Neirynck*, vol. 1, ed. F. van Segbroek et al. (Louvain: Leuven University Press, 1992), 388.

7. James M. Robinson, "The Sayings of Jesus: 'Q,' " *Drew Gateway*, Fall 1983, 28.

8. That Luke used Matthew is common ground uniting the following major hypotheses: (1) Mark first, Matthew second, and Luke third; (2) Matthew first, Mark second, and Luke third; and (3) Matthew first, Luke second, and Mark third. Only one of these hypotheses—Matthew first, Luke second, and Mark third—will be compared with the Two-Source Hypothesis in this discussion. This is known today as the Two-Gospel Hypothesis. Of all the major alternatives to the Two-Source Hypothesis, the Two-Gospel Hypothesis is most fully explained and defended in contemporary scholarly literature. It is important, however, that many if not most of the arguments for the Two-Gospel Hypothesis and against the Two-Source Hypothesis would also apply to a solution based on a Matthew-Mark-Luke order of composition. As far as dispensing with Q, everything said in favor of that in this book would hold equally well for any of the three alternative hypotheses mentioned above. In other words, the argument of this book required foremost that we dispense with Q on grounds that Luke used Matthew as a source and that Mark was later than Matthew. A case for Matthew-Mark-Luke can be made along the same lines. A chief weakness of this hypothesis, however, is that it fails to explain satisfactorily why, if Luke copied Mark, literary characteristics of Mark never show up in Luke. If Luke had copied Mark, one would have expected characteristics of Mark to show up inadvertently in Luke's text, at least in fragmentary form. This does not happen, and it is clear literary evidence that Luke did not copy Mark. On the other hand, traces of Luke's literary characteristics show up in Mark's text.

9. E. Earle Ellis, "Gospel Criticism: A Perspective on the State of the Art," in *Das Evangelium und die Evangelien: Vorträge vom Tübinger Symposium*, 1982, ed. P. Stuhlmacher (Tübingen: J.C.B. Mohr [Paul Siebeck], 1983, 24–54. Wissenschaftliche Untersuchungen zum Neuen Testament 28).

10. Eta Linnemann, *Is There a Synoptic Problem? Rethinking the Literary Dependence of the First Three Gospels*, trans. Robert W. Yarbrough (Grand Rapids: Baker Book House, 1992), 43–66. Linnemann's analysis of the critical tradition has led her to question whether sufficient evidence exists for any literary dependence among the Gospels. While some of her arguments fail to convince this reader, Linnemann's book has much to offer. The recent study she cites is the book by Hans Herbert Stoldt, *Geschichte und Kritik der Markus Hypothese* (Göttingen: Vandenhoeck & Ruprecht, 1977); English translation, *The History and Criticism of the Marcan Hypothesis*, trans. and ed. Donald Niewyk (Macon, Ga.: Mercer University Press, and Edinburgh: T. & T. Clark, 1980). Stoldt was not a university professor but a retired preparatory school administrator who specialized in eighteenth- and nineteenth-century German literature and had made himself an expert on the synoptic problem.

11. See especially William R. Farmer, *Jesus and the Gospels: Tradition, Scripture, and Canon* (Philadelphia: Fortress Press, 1983).

12. William R. Farmer, "Peter and Paul and the Tradition concerning the Lord's Supper in 1 Corinthians 11:23–26," in *One Loaf, One Cup: Ecumenical Studies of 1 Corinthians 11 and Other Eucharistic Texts*, ed. Ben F. Meyer (Macon, Ga: Mercer University Press, 1993), 35–46.

13. For books on that subject, consult Dungan's bibliography (note 5).

14. Helmut Koester, "History and Development of Mark's Gospel: From Mark to Secret Mark and 'Canonical' Mark," in *Colloquy on New Testament Studies: A Time for Reappraisal and Fresh Approaches*, ed. Bruce Corley (Macon, Ga.: Mercer University Press, 1983), 35–57.

15. See David B. Peabody, "The Late Secondary Redaction of Mark's Gospel and the Griesbach Hypothesis: A Response to Helmut Koester," in *Colloquy on New Testament Studies*, 87–132.

16. "It is widely assumed that Q is composed of several layers of material, and/or that it underwent a series of redactions," wrote Arland D. Jacobson in "Apocalyptic and the Saying Source Q," in *The Four Gospels: 1992 Festschrift Frans Neirynck*, vol. 1, ed. F. van Segbroeck et al. (Louvain: Leuven University Press, 1992), 412.

2. A Systematic Overview of the Two-Gospel Hypothesis

1. See Denis Farkasfalvy, O.Cist., "The Presbyter's Witness on the Order of the Gospels as Reported by Clement of Alexandria," *Catholic Biblical Quarterly* 54 (April 1992): 260–70. Farkasfalvy has correctly presented the way in which the Clement testimony should be discussed, and all subsequent discussion should proceed from the new point of departure that he has laid down.

2. Augustine of Hippo, *The Harmony of the Gospels* 4.10.11.

3. See David B. Peabody, "Augustine and the Augustinian Hypothesis: A Reexamination of Augustine's Thought in *De consensu evangelistorum*," in *New Synoptic Studies:*

The Cambridge Gospel Conference and Beyond (Macon, Ga.: Mercer University Press, 1983), 37–64.

4. See Bernard Orchard, *Matthew, Luke, and Mark* (Manchester: Koinonia Press, 1976).

5. *Theologische Jahrbücher* (1843), 443–543.

6. Cf. Philip L. Shuler, *A Genre for the Gospels: The Bibliographical Character of Matthew* (Philadelphia: Fortress Press, 1982).

3. The Two-Gospel Hypothesis Illustrated by Texts

1. Although there is only one Gospel and each of the church's four canonical Gospels is actually that one Gospel "according to" the person named in the title, in this discussion the commonly accepted shorthand expressions, such as "the Gospel of Matthew" or even "Matthew," will be used.

2. See Austin Farrer, "On Dispensing with Q," in *Studies in the Gospels: Essays in Memory of R. H. Lightfoot*, ed. Dennis E. Nineham (Oxford: Basil Blackwell Publisher, 1955), 55–88; Bernard Orchard, *Matthew, Luke, and Mark* (Manchester: Koinonia Press, 1976); Michael D. Goulder, *Luke: A New Paradigm*, 2 vols., Journal for the Study of the New Testament—Supplement Series 20 (Sheffield: Sheffield Academic Press, 1989). While Mark contains no parallel to Luke 10:1–10, and while no Markan parallel exists for most of the verbatim material in Matthew and Luke in the other two passages, a few lines in both Luke 3:2b–9 and Luke 7:18–35 are verbatim in all the Gospels. These triple agreements in long passages where there is extensive agreement between Matthew and Luke constitute major difficulties for the Two-Source Hypothesis. For an argument against any direct literary dependence among the Gospels, see Eta Linnemann, *Is There a Synoptic Problem? Rethinking the Literary Dependence of the First Three Gospels*, trans. Robert W. Yarbrough (Grand Rapids: Baker Book House, 1992).

3. The writers in note 2 agree with this statement. For the classic arguments for and against Q, see *The Two-Source Hypothesis: A Critical Appraisal*, ed. Arthur J. Bellinzoni, Jr. (Macon, Ga.: Mercer University Press, 1985), 319–433.

4. See Thomas R. W. Longstaff, *Evidence of Conflation in Mark? A Study of the Synoptic Problem* (Missoula, Mont.: Scholars Press, 1977); J. J. Griesbach, "A Demonstration That Mark Was Written after Matthew and Luke," trans. Bernard Orchard, in *J. J. Griesbach: Synoptic and Text-Critical Studies, 1776–1979*, ed. Bernard Orchard and Thomas R. W. Longstaff (Cambridge: Cambridge University Press, 1978), 103–35; Roland Mushat Frye, "The Synoptic Problems and Analogies in Other Literatures," in *The Relationship among the Gospels: An Interdisciplinary Dialogue*, ed. William O. Walker, Jr. (San Antonio: Trinity University Press, 1978); William R. Farmer, "The Statement of the (Two-Gospel) Hypothesis," in *The Interrelation of the Gospels*, a symposium led by M. E. Boisonard, W. R. Farmer, and F. Neirynck, ed. David L. Dungan (Louvain: Leuven University Press, 1990), 132–36, 141–43; David Neville, *Arguments from Order*, New Gospel Studies Monograph Series (Macon, Ga.: Mercer University Press, 1994).

5. Eta Linnemann does not discuss this evidence.

6. Mark 1:1, 11, 14, 15, 29, 33, 35; 2:3; 4:31–32; 6:3, 8–9, 13; 7:24–31; 8:27–33; 9:14; 9:30f.; 9:35–37, 43–47; 10:11, 37, 43–45; 11:17, 25; 12:25, 28–34, 36; 13:1–2, 11, 13b; 14:17–21, 22–25, 30, 58, 62, 72; 15:5, 25, 44–45. This constitutes very telling evidence against the priority of Mark because the scholars making their critical judgments are effectively hostile witnesses in that they are drawing attention to evidence that is anomalous to their own theory. Of course, no single adherent of Markan priority is aware of all this evidence. Such a person probably would look for another theory. (There is no similar list of passages that witness against the view that Mark was written third.) Cf. "Suggested Exceptions to the Priority of Mark," in *Tendencies of the Synoptic Tradition* (Cambridge: Cambridge University Press, 1969), 290–93. Sanders gives a brief explanation for each passage and the relevant bibliographical references. A multiple-source hypothesis can also explain Sanders's data. In this case, though, the Two-Gospel Hypothesis explains the agreements and disagreements among the three Gospels equally well without appealing to hypothetical sources.

7. See Helmut Koester, who concludes that the text of canonical Mark was composed after Matthew and Luke. "History and Development of Mark's Gospel: From Mark to Secret Mark and 'Canonical' Mark," *Colloquy on New Testament Studies: A Time for Reappraisal and Fresh Approaches*, ed. Bruce Corley (Macon, Ga.: Mercer University Press, 1983), 35–57.

8. A growing number of Two-Source Hypothesis adherents, including Helmut Koester, propose that the apocryphal *Gospel of Peter* and *Thomas* draw upon sources that are earlier than the immediate sources of Matthew and Luke. See the discussion of Koester, "The Synoptic Problem and the Sources of the Gospels," in his *Introduction to the New Testament*, vol. 2: *History and Literature of Early Christianity* (Philadelphia: Fortress Press, 1980), 44–49. In the same section of his textbook, Koester repeats for his readers what they will find in many other texts about the priority of Mark. However, elsewhere Koester published work arguing that the text of canonical Mark is later than Matthew and Luke. See "History and Development of Mark's Gospel: From Mark to Secret Mark and 'Canonical' Mark," 35–57. Rarely, if ever, in scientific literature are inconsistencies between the conclusions to which a scholar has been led in his research and what he has published in a textbook for students more misleading than in these two publications of Professor Koester.

4. The Lord's Prayer

1. It is clear from comparing this reconstruction of the Q text for the Lord's Prayer and the texts in Matthew and Luke that the Q reconstruction effectively combines the texts of the two evangelists, adhering generally to the common text to which they bear concurrent testimony.

5. The Lord's Supper

1. See *One Loaf, One Cup: Ecumenical Studies of 1 Corinthians 11 and Other Eucharistic Texts*, ed. Ben F. Meyer (Macon, Ga.: Mercer University Press, 1993).

2. "Christ in his Eucharist is truly the heart of the church." Henri de Lubac, *The Splendor of the Church* (London: Sheed & Ward, 1956), 113.

3. Morna Hooker, *Jesus and the Servant: The Influence of the Servant Concept of Deutero-Isaiah in the New Testament* (London: SPCK, 1959).

4. Rudolf Bultmann, *History of the Synoptic Tradition*, trans. John Marsh (Oxford: Basil Blackwell Publisher, 1963), from *Die Geschichte der synoptischen Tradition*, 3d ed. (Göttingen: Vandenhoeck & Ruprecht, 1958). This work was dedicated to Wilhelm Heitmüller.

5. See William R. Farmer, "Peter and Paul and the Tradition concerning the Lord's Supper," in *One Loaf, One Cup*.

6. Justification by Faith

1. In this chapter we begin with a scripture passage, but we must depart from the practice of comparing it with different versions of the same passage because this key parable occurs only in Luke.

2. Our interpretation is congruent with the recent understanding of "works of the law" in Paul as a protest not against the idea that the law could and should be obeyed, but that Israel had claimed Torah as its own special property and had mistakenly viewed the special badges of the law (circumcision, keeping the Sabbath, and other practices) as the exclusive domain of the righteousness of God. Cf. James D. G. Dunn, *Jesus, Paul, and the Law: Studies in Mark and Galatians* (Louisville, Ky.: Westminster/ John Knox Press, 1990), 183–214.

3. For a different view, see Ernst Käsemann, "A Critical Analysis of Philippians 2:5–11," in *God and Christ: Existence and Province*, ed. Robert W. Funk and Gerhard Ebeling (New York: Harper & Row, 1968), 45–88. Käsemann contends that the references to "the mind which is yours in Christ Jesus," "emptying himself," and "humbling himself" in these points belong to a wider metaphysical framework within Hellenistic religion and *have nothing to do with the actual life of the earthly Jesus*. In any case, it seems rather obvious that in some sense a remembrance of Jesus' life is held up to the readers as a model for ethical living.

7. The Faithful Witness of Women

1. See Michael D. Goulder, *Luke: A New Paradigm*, vol. 1, Journal for the Study of the New Testament—Supplement Series 20 (Sheffield: Sheffield Academic Press, 1989), 2–11.

2. Adherents of the Two-Gospel Hypothesis generally accept the majority view of text critics on this question. In fact, the first text critic to question the authenticity of these verses was Joachim Jacob Griesbach, the scholar who brought the view that Mark used both Matthew and Luke into the mainstream of Gospel criticism. The fullest discussion of these verses finds the evidence on their authenticity rather evenly divided, with the balance slightly toward including these verses as part of Mark's Gospel. Few scholars, however, question the propriety of bracketing these verses because of the well-recognized inconclusiveness of the manuscript evidence. See William R. Farmer, *The Last Twelve Verses of Mark* (Cambridge: Cambridge University Press, 1974).

3. *The Women's Bible Commentary*, ed. Carol A. Newsom and Sharon H. Ringe (Louisville, Ky.: Westminster/ John Knox Press, 1992), 395. All subsequent references in this chapter are to this volume, and page numbers are enclosed in parentheses.

4. Cf. Gal. 3:28, and the discussion of this text by Jouette M. Bassler, *Divine Impartiality: Paul and a Theological Axiom*, SBL Dissertation Series (Missoula, Mont.: Society of Biblical Literature, 1982).

8. God's Special Commitment to the Poor

1. This chapter's title, God's special commitment to the poor, is taken from paragraph 69, section 4, "Our Theological Task," of the *Book of Discipline of the United Methodist Church* (Nashville: United Methodist Publishing House, 1988), to emphasize that the South American Bishops Council's preferential "option for the poor" has led to a corresponding legislative enactment by a major Protestant church. The wording is probably that of the late Professor Albert C. Outler, an ecumenical theologian to whose memory this chapter is dedicated.

2. Cf. John Dominic Crossan, *The Historical Jesus: The Life of a Mediterranean Jewish Peasant* (San Francisco: HarperCollins, 1991), and Burton L. Mack, *The Lost Gospel: The Book of Q and Christian Origins* (San Francisco: HarperCollins, 1993).

3. For an authoritative account of 100 years of Vatican social teaching beginning with the call for justice in Pope Leo XIII's *Rerum Novarum*, the first great social encyclical, see Donald Dorr, *Option for the Poor* (Maryknoll, N.Y.: Orbis Books, 1992). For the most comprehensive collection of primary documents, see *Catholic Social Thought, the Social Heritage*, ed. David J. O'Brien and Thomas A. Shannon (Maryknoll, N.Y.: Orbis Books, 1992).

4. See Paul Ramsey, *Basic Christian Ethics* (New York: Charles Scribner's Sons, 1950), reprinted in Library of Theological Ethics (Louisville, Ky.: Westminster/ John Knox Press, 1993).

9. The Keys of the Kingdom

1. See William R. Farmer and Roch Kereszty, O.Cist., *Peter and Paul in the Church of Rome: The Ecumenical Potential of a Forgotten Perspective* (Mahwah, N.J.: Paulist Press, 1990), 186. This book builds upon earlier European scholarship, both Catholic and Protestant. See bibliography, 138. The later Tertullian is the first to use Matt.16:17–19 in an argument for the bishop of Rome as the successor of Peter.

2. Edouard Massaux, *Influence de l'Evangile de Saint Matthieu sur la littérature Chrétienne avant Saint Irénée*, 1950, Bibliotheca Ephemeridum Theologicarum Lovaniensium 75, reprinted with new introduction by Frans Neirynck and with a supplementary bibliography in 1985. Translation into English by Norman J. Beval and Suzanne Hecht, edited with an introduction and addenda by Arthur J. Bellinzoni, *The Influence of the Gospel of Saint Matthew on Christian Literature before Saint Irenaeus*, 3 vols. (Macon, Ga.: Mercer University Press, 1990–1993). See also P. Batiffol, *Cathedra Petri: Etude d'histoire ancienne de l'Eglise* (Paris: Cerf, 1938), and J. Ludwig, *Die Primatworte Matt. 16: 18–19 in der altkirchlichen Exegese*, Neutestamentliche Abhandlungen 19, Band 4 (Münster: Aschendorffsche Verlagsbuchhandlung, 1952).

3. Von Allmen, "L'Eglise locale parmi les autres églises locales," *Irenikon* 43 (1970), 512–37, noted in *The Eucharist Makes the Church: Henri du Lubac and John Zigioulas in Dialogue*, ed. Paul McPartlan (Edinburgh: T. & T. Clark, 1993), 115.

4. See David B. Peabody, *Mark as Composer* (Macon, Ga.: Mercer University Press, 1987), 55, table 69. "It is characteristic of Mark to use 'word' absolutely as 'the word.' "

5. For a different way of understanding these texts, see John S. Kloppenborg, "The Theological Stakes in the Synoptic Problem," in *The Four Gospels: 1992 Festschrift Frans Neirynck*, vol. 1, ed. F. van Segbroeck et al. (Louvain: Leuven University Press, 1992), 93–120.

6. Peabody, *Mark as Composer*, 69, table 107.

7. Ibid., 38, tables 14 and 193. See also tables 11 and 242.

8. Ibid., 70, table 111.

9. Rudolf Bultmann, *History of the Synoptic Tradition*, trans. John Marsh (Oxford: Basil Blackwell, 1963), 258. Cf. Charles Fox Burney, *The Poetry of Our Lord: An Examination of the Formal Elements of Hebrew Poetry in the Discourses of Jesus Christ* (Oxford: Clarendon Press, 1925). Burney renders these verses back into Aramaic on 117.

10. Bultmann, *Synoptic Tradition*, 257–58.

11. Rudolf Bultmann, "Die Frage nach der Echtheit von Matt. 16, 17–19," *Theologische Blätter* 20 (1941): 265–79. Bultmann argues against the authenticity of these verses mainly on the basis of the unlikelihood that Jesus would have used the term *ekklesia*. As a criterion he appeals to the Two-Source Hypothesis. Authentic sayings of Jesus "should fit together in language, conceptuality, and interest with the sayings of Jesus which can be regarded as early on the basis of their having been preserved in Mark and the sayings source [Q]. For Matt. 16: 17–19, this is clearly not the case." See Appendix.

12. Bultmann, 259.

13. Bultmann, 138–41. Cf. Otto Betz, *Jesus der Messias Israels* (Tübingen: J.C.B. Mohr [Paul Siebeck], 1987), 99–126, for further evidence from Qumran texts to support the conclusion that Matt. 16:17–19 had a Palestinian origin.

14. Some scholars argue for or against the historicity of the keys of the kingdom saying on grounds other than whether Matthew used Mark or vice versa. But on the more decisive point of the effect of source analysis itself upon the question of historicity, the consequence of the Two-Source Hypothesis is clear: In relation to the Two-Gospel Hypothesis, the Two-Source Hypothesis serves to weaken the case for historicity by requiring the additional hypothesis that Mark has omitted from a hypothetical Ur-Markus the verses preserved in the supposedly later Gospel of Matthew, as well as requiring the hypothesis that Matthew has copied this hypothetical source more faithfully than the earlier evangelist Mark. It should also be said that much if not most of what has been said in favor of the Two-Gospel Hypothesis could also be said in favor of any hypothesis that recognizes that Mark is secondary to Matthew, for example, the view that Mark was written after Matthew but before Luke.

15. *1 Clement to the Corinthians* 7.

16. Gal. 6:14.

17. Eusebius, *Church History* 5.2.4–5. Cf. William R. Farmer, *Jesus and the Gospel: Tradition, Scripture, and Canon* (Philadelphia: Fortress Press, 1982), 204–27.

18. Because, according to Matthew, Jesus sent Mary Magdalene and the other Mary to carry the good news of his resurrection to his disciples (Matt. 28:9–10), it was a

common theme in medieval literature to refer to these women as apostles to the apostles (*apostolae apostolorum*). When we see the mission of evangelization (Mary Magdalene and the other Mary) in relationship to the mission of martyrdom (Blandina and other women martyrs) and recognize that these are but dual witnesses to the one apostolic mission of Peter and Paul and the other apostles, then it is fitting to ask, by what logic can women be excluded from any office in the church and specifically banned from representing Christ at the altar of sacrifice if their mission of evangelization and their mission of martyrdom is as essential to the church as that of men? Certainly the tradition that men and women contending for the faith were able to see Jesus Christ crucified in the form of Blandina works against the argument that a woman cannot be an icon of Christ. The criterion for being an icon of Christ is less gender than faithfulness to his example.

19. "Renounce once and for all the chase of the phantom Ur-Markus, and the study of the minor agreements becomes a highway to the recovery of the purest text of the Gospels." Burnett Hillman Streeter, *The Four Gospels: A Study of Christian Origins* (1924; London: Macmillan & Co., 1953), 331.

20. *Peter in the New Testament*, ed. R. E. Brown, K. P. Donfried, and J. Reumann (Maryknoll, N.Y.: Paulist Press, 1973), is viewed in some circles as a valuable contribution to ecumenical discussion. This book has the value of introducing the reader to a wide range of New Testament passages that need to be taken into consideration in understanding "Peter in the New Testament." However, since all participants in the discussion understood that their work would presuppose the Two-Source Hypothesis, this needs to be taken into account in evaluating the long-term usefulness of this work. See also *Lutherans and Catholics in Dialogue* (New York: National Committee of the Lutheran World Federation and the Bishops' Commission for Ecumenical Affairs, 1965). In these discussions, promising avenues for ecumenical dialogue are being opened.

10. The Idea and Reality of Markan Priority

1. In May 1977, Roland Mushat Frye, then professor of English literature at the University of Pennsylvania, at the Colloquy on the Relationships among the Gospels at Trinity University in San Antonio, Texas, disclosed that his study of comparable works in English literature demonstrated that, when he found a work where the author had conflated earlier sources, the author of the later work typically condensed the overall length of his sources, while often expanding individual pericopes with "the addition of lively details to provide a fresher and more circumstantial narrative." "The Synoptic Problems and Analogies in Other Literatures," in *The Relationship among the Gospels: An Interdisciplinary Dialogue*, ed. William O. Walker, Jr. (San Antonio: Trinity University Press, 1978), 261–302.

2. Augustine, *The Harmony of the Gospels* 4.10.11. See David B. Peabody, "Augustine and the Augustinian Hypothesis: A Reexamination of Augustine's Thought in *De consensu evangelistarum*," in *New Synoptic Studies: The Cambridge Gospel Conference and Beyond*, ed. William R. Farmer (Macon, Ga.: Mercer University Press, 1983).

3. This dream of a national Christian consensus caused havoc a century later in the

hands of the German Christians, although by then the larger Germany, including Austria, was in the mind of Germany's rulers.

4. Hajo-Uden Meijboom, *A History and Critique of the Origin of the Marcan Hypothesis* (Macon, Ga.: Mercer University Press, 1993), 228.

5. Bo Reicke, "From Strauss to Holtzmann and Meijboom: Synoptic Theories Advanced during the Consolidation of Germany, 1830–1870," *Novum Testamentum* 29, no. 1 (1987): 1–21.

6. Symposium on the Minor Agreements, organized by Professor Georg Strecker of Göttingen University.

7. Symposium on Presuppositions, Paradigm Shifts, and Conveyance of Opinion to the Public in Biblical Studies, 1850–1914. Organized by Professor H. Graf Reventlow of Ruhr University Bochum.

8. For a comprehensive analysis of Streeter's influential contribution to the Two-Source Hypothesis, see William R. Farmer, *The Synoptic Problem: A Critical Analysis* (New York: Macmillan Co., 1964), 118–77. For a well-reasoned defense of Streeter in light of Farmer's critique, see Joseph A. Fitzmyer, "The Priority of Mark and the 'Q' Source in Luke," in *Jesus and Man's Hope*, ed. D. G. Buttrick (Pittsburgh: Pittsburgh Theological Seminary, 1970), 1:131–70. For a point-by-point response to Fitzmyer's defense of Streeter, see William R. Farmer, "A Response to Joseph Fitzmyer's Defense of the Two-Document Hypothesis," in *New Synoptic Studies: The Cambridge Gospel Conference and Beyond*, ed. William R. Farmer (Macon, Ga.: Mercer University Press, 1983); and "Modern Developments of Griesbach's Hypothesis," *New Testament Studies* 23 (1977): 275–95. Scheduled for publication in 1994 is David Neville, *Arguments from Order in Synoptic Source Criticism: A History and Critique* (Macon, Ga.: Mercer University Press). For further details of some of the history of the arguments from order see the Appendix of Neville's book; and for further discussion of the literary evidence bearing on the phenomenon of order, see chapter 2.

9. David B. Peabody, *Mark as Composer* (Macon, Ga.: Mercer University Press, 1987), 55. Cf. table 70 for "again" used retrospectively uniting two or more separate, smaller literary units; table 15 for "by the sea"; table 85 for "all the crowd"; table 84 for "and he taught them." This is no more than half of Mark's literary characteristics that overlap with "again" used retrospectively in Mark 2:13. For a complete listing, see William R. Farmer, "The Minor Agreements of Matthew and Luke against Mark and the Two-Gospel Hypothesis: A Study of These Agreements in Their Compositional Contexts," in *Symposium on Minor Agreements*, ed. Georg Strecker (Göttingen: Vandenhoeck & Ruprecht, 1993), 175. Farmer's listing is drawn from *Mark as Composer*.

10. Mark 2:1; 2:13; 3:1; 3:20; 4:1; 5:21; 7:14; 7:31; 8:1; 8:13; 10:1; 10:10; 10:32; and 11:27.

11. For instance, Gottlob Christian Storr, as early as 1786.

12. Notably, Gotthold Ephraim Lessing, as early as 1784.

13. The great Berlin theologian Friedrich Schleiermacher, who followed Bleek and De Wette in placing Mark third, first proposed that Papias's *Logia* of Matthew referred not to the Gospel of Matthew, as had been previously supposed, but to a collection of Jesus' sayings.

14. I am indebted in part to my colleague Abbot Denis Farkasfalvy for this description of what can be designated as an important potential "third force" on the

international scene of Gospel exegesis. Abbot Farkasfalvy has also drawn to my attention the special importance of the book: Raymond E. Brown, S.S., and John P. Meier, *Antioch and Rome: New Testament Cradles of Catholic Christianity* (Mahwah, N.J.: Paulist Press, 1983). Farkasfalvy analyzes a basic argument of Meier as follows: Step 1: Axiom: Mark is the source of Matthew. Step 2: Matthew is late because of the complicated process of textual combinations of Mark, Q, and Special Matthew source material. Step 3: In Antioch, the Jewish Christians opened themselves to Gentile missionaries (absurd conclusion), 15–16. Farkasfalvy concludes that this is a classical case for proving that the "axiom" must be false because it leads to a false conclusion. Farkasfalvy notes that Brown observes that Paul in Rom. 1:1 offers "a gospel formulation that is not his own but is already known" to his readers in Rome. It is known to the readers "almost as a creedal expression, with the hallmark of Jewish origin" (118). Farkasfalvy justifiably complains that Brown does not continue the reflection by stating: "a gospel presenting evidences about Jesus as Son of David" (Rom. 1:1) must reflect a pre-Pauline origin, a state of affairs preceding the exclusive Gentile missionary orientation of Mark and Luke. All this is in correspondence and is cited with the author's permission.

15. Also recommended is the earlier *The Two-Gospel Hypothesis: A Critical Appraisal*, ed. Arthur Bellinzoni (Macon, Ga: Mercer University Press, 1985). Here one finds the classic essays for and against Markan priority, and for and against the existence of Q.

16. *A History and Critique of the Marcan Hypothesis: 1835–1866: A Contemporary Report Rediscovered*, a translation with introduction and notes of *Geschiedenis en Critiek der Marcushypothese* by Hajo-Uden Meijboom, 1866, trans. and ed. John J. Kiwiet (Macon, Ga.: Mercer University Press, 1992).

17. *The New Testament: The History of the Investigation of Its Problems*, trans. S. MacLean Gilmour and Howard Clark Kee (Nashville: Abingdon Press, 1972), 151. Professor Helmut Koester cites Holtzmann as "the classic advocate" of the Two-Source Hypothesis in his latest book: *Ancient Christian Gospels: Their History and Development* (Philadelphia: Trinity Press International, 1990), 128. Eta Linnemann chastises her German colleagues for not recognizing that Holtzmann has been effectively refuted in recent scholarly literature. In her book, *Is There A Synoptic Problem? Rethinking the Literary Dependence of the First Three Gospels*, trans. Robert W. Yarbrough (Grand Rapids: Baker Book House, 1992), 47–66, Linnemann notes the problem of explaining Luke's use of Matthew and argues against literary dependence not only between Matthew and Luke but between any of the Gospels. Linnemann is the first German university professor to break ranks with those who accept the Two-Source Hypothesis. Her book is full of valuable insights, but her basic argument against literary dependence fails. For example, at decisive points she denies to the evangelists the authorial freedom that would be extended to any other author. This is the death of literary criticism and of sound exegesis.

18. David B. Peabody, "Chapters in the History of the Linguistic Argument for Solving the Synoptic Problem: the Nineteenth-Century Context," *Jesus, the Gospels, and the Church*, ed. E. P. Sanders (Macon, Ga.: Mercer University Press, 1987).

19. This group numbers more than one hundred scholars, and at the society's annual meeting, the work of members is submitted for peer review. Publication of research by this group on all three synoptics is projected for 1996. The preliminary

working papers on Luke were published in the seminar papers of the Society of Biblical Literature for 1992 and 1993 and will reach completion in 1994.

20. Cf. William R. Farmer, "Luke's Use of Matthew: A Christological Inquiry," *Perkins School of Theology Journal*, July 1987, 39–42. See especially the section, "The Order of Discourse Material in Luke Relative to Matthew."

11. A Social History of Markan Primacy

1. Hans Herbert Stoldt, *The History and Criticism of the Marcan Hypothesis*, trans. and ed. Donald L. Niewyk (Macon, Ga.: Mercer University Press, 1980). See note 10 of chapter 1, above.

2. Griesbach, Hug, Palus, Saunier, Fritzsche, Meyer, Sieffert, Schwartz, DeWette, Bleek, Schleiermacher, F. C. Baur, Schwegler, Köstlin, Delitzsch, Keim, Davidson, Nösgen, D. F. Strauss, Zeller, Hilgenfeld, and Zahn. All but Hug, Hilgenfeld, and Zahn regarded Mark as third. DeWette and Bleek decided Matthew and Luke were independent of each other and posited an Ur-Gospel behind these two Gospels.

3. Christopher Tuckett, "The Griesbach Hypothesis in the Nineteenth Century," *Journal for the Study of the New Testament* 3 (1979): 29–60.

4. See Werner Georg Kümmel, *The New Testament: The History of the Investigation of Its Problems*, trans. S. MacLean Gilmour and Howard Clark Kee (Nashville: Abingdon Press, 1972), and the pertinent reference in the previous chapter.

5. Hajo-Uden Meijboom, *A History and Critique of the Marcan Hypothesis: 1835–1866: A Contemporary Report Rediscovered*, trans. John J. Kiwiet (Macon, Ga.: Mercer University Press, 1992).

6. For an earlier version of this discussion, see William R. Farmer, "State *Interesse* and Markan Primacy 1870–1914," in *The Four Gospels: 1992 Festschrift Frans Neirynck*, vol. 3, ed. F. van Segbroeck et al. (Louvain: Leuven University Press, 1992), 2477–98.

7. Sir Adolphus William Ward, *Cambridge History Series: Germany 1815–1890*, vol. 3 (Cambridge: Cambridge University Press, 1918), 56–57.

8. Ibid., 57.

9. Ibid.

10. Karl von Hase, *Handbook to the Controversy with Rome* (translated from the seventh edition of *Handbuch der protestantischen Polemik gegen die römisch-katholische Kirche*), vol. 1, ed. A. W. Streane (London, 1906), 311–12.

11. Lillian Parker Wallace, *The Papacy and European Diplomacy* (Chapel Hill, N.C.: University of North Carolina Press, 1948).

12. Ibid., 154. The enumeration is mine.

13. Georges Goyau, *L'Allemagne religieuse, le Catholicisme 1800–1870*, vol. 4 (Paris, 1872), 229f., as translated and commented upon by Wallace, *The Papacy*, 154–55. Germany had no papal representative at this time. "The nuncio was to the kingdom of Bavaria, a post that Eugenio Pacelli held during the First World War, and he subsequently became the first nuncio to Germany after it became a republic," Winthrop Brainerd wrote in a letter to me on May 4, 1987.

14. Ellen Lovell Evans, *The German Center Party 1870–1933: A Study in Political Catholicism* (Carbondale, Ill.: Southern Illinois University Press, 1981), 76.

15. Wallace, *The Papacy*, 193.

16. Ibid., 194.

17. Ibid., 194–95.

18. This simple and unqualified identification of Catholic as "ultramontane" represents an extreme view.

19. *Frankfurter Zeitung*, February 1875, as cited in Wallace, *The Papacy*, 193.

20. Ludwig Hahn, *Geschichte des Kulturkampf in Preussen* (Berlin, 1881), 102f. English translation by Wallace, *The Papacy*, 201.

21. Wallace, *The Papacy*, 201.

22. Ward, *Germany*, 63–64. A distinction should be noted between the imperial parliament, the Reichstag, and the Prussian legislature, the Prussian Landtag. The May Laws were Prussian, not imperial. But, because of its enormous size, Prussia dominated the German empire, exercising a virtual veto in the Reichstag.

23. January 9, 1873.

24. Ward, *Germany*, 65–66.

25. Wallace, *The Papacy*, 215.

26. Ibid., 216.

27. Jaroslav Pelikan, *The Riddle of Roman Catholicism* (Nashville: Abingdon Press, 1959), 79.

28. Wallace, *The Papacy*, 241.

29. Ibid.

30. Ibid., 241–42.

31. Ibid., 247. "The consequences of the *kulturkampf* were extremely serious for the Church. More than a million Catholics were deprived of the sacraments because thousands of priests were in exile or in prison. There were no bishops available to ordain new priests, because they had been relieved by the state of their sees after their failure to secure the approval of the prefects to their ordination; two archbishops (Cologne and Posen) had been exiled. The government forbade parish priests to visit other parishes than their own to give the sacraments. And, as a sort of crowning insult, priority in the use of the churches was given to the handful of anti-Roman Old Catholics, and the government created a new bishopric which it bestowed upon the leader of that sect" (E.E.Y. Hales, *The Catholic Church in the Modern World: A Survey from the French Revolution to the Present* [London: Eyre & Spottiswoode and Burns & Oates, 1958], 235). This undocumented summary paragraph represents how a twentieth-century Catholic historian could look back on the *Kulturkampf* from a post–Third Reich perspective, and yet leave unnoted in his book how Bismarck paved the way for Hitler. Apparently because Bismarck "believed in the value of the Church and was concerned to gain control over it, so as to make sure it gave support to his regime," whereas "Hitler's personal standpoint was fundamentally antithetical to Christianity as such" (296), justified in this historian's mind not drawing his reader's attention to the way in which Bismarck's actions provided Hitler with legal precedents to consider. Differences between Bismarck and Hitler existed and were decisive, but that fact does not justify a failure to take continuity seriously, as well as discontinuity, in the modus operandi of the leaders of the Second and Third Reichs. A main difference between Bismarck and Hitler is their relationships with Jews. Bismarck chose for his personal banker a Jew. Hitler believed international Jewish financial circles had stabbed Germany in the back.

32. *Provinzial-Korrespondenz.*

33. The appointment of Bernhard Weiss as professor in the University of Berlin two years later in 1876 would have further strengthened the hand of Bismarck because he too was an influential proponent of Markan primacy. The preliminary decisions leading to this important appointment would have been initiated while the *Kulturkampf* was still at white heat. The appointments of Holtzmann and Weiss at these two influential Prussian universities within a two-year period while the *Kulturkampf* was especially conflictive suggests some measure of state interest in the Petrine question because these two professors became the most influential proponents of what came to be known as the Two-Source Hypothesis. The realistic but subtle relationship between the professorate and state *interesse* emerges clearly in two excellent books on the German universities. These are C. E. McClelland, *State, Society, and University in Germany, 1700–1914* (Cambridge: Cambridge University Press, 1980), and F. K. Ringer, *The Decline of the German Mandarins: The German Academic Community, 1890–1933* (Cambridge, Mass.: Harvard University Press, 1969). For documentation of the anti-Catholic ethos of the Prussian-controlled universities in the imperial period, see Konrad H. Jarausch, *Students, Society, and Politics in Imperial Germany* (Princeton, N.J.: Princeton University Press, 1982), and John E. Craig, *Scholarship and Nation Building: The University of Strasbourg and Alsatian Society, 1870–1939* (Chicago: University of Chicago Press, 1984).

34. I learned this from Emanuel Hirsch in an interview, arranged by his neighbor, Professor Emeritus Friedrich Gogarten, during the summer of 1958. Hirsch told me that, by way of contrast, young theologians were advised that they needed to consider Holtzmann's views seriously.

35. Gordon A. Craig, *Germany: 1866–1945* (Oxford: Oxford University Press, 1988), 168.

36. Farmer, *The Synoptic Problem: A Critical Analysis* (New York: Macmillan Co., 1968), 48–198.

37. Eta Linnemann, referring to the lamentable consequences of this legacy for German pastors, writes: "They have been required by church authorities to be schooled in historical and critical theology. As a result of this forced march through years of pseudoscientific study, pastors usually lack all missionary or evangelistic competence. The same forced march was made, however, by the church authorities themselves years ago. The desolation is total and comprehensive." *Is There a Synoptic Problem?* 210.

12. A Dismantling of the Church's Canon

1. James M. Robinson and Helmut Koester, *Trajectories Through Early Christianity* (Philadelphia: Fortress Press, 1971); *Entwicklungslinien durch die Welt des frühen Christentums* (Tübingen: J.C.B. Mohr [Paul Siebeck], 1971).

2. Robinson's essay, LOGOI SOPHON (Greek for "wisdom sayings"), on the *Gattung* (German for "literary category") of Q, was first published by Mohr in 1964 in a volume celebrating Rudolf Bultmann's eightieth birthday, *Zeit und Geschichte*.

3. *The Future of Our Religious Past*, ed. James M. Robinson, was copublished by Harper & Row in New York and by SCM Press in London in 1971, in the same year

that Robinson and Koester's *Trajectories* was published by Fortress Press in Philadelphia and by Mohr in Tübingen.

4. See John Drury, *Tradition and Design in Luke's Gospel* (Atlanta: John Knox Press, 1976); Edward C. Hobbs, "A Quarter Century without Q," *Perkins School of Theology Journal* 30 (Summer 1980): 12; James Hardy Ropes, *The Synoptic Gospels* (Cambridge: Cambridge University Press, 1934), 67.

5. Robinson and Koester, *Trajectories*, 270. As noted in the opening chapter, more recently Professor Koester has written: "One of the most striking features of the *Gospel of Thomas* is its silence on the matter of Jesus' death and resurrection—the keystone of Paul's missionary proclamation. But Thomas is not alone in this silence. The synoptic Sayings Source Q used by Matthew and Luke, also does not consider Jesus' death a part of the Christian message. . . . The Gospel of Thomas and Q challenge the assumption that the early Church was unanimous in making Jesus' death and resurrection the fulcrum of Christian faith." *Ancient Christian Gospels: Their History and Development* (Philadelphia: Trinity Press International, 1990), 86.

6. Robinson and Koester, *Trajectories*, 16. An English edition of Bauer's book appeared in a timely fashion in the same year as *Trajectories*. The German title of Bauer's book was *Rechtgläubigkeit und Ketzerei im ältesten Christentum*. It first appeared in 1934 as the tenth volume in the series Beiträge zur historischen Theologie (Tübingen: J.C.B. Mohr [Paul Siebeck]), and was reprinted with minor additions and corrections, plus two supplementary essays by Georg Strecker in 1964. Bauer's work, as corrected and supplemented by Strecker, was translated into English and published by Fortress Press in 1971.

7. Robinson and Koester, *Trajectories*, 85–95. Space does not permit repeating all of the valid considerations in Robinson's argumentation. But with *Thomas* we now have a document that resembles what Q is supposed to have been, primarily a collection of the sayings of Jesus. However, the selection and order of the sayings of Jesus in *Thomas* is so different from Q that it could be argued that *Thomas* raises more questions than it answers. For example, if Q ever existed, it must have been a very important document. Why then in the arrangement of the sequence of the many sayings of Jesus that are found both in *Thomas* and in the hypothetical Q source, does *Thomas* not reflect some clear influence from Q? Professor Koester may be aware of the problem, but he says only: "What is most puzzling about the composition of sayings in this wisdom book is the arrangement and order of the sayings. There is seemingly no rhyme or reason for the odd sequence in which the sayings occur in the *Gospel of Thomas*." Koester, *Ancient Christian Gospels*, 81.

8. Matt. 7:28; 11:1; 13:53; 19:1; 26:1.

9. Robinson and Koester, *Trajectories*, 95.

10. Ibid., 94–95.

11. Fortunately, we can test whether there was a "trend toward alluding, near its end, to such a collection as *logoi*" by examining each of the *other four* collections in Matthew. While *logoi* occurs in Matt. 7:28; 19:1; and 26:1, it is very important to note that none of the "concluding sayings" in the other four Matthean collections uses *logoi*. Thus, contra Robinson, there appears to be no discernible trend. So when he says: "It would be the same trend at work in Matthew that leads to the fixed formula with which he concludes his five sayings collections," we can see him building on a "trend" that is illusory.

12. An early Christian letter from Clement, Bishop of Rome, ca. 90 C.E.

13. Robinson and Koester, *Trajectories*, 97.

14. In *Ancient Christian Gospels*, his latest book, Koester makes no reference to his earlier *Trajectories* project, as is noted by his reviewers, Fred W. Burnett and Gary A. Phillips. See "Palm Reading and the Big Bang: Origins and Development of Jesus Traditions," *Religious Studies Review* 18 (October 1992): 299. He does, however, continue to assume the Q hypothesis. His continued assumption of the existence of Q and some modified form of the Ur-Markus hypothesis lie at the basis of a highly speculative reconstruction of Christian origins that will only be credited by those who believe that he has "assured" securities to cover his bets. A case in point is Koester's conclusion that "the Gospel of Peter [a Docetist writing—W.R.F.] has preserved the most original narrative version of the tradition of scripture interpretation" (230).

15. Robinson and Koester, *Trajectories*, 98.

16. A construction in Greek that roughly translates as "various thoughts" or "different thoughts."

17. Robinson and Koester, *Trajectories*, 135.

18. James M. Robinson, "The Problem of History in Mark Reconsidered," *Union Seminary Quarterly Review* 20 (1965): 135.

19. Nag Hammadi is the place in Egypt associated with the discovery of *Thomas* and other Coptic documents.

20. See J. S. Kloppenborg, "The Theological Stakes in the Synoptic Problem," in *The Four Gospels: 1992 Festschrift Frans Neirynck*, vol. 1, ed. F. van Segbroeck et al. (Louvain: Leuven University Press, 1992), 93–120. See also Arland D. Jacobson, *The First Gospel: An Introduction to Q* (Sonoma, Calif.: Polebridge Press, 1992), 13ff. Jacobson correctly notes the importance of the problem of explaining Luke's use of Matthew. But he is mistaken in stating that Farmer assumes that one of the eighteen fundamental ways that the Gospels may be related to one another "must" be the correct one. I assume that one of these "may" be the correct one, and lay out in detail the evidence and argumentation that lead me to the conclusion that one of these eighteen probably is the correct one. Jacobson grants that appeal to a hypothetical source should not be made in solving the synoptic problem, unless that becomes necessary to explain the data. The question to be put to Jacobson is this: "Is Q really necessary to explain the data?" An increasing number of scholars are prepared to say no in answer to this question.

21. David Dungan, "Mark and the Abridgment of Matthew and Luke," *Jesus and Man's Hope*, ed. D. G. Buttrick (Pittsburgh: Pittsburgh Theological Seminary, 1970), 1:77.

22. Dungan, when quoting Petrie, cites "Q Is Only What You Make It," *NovT* 3 (1959): 28–33; the quotation is on 31. A review of the question of Q has been made by Earle Ellis in his essay on the state of the art of Gospel criticism. Ellis cites Petrie's judgment against the Q hypothesis favorably and then, to make clear that no one can decide what Q really was, he summarizes Petrie's findings in these memorable words:

Q is a single document, a composite document, several documents. It incorporates earlier sources; it is used in different redactions. Its original language is Greek; it is Aramaic; Q is used in different translations. It is the Matthean *logia*; it is not. It has shape and sequence; it is a collection of fragments. It is a Gospel;

it is not. It consists wholly of sayings; it includes narrative. It is all preserved in Matthew and Luke; it is not. Matthew's order of Q is correct. Luke's is correct; neither is correct. It is used by Mark; it is not used by Mark. ("Gospel Criticism: A Perspective on the State of the Art," in *Das Evangelium und die Evangelien: Vorträge vom Tübinger Symposium* 1982, ed. P. Stuhlmacher [Tübingen, J.C.B. Mohr (Paul Siebeck), 1983], 37.)

23. Edward C. Hobbs reviews the evidence for this with regard to Q in "A Quarter Century without Q," in the *Perkins School of Theology Journal* 30 (1980): 10–19. Evidence for this with regard to Markan priority may be found in *New Synoptic Studies: The Cambridge Gospel Conference and Beyond*, ed. William R. Farmer (Macon, Ga.: Mercer University Press, 1983). See in particular Pierson Parker, "The Posteriority of Mark," 67–142; Lamar Cope, "The Argument Revolves: The Pivotal Evidence for Marcan Priority Is Reversing Itself," 143–59; Phillip Sigal, "Aspects of Mark Pointing to Marcan Priority," 185–208; Bo Reicke, "A Test of Synoptic Relationships: Matthew 10:17–23 and 24:9–14 with Parallels," 209–29; and William R. Farmer, "A Response to Joseph Fitzmyer's Defense of the 'Two Document Hypothesis,' " 501–23.

24. See especially Helmut Koester, "History and Development of Mark's Gospel," in *Colloquy on New Testament Studies: A Time for Reappraisal and Fresh Approaches*, ed. Bruce C. Corley (Macon, Ga.: Mercer University Press, 1983), 35–57. Koester argues on the basis of sound linguistic evidence that the text of the Gospel of Mark is later than the text of Matthew and Luke (while holding to a complex theory of Ur-Markus and Q). David Peabody, in a detailed response, confirms Koester's linguistic evidence and points out additional linguistic evidence to support Koester. Peabody then shows how Koester's evidence is more easily explained based on the Two-Gospel Hypothesis ("The Late Secondary Redaction of Mark's Gospel and the Griesbach Hypothesis: A Response to Helmut Koester," 87–132). The Robinson-Koester *Trajectories* project can thus be viewed on critical grounds as collapsing from within.

25. *Drew Gateway*, Fall 1983, 26–38.

26. Ibid., 28.

27. At the conclusion of his lecture, Professor Robinson refers to Q as a "lost collection of Jesus' sayings, which in my opinion is the most important book ever written by a Christian, if he or she can be called a Christian." Though still not acknowledging Q's hypothetical character, Robinson concedes that his canonical claims for Q, which place it above all other Christian books, was a personal opinion and not a scholarly consensus.

28. Robinson, "Sayings of Jesus: Q," 32.

29. Ibid., 32.

30. Among these scholars were David L. Dungan, David B. Peabody, Alan McNicol, Philip Shuler, and Lamar Cope.

31. Cf. Edward Simons, *Hat der dritte Evangelist den kanonischen Matthäus benutzt?* (Bonn, 1880).

32. Hobbs, in "A Quarter Century without Q," traces the essential development between Simons and Farrer (11–12) and then restates Farrer's case against Q (12–17).

33. Robert Morgenthaler, *Statistische Synopse* (Zurich, 1971), 300–305.

34. Frans Neirynck, *The Minor Agreements of Matthew and Luke against Mark, with a Cumulative List* (Louvain: Leuven University Press, 1974).

35. Most recently, Robert Gundry has joined with Goulder in concluding that Luke knew Matthew, while disagreeing with Goulder (and Streeter) that this conclusion would mean that Q is unnecessary. Robert Gundry, "Matthean Foreign Bodies in Agreements of Luke with Matthew against Mark: Evidence That Luke Used Matthew," in *The Four Gospels: 1992 Festschrift Frans Neirynck*, vol. 2, ed. F. van Segbroeck et al. (Louvain: Leuven University Press, 1992), 1467–95.

36. E. P. Sanders, *The Tendencies in the Synoptic Tradition*, Society for New Testament Synoptic Studies Monograph Series 9 (Cambridge: Cambridge University Press, 1969).

37. E. P. Sanders and Margaret Davies, *Studying the Synoptic Gospels* (Philadelphia: Trinity Press International, 1989).

38. See ibid., especially 67ff.

39. See particularly the works of Kosch, Zeller, and Sevenich-Bax.

13. The Gospel of the Lord Jesus

1. Rom. 8:22.

2. 2 Cor. 5:17.

3. Gal. 2:1–21.

4. Cf. Isa. 14:24–26.

5. Gal. 2:1–21.

6. Denis Farkasfalvy has provided me the following note which I gratefully pass along with his permission: "The 'blood of the new covenant' is not just a matter pertaining to the exegesis of Isaiah, but, more importantly introducing the whole heredity of Moses—the Law and the covenant—into the fulfillment of the prophesy on the suffering servant. Isaiah 53 is a base too narrow for the Pauline theology as it establishes the *proper link* between the Law and the Prophets. . . . In Romans 10, around a quotation of Isaiah, you have Deut. 30:12–14 (Rom. 10:6–8) and Deut. 32:21 (Rom. 10:19). The cross-referencing of Deuteronomy with Isaiah is quite skillfully done by Paul. It assures that Moses would be interpreted in the light of Isaiah and both (Moses and Isaiah) in the light of the death and resurrection of Christ." I hold that Isaiah 53 by itself is too narrow a base for anything. But by cross-referencing this central text with Deuteronomy, as Paul does here, and by cross-referencing related texts from Isaiah with Psalms and other books of the Law and the Prophets, Paul is able to draw upon a compellingly convincing set of scriptures for his theology. Were Paul's theology the focus of my book I would be writing it very differently. As it is, one purpose in writing this book is to document the importance of Isaiah 53 for Paul and for Jesus. The need for this documentation may be measured by how frequently adherents of the Two-Source Hypothesis ignore the importance of Isaiah 53 for understanding Jesus or the gospel in relation to Jesus. Cf. John Dominic Crossan, *The Historical Jesus: The Life of a Mediterranean Jewish Peasant* (San Francisco: Harper-Collins, 1991), who treats more than one hundred different authors and books from antiquity but never refers to the book of Isaiah, let alone Isaiah 53.

7. All underlining in this and following texts focuses attention on evidence suggesting the influence of Isaiah 53.

8. Matt. 20:28 and Mark 10:45.

9. Matt. 26:28 and Mark 14:24.

10. 2 Cor. 5:15.

11. "In laments and declarative praise the suffering brought to God's notice always has limits set to it. Here, however, the drift (of the report on the servant's suffering) involves an entire lifespan: he grew up . . . he was buried. On the other hand, here there is point-for-point correspondence with the church's confession as it is given in the Apostles' Creed—born, suffered, died, and was buried. This similarity in structure . . . is far more important than quotations from Isa. 53f. here and there in the New Testament." Claus Westermann, *Isaiah 40–66, A Commentary* (Philadelphia: Westminster Press, 1969), 257.

12. 1 Cor. 15:1–3.

13. This Pauline-like formula is close to the opening words of Mark's text "here begins the Gospel of Jesus Christ, the Son of God." It may well have been the Markan formulation that influenced those who formed the canon to adopt the uniform assumption: "The Gospel according to . . . " for all four canonical Gospels.

14. Cf. Gal. 2:11–21.

15. Cf. Gal. 1:3: "Our Lord Jesus Christ who gave himself for our sins. . . ."

16. Cf. Gal. 2:11–21.

17. All underlining in this and succeeding text is intended to focus attention on evidence indicating Isaiah's concern for the nations.

18. 2 Cor. 5.

19. See especially Isa. 42:1–4 with Isa. 49:6 and Isa. 66:18.

20. That Jesus focused his ministry on the eschatological gathering of Israel did not preclude his knowledge of God's will to save the nations as well as Israel. On the contrary, the salvation of Israel was inextricably bound up with the gathering of the nations.

21. Cf. Marinus de Jonge, *Jesus, the Servant Messiah* (New Haven, Conn.: Yale University Press, 1991). He states his conclusion after reviewing the work of T. W. Manson, J. Jeremias, O. Cullmann, C. K. Barrett, Morna Hooker, G. N. Stanton, and Martin Hengel. Since Morna Hooker's book *Jesus and the Servant: The Influence of the Servant Concept on Deutero-Isaiah in the New Testament* (London: SPCK, 1959) is where this position is most fully developed, we must conclude that Hooker's book still continues to exercise great influence despite the contrary position argued by M. Hengel in his book, *The Atonement: The Origin of the Doctrine in the New Testament* (London: SCM Press, 1981). Hengel does not answer Hooker's arguments. His evidence is sound, but it remains to be seen whether Hengel's position can be convincingly argued, assuming the Two-Source Hypothesis. This is an example of the difference it makes. Hengel's evidence is very convincing under the Two-Gospel Hypothesis or any hypothesis that recognizes the primary character of the Matthean account.

Appendix

1. This appendix is an abbreviated form of the article "The Two-Document Hypothesis as a Methodological Criterion in Synoptic Research," published in the *Anglican Theological Review*, October 1966. It has been edited for its present use with

the assistance of Luis A. Payan. (Note: "Two-Document" and "Two-Source" are equivalent terms, the latter now being preferred.)

2. Rudolf Bultmann, "Die Frage nach der Echtheit von Matt. 16, 17–19," *Theologische Blätter* 20 (1941): 265–79.

3. "Die Frage," col. 268 (my translation).

4. Christian Hermann Weisse, *Die evangelische Geschichte kritisch und philosophisch bearbeitet* (Leipzig, 1838), 28ff.

5. Heinrich Julius Holtzmann, *Die synoptischen Evangelien: Ihr Ursprung und ihr geschichtlicher Charakter* (Leipzig, 1863).

6. Rudolf Bultmann, *Jesus and the Word*, trans. L. P. Smith and E. H. Lantero (New York, 1934).

7. Rudolf Bultmann, *History of the Synoptic Tradition*, trans. John Marsh (Oxford: Basil Blackwell Publisher, 1963), 32–37.

8. Karl Lachmann, "De ordine narrationum in evangeliis synopticis," *Theologische Studien und Kritiken* 8 (1835): 570–90.

9. "How anyone who has worked through . . . [the immense mass of details that J. C. Hawkins collected, analyzed, and tabulated in *Horae Synopticae*] with a synopsis of the Greek text can retain the slightest doubt of the original and primitive character of Mark I am unable to comprehend. But since there are, from time to time, ingenious persons who rush into print with theories to the contrary, I can only suppose, either that they have not been at pain to do this, or else that—like some of the highly cultivated people who think that Bacon wrote Shakespeare, or that the British are the Lost Ten Tribes—they have eccentric views of what constitutes evidence" (B. H. Streeter, *The Four Gospels* [London, 1924], 164). Actually, Hawkins did not regard his work as providing evidence for Markan priority. He thought that the argument from order as developed and defended F. H. Woods led "irresistibly" to the view that Matthew and Luke copied a Gospel substantially identical with Mark. Hawkins, therefore, made Markan priority a basic presupposition of his work and built on it. Thus, it is clear that, behind Streeter and Hawkins, it is the argument from order that is decisive for this whole development in synoptic research. This matter is discussed in detail in my *The Synoptic Problem: A Critical Analysis* (New York: Macmillan Co., 1964), 63–67 and 153–58.

10. H. G. Jameson, *The Origin of the Synoptic Gospels* (Oxford, 1922), 9–11.

11. J. F. Springer, "The Synoptic Problem, II: Facts and Conclusions as to the Synoptic Order of Events," *Bibliotheca Sacra* 81 (1924): 59–80.

12. John Chapman, *Matthew, Mark and Luke: A Study in the Order and Interrelation of the Synoptic Gospels* (London, 1937).

13. G. M. Styler, "The Priority of Mark," published as an excursus in C.F.D. Moule, *The Birth of the New Testament* (London, 1962), 223–32.

14. Pierson Parker, *The Gospel before Mark* (Chicago: University of Chicago Press, 1953).

15. B. C. Butler, *The Originality of Matthew* (Cambridge: Cambridge University Press, 1951).

16. Austin M. Farrer, "On Dispensing with Q," in *Studies in the Gospel: Essays in Memory of R. H. Lightfoot*, ed. D. E. Nineham (Oxford, 1955): 55–86. See also Léon Vaganay, *Le Problème Synoptique* (Tournai, 1954); X. Léon Dufour, "L'Episode de l'enfant épileptique (Matt.17,14–21)," in *La Formation des Evangiles: Problème Synop-*

tique et Formgeschichte, Recherches Bibliques 2 (Bruges, 1957), 85–115; R. L. Lindsey, "A Modified Two-Document Theory of the Synoptic Dependence and Interdependence," *Novum Testamentum* 6 (1963): 239–63; Stefan Porúbcan, S.J., "Form Criticism and the Synoptic Problem," *Novum Testamentum* 7 (1964): 81–118.

17. Against this argument is the fact that a comparative linguistic analysis of the Gospels indicates that Matthew's text is closer to the Jewish and Palestinian form of the earliest tradition than is the text of Mark. The text of Mark is often more primitive than the text of Luke, but in such instances Mark's text is generally the same as that of Matthew. Therefore, primitive features in Mark's Gospel are not evidence for the priority of Mark to Matthew. The argument that Mark's text is more primitive than those of Matthew and Luke is treated in detail in my book *The Synoptic Problem*, 120–24, 159–69. See especially "Streeter's Misconception of Hawkins' *Horae Synopticae*," 153–58. Through this misconception, many scholars have assumed incorrectly that Hawkins' detailed linguistic analysis of the synoptic Gospels constitutes evidence for the priority of Mark. See, e.g., Kümmel, *Introduction*, 48.

18. Liberal theology was significantly shaped by adherence to the Markan hypothesis beginning with Albrecht Ritschl's conversion to the idea of Markan priority in the period of political and ecclesiastical reaction that led to the downfall of the Tübingen school.

19. Albert Schweitzer, *The Quest of the Historical Jesus*, trans. W. Montgomery (1910; New York, 1948), 203–4.

20. The reader may discern the direction of historical investigation in chapter 11 of this book.

Index of Scripture

Index of Names and Subjects